RECIPES ON PARADE

favorite recipes of [R]
MILITARY OFFICERS' WIVES

DEAR HOMEMAKER

The social know-how of officers' wives has always been the basis of the popular Recipes On Parade series, and this latest edition is no exception. It is devoted to something that military couples do with expertise: entertaining.

Turn the pages of this out-of-the-ordinary cookbook to discover party-proven drinks and punches, planning tips, and reliable party food recipes — all shared with us by officers' wives. The result of their contributions is the Recipes On Parade PARTY BOOK.

We feel certain this volume will become the one you turn to when planning a fun-filled evening for friends. By combining modern party etiquette with home-tested recipes, a truly complete party book has been produced.

We appreciate the participation of officers' wives stationed all over the world who contributed recipes for party drinks and food creations. Their enthusiastic response brought this book to materialization.

And thanks, too, to you homemakers who have added this new Recipes On Parade edition to your kitchen libraries. In so doing you are supporting the numerous worthwhile service projects that are sponsored by the officers' wives club.

Sincerely yours,

Mary Anne Richards

BOARD OF ADVISORY EDITORS

Mrs. Von Dean Clark
B. S. Home Economics
Blum, Texas

Mrs. Kay Gueymard
M. A. Home Economics
Atlanta, Georgia

Mrs. Mary Prager
B. S. Home Economics
Fullerton, California

Mrs. Lorraine Cummins
B. S. Home Economics
Honolulu, Hawaii

Mrs. Stella Marquez
B. S. Home Economics
Hampton, Virginia

Mrs. Rhoda Serrin
B. S. Home Economics
Alexandria, Virginia

©Favorite Recipes Press MCMLXXIII
Post Office Box 3396, Montgomery, Alabama 36109
Library of Congress Catalog Card No. 73-82898
ISBN O-87197-049-X

PREFACE

Entertaining should begin with the welfare of the guests as the foremost
concern. When a hostess genuinely desires to see that her guests have
a good time, everyone from the life-of-the-party extrovert to the retiring
individual comes away feeling that it was a warm, friendly evening.

Such a hostess makes successful entertaining look completely effortless.
But you may be assured that no memorable party just happens. Careful pre-
planning is always behind the smile of a relaxed hostess.

If you would like to give your friends an unforgettable evening but
don't quite know where to begin, then begin here — with the Recipes
On Parade complete PARTY BOOK. An up-to-date guide to entertaining,
it places every needed detail at your fingertips.

First, you will find hundreds of party drink recipes: mixed drinks, aperitifs,
delicious punches with and without spirits. Then, in an information-packed
planning section, there is complete advice on issuing invitations, making
your guest list, preparing the menu, and solving particular problems of
entertaining. To finish your party arrangements, choose from innumerable
guest-pleasing recipes for appetizers, soups, entrees, vegetables and desserts.

Now you are ready to give a party that friends will talk about for long
afterward. Plan it thoroughly . . . then relax and have a wonderful time.

Mrs. Richard M. Nixon
The White House
Washington, D. C.

WHITE HOUSE FRUIT PUNCH

2 gal. orange base
2 gal. lemon base
1 qt. ReaLemon juice
3 46-oz. cans grapefruit juice
3 46-oz. cans pineapple juice
10 1/2 gal. water
12 qt. ginger ale

This will make 20 gallons of punch.

CONTENTS

THE DRINK BOOK

APERITIFS AND AFTER DINNER DRINKS

Aperitifs and after dinner drinks are the "alpha and omega" of a good meal. Aperitifs wake up our palates for an evening of good food, and after dinner drinks pamper us after we've completed the final course.

"Aperitif" is a French expression meaning any drink taken before a meal as a stimulant to the appetite. Sherry, champagne, white wines and mixed drinks are commonly served before dinner to relax guests and perk up their appetites.

After dinner drinks are smooth in taste and seem to crown a meal with a final, glorious richness. They help us sink into the contentment of a completely satisfied appetite.

This section of recipes will give you some wonderful suggestions for tangy aperitifs as well as liqueurs, dessert wines and other after dinner drinks. Enjoy trying them when you entertain.

APRICOT CORDIAL

1 lb. rock candy
1 lb. dried apricots or peaches
1 fifth vodka

Place candy in bottom of wide-mouth gallon jar; place dried apricots on candy. Pour vodka over apricots. Place clear plastic wrap over top of jar; hold down with rubber band. Let set for 45 days in dark place such as back of linen closet. Pour off liquid into bottle, using nylon stocking for strainer.

Mrs. James N. Posey, W and M Chm., OWC
Ellsworth AFB, South Dakota

BRANDY ALEXANDER FRAPPES

1 qt. vanilla ice cream
1/2 c. brandy
1/2 c. creme de cacao
1 sq. chocolate

Chill 8 sherbet glasses. Allow ice cream to soften. Combine ice cream, brandy and creme de cacao in blender container; blend at high speed until smooth. Pour into chilled glasses. Let chocolate warm to room temperature. With sharp paring knife or vegetable parer, cut thin curls. Garnish drinks with curls. Serve in sherbet glasses. Yield: 8 servings.

Mrs. Charles N. Reed, Corr. Sec., OWC
Great Lakes Naval Hospital, Illinois

FROZEN BRANDY ALEXANDER

3 oz. Kahlua
3 oz. brandy
1 1/2 qt. vanilla ice cream

Place Kahlua, brandy and 1 pint ice cream in blender container; blend until smooth. Add more ice cream; blend. Repeat process until consistency of very thick milk shake. Serve in wine glasses. Yield: 4 servings.

Mrs. R. K. Bowers, 1st VP, O and CWC
Ft. Huachuca, Arizona

APRICOT BRANDY

1 qt. vodka
3 c. dried apricots, chopped
2 1/2 c. sugar

Mix vodka, apricots and sugar well. Seal tightly. Allow to stand for 2 months. Strain, bottle and seal. Serve in liqueur glasses.

Mrs. Robert E. Boughn, Hon. Pres., OWC
Ft. MacArthur, San Pedro, California

THIRTY-DAY APRICOT BRANDY

1 fifth vodka
1 lb. rock candy
1 pkg. dried apricots, chopped

Combine all ingredients in large glass container; mix well. When rock candy dissolves, remove string. Store for 30 days. Strain into decanter. Serve in liqueur glasses. Yield 16 servings.

Mrs. Robert L. Giese, Pres., OWC
Duluth AFB, Minnesota

CRICKETS

2 jiggers creme de cacao or Kahlua
1 jigger brandy
1/2 pt. vanilla ice cream
4 ice cubes

Combine creme de cacao, brandy, ice cream and ice cubes in blender container; blend thoroughly. Serve in punch cups. Yield: 4 servings.

Mrs. Carolyn A. Lyon, Reservation Chm., OWC
Andersen AFB, Agana, Guam

CHAUDEAU

4 egg yolks
1/4 c. sugar
1 tbsp. Cointreau, brandy or rum
1 c. dry white wine

Combine egg yolks and sugar in top of 1 1/2-quart double boiler; add Cointreau and wine gradually, beating until smooth. Place over simmering water; beat constantly with electric mixer. Mixture will foam and increase in volume as heated. Beat for 4 minutes or until mixture reaches top of boiler. Serve in wine glasses. Yield: 5 servings.

Mrs. David C. Robinson, Pres., OWC
Storck Barracks, Illesheim, Germany

CAPPUCINO

1 c. milk
1 tsp. instant coffee
2 tbsp. instant cocoa
1 jigger brandy
1 jigger rum
Cinnamon stick

Heat milk; add coffee and cocoa. Add brandy and rum; pour into large, heated mug. Add cinnamon stick. Yield: 1 serving.

Mrs. Henry H. Mauz, Jr., Pres., NOWC
USNB, Charleston, South Carolina

CAFE DIABLE

3 sm. sugar cubes
1/4 c. butter or margarine
1 c. whole coffee beans
Grated rind of 1 orange
Chopped peel of 1 apple
1   2-in. piece of cinnamon stick
12 cloves
6 tbsp. cognac
6 tbsp. kirsch
6 tbsp. curacao
1 1/4 c. freshly made coffee
Juice of 1 orange

Place sugar and butter in chafing dish or diable pan over direct flame; melt butter but do not

brown. Add coffee beans, orange rind, apple peel, cinnamon and cloves. Pour in cognac, kirsch and curacao; stir and heat. Tilt pan; touch match to edge. Hold match at arm's length as alcohol flames instantly. Stir constantly to prolong flames until all alcohol has been consumed; never add more liqueur during flaming or stream of liquid could ignite. Add coffee and orange juice when flame dies out. Heat to steaming; pour through strainer into demitasse cups. Yield: 4-6 servings.

COFFEE CARROLL

1 jigger creme de cacao
Coffee
1 1/2 tbsp. brandy
Whipped cream

Place creme de cacao in Irish coffee cup or wine glass; fill almost to top with coffee. Pour brandy in over a spoon so it will float on top; top with whipped cream.

Mrs. John R. Johnson, Pres., OWC
Naval Missile Center, Pt. Mugu, California

MEXICAN COFFEE

1 jigger tequila
1/2 jigger Kahlua
Freshly brewed hot coffee
Whipped cream

Pour tequila and Kahlua into coffee cup or mug. Fill cup with hot coffee, then top with whipped cream.

Lt. Cmdr. Edward R. Kuhn
DATC, Long Beach NS, Long Beach, California

COFFEE ESPECIEL

2 tbsp. lime juice
2 tbsp. sugar
1 oz. Kahlua
1 oz. brandy
Strong coffee
Whipped cream

Rim 4-ounce Irish coffee glass by dipping rim in lime juice, then in sugar. Crystallize sugared rim by twirling in flame if glass is heatproof. Pour Kahlua and brandy into glass; fill glass with coffee, leaving 1/2-inch space at top. Crown with dollop of whipped cream.

Mrs. Larry P. Anderson, W and M Chm., OWC
Kelly AFB, San Antonio, Texas

PAT'S SPECIAL

Hot coffee
1 jigger Kahlua
1 jigger brandy
1 jigger creme de cacao
Whipped cream

Pour coffee into mug; add Kahlua, brandy and creme de cacao. Top with whipped cream.

Mrs. Pat Pickett, Corr. Sec., Cookbook Chm., OWC
NAS, Lemoore, California

DESSERT DRINK

1 pt. vanilla ice cream
1 1/2 to 2 oz. Hiram Walker's Chocolate
  Mint

Soften ice cream slightly; whip with Chocolate Mint. Freeze until ready to serve. Serve in sherbet or champagne glasses. Yield: 4 servings.

Mrs. Dale R. Brummund, 1st VP, OWC
Wurtsmith AFB, Michigan

COLONEL'S GRASSHOPPER

1 jigger creme de menthe
1 jigger brandy
1 scoop vanilla ice cream

Combine creme de menthe, brandy and ice cream in blender container; blend well. Serve immediately. Yield: 1 serving.

Col. David W. Meyer
Defense Elec. Supply Center, Dayton, Ohio

FAVORITE GRASSHOPPER

1 oz. white creme de cacao
1 oz. green creme de menthe
Green food coloring
1 lg. scoop vanilla ice cream

Place creme de cacao, creme de menthe, 1 or 2 drops of food coloring and ice cream in electric

blender container; blend. Serve immediately. Yield: 1 or 2 servings.

Mrs. Joel M. Couch, Pres., OWC
Bolling AFB, Washington, D. C.

NORTH CAROLINA GRASSHOPPER

4 oz. white creme de cacao
4 oz. green creme de menthe
4 oz. whipping cream
1 c. (about) cracked ice

Place all ingredients in an electric blender container; blend for several seconds, then strain. Serve in champagne glasses. Brown creme de cacao was originally used in this drink, but, while taste was excellent, color was undesirable. Yield: 4 servings.

Mrs. J. B. McIlhenny, Past Co-Chm., Gp. VI, OWC
Camp Lejeune, North Carolina

HOT TODDY

1 jigger blended whiskey
1 tsp. sugar
3 whole cloves
1 lemon wedge
1 stick cinnamon

Pour whiskey into a mug; add sugar. Insert cloves in lemon wedge; place in mug. Add cinnamon and boiling water; stir well. Yield: 1 serving.

Maj. Edward B. Hanrahan
USAF Academy, Colorado

HOMEBREW KAHLUA

8 c. sugar
2 vanilla beans
1   4-oz. jar freeze-dried coffee
2 fifths bourbon

Mix sugar with 6 cups water; bring to a boil. Boil for 6 minutes; divide into 2 parts. Chop vanilla beans into small pieces; add to 1 part sugar syrup with coffee. Add bourbon to second half; stir well. Combine coffee mixture with bourbon mixture; blend well. Age for 6 weeks. Serve in liqueur glass. Yield: 1 gallon.

Mrs. Roger E. Wills, Jr., W and M Chm., OWC
Loring AFB, Maine

HOMEMADE KAHLUA

4 c. sugar
2 oz. Spice Islands Antigua instant coffee
1 vanilla bean, split in half
1 fifth brandy

Mix sugar and coffee in 2 cups boiling water; cool. Add vanilla bean and brandy. Let stand for 30 days in covered container; pour into wine bottles or decanters.

Mrs. Robert L. Giese, Pres., OWC
Duluth AFB, Minnesota

ISLANDS KAHLUA

4 c. sugar
2 oz. instant coffee
1 fifth vodka
1 vanilla bean, split lengthwise

Bring sugar and 4 cups water to a boil; boil for 5 minutes. Blend coffee with small amount of water; stir into sugar syrup. Bring to a boil, stirring until coffee is dissolved. Remove from heat; cool. Pour into gallon glass jug; add vodka and vanilla bean. Allow to age for 2 weeks, shaking contents well every day; remove vanilla bean. Serve in liqueur glass. Yield: 2 quarts.

Mrs. Donald B. Koch, VT-3 OWC
Whiting Field, Pensacola, Florida

KAHLUA HAWAIIAN

3 c. sugar
2 oz. instant coffee
1 fifth vodka or gin
1 vanilla bean

Bring sugar and 4 cups water to a boil; boil for 5 minutes. Cool slightly, add instant coffee. Heat, stirring, for 1 minute; add vodka. Cut vanilla bean into 4 pieces; add to vodka mixture in 1/2-gallon container. Let stand for 36 days; shake mixture periodically. Serve in liqueur glasses. Yield: 60 servings.

Cmdr. Charles W. Lord
Ships Parts Control Ctr.
Mechanicsburg, Pennsylvania

SOUTH SEAS KAHLUA

2 oz. instant coffee
3 1/2 c. sugar

2 1/4 c. brandy
1 vanilla bean, cut in half

Combine instant coffee, sugar and 2 cups boiling water; stir in brandy. Pour into 2 bottles; add vanilla bean to each bottle. Seal and let age for at least 30 days. Serve in liqueur glasses. Yield: 2 fifths.

Mrs. Kieth G. Wilson, Parliamentarian, OWC
Aviano AFB, Italy

EASY HOT BUTTERED RUM

1 tsp. brown sugar
2 whole allspice
1 whole clove
1 cinnamon stick
1/2 tsp. butter
2 oz. rum

Bring 1 cup water to boiling point. Place brown sugar, spices, butter and hot water in mug. Add rum; cover with pot holder or lid to steep briefly. Yield: 1 serving.

Mrs. Keith E. Phillips, OWC
USMTM, Saudi Arabia

HOLIDAY HOT BUTTERED RUM

1/4 lb. butter
1 1-lb. box brown sugar
1/8 tsp. salt
1/2 tsp. nutmeg
1/2 tsp. cinnamon
1/2 tsp. cloves
Dark rum
Cinnamon sticks

Cream butter and sugar together until smooth and fluffy. Add salt and spices; mix well. Mixture may be stored for long time in refrigerator. Place heaping teaspoon spice mixture in cup; add 1 1/2 ounces rum. Fill cup with hot water; add cinnamon stick. Yield: 12-16 servings.

Mrs. Albert E. Manning
Luncheon Club Hostess, NPFC, OWC
Defense Industrial Supply Center
Philadelphia, Pennsylvania

SPELUNKER SPECIAL

1 tsp. butter
1 tsp. sugar
5 cloves
1 1/2 oz. bourbon

Place butter, sugar, cloves and bourbon in a mug. Fill mug with boiling water. Stir to mix.

Cmdr. Roger P. Hartgen
Tracen, Petaluma, California

SOL Y SOMBRA

1 1/2 jiggers anisette
1 1/2 jiggers brandy

Pour anisette and brandy into small brandy snifter or liqueur glass; do not stir. May be served over ice, if desired.

Mrs. Donald D. Dunton, 1st VP, OWC
Sheppard AFB, Wichita Falls, Texas

MARYLAND TOM AND JERRY

3 eggs, separated
3 tbsp. (heaping) powdered sugar
3 oz. rum
1 1/2 oz. brandy
Freshly ground nutmeg

Beat egg whites until stiff. Add powdered sugar. Fold in beaten egg yolks. Pour rum and brandy into 6-ounce cup. Fill cup almost full with boiling water, then spoon 2 or 3 tablespoons egg mixture on top. Sprinkle with nutmeg. Yield: 6 servings.

Cmdr. Bruce I. Williams
Washington Science Center, Rockville Maryland

ANTIQUE BOMB

1 1/2 c. sugar
1 qt. dark rum
1 c. fresh lime juice or 1 sm. bottle
*   lime juice*

Mix sugar with 2 1/2 cups water, rum and lime juice until sugar is dissolved. Bottle in stone or dark glass bottles; age for at least 7 days. Serve on the rocks in old-fashioned glasses. Yield: 10 servings.

Mrs. Robert C. Hawlk
Aberdeen Proving Ground, Maryland

NEW YEAR'S DAY LONDON FOG

1 qt. vanilla ice cream
1 qt. cold black coffee
2 c. blended whiskey
Dash of rum

Combine ice cream, coffee, whiskey and rum in punch bowl; blend well. Serve in punch cups. Yield: 8 servings.

Mrs. James M. Keck, Adv., Hon. Pres., OWC
Barksdale AFB, Louisiana

DIFFERENT LONDON FOG

1 qt. brewed coffee
1 qt. vanilla ice cream
1 qt. bourbon or blended whiskey

Combine coffee, ice cream and bourbon; blend well. Serve in punch cups or wine glasses. For a sweeter punch, add ice cream and lessen amount of coffee in proportion. Yield: 24 servings.

Mrs. Robert B. Polk, Pres.
North Island Wives Club
NAS, San Diego, California

FIN DE SIECLE AVOCADO FRAPPES

1 fully ripe California avocado
1 c. light cream
1/2 c. milk
1/3 c. white creme de cacao
1/4 c. cognac

Halve avocado lengthwise, twisting gently to separate halves. Whack sharp knife directly into seed; twist to lift out. Peel halves; puree with cream, milk, creme de cacao and cognac, using fine sieve or electric blender. Chill. Half fill tall glasses with crushed or shaved ice; fill to top with avocado puree. Garnish with mint and lime and lemon slices. Glasses may be frosted by dipping into lightly beaten egg white, then into salt and/or lemon or lime juice. Serve with straws or sippers.

SOURS, COLLINS, FIZZES AND COOLERS

If you are anxious to break out of the monotony of ordinary mixed drinks, explore through the following pages. You'll find a wealth of recipes for zingy, refreshing sours, collins, fizzes and coolers.

For your summer barbecues, delight your friends with a frosty whiskey sour, rum collins, gin fiz or a selection of icy liquor and fruit combinations. These drinks can help cool even the hottest summer afternoon.

DARLING SPECIAL

Juice of 1 lemon
Juice of 1 orange
3 tsp. sugar
2 parts vodka
1 part brandy

Combine all ingredients in shaker; shake vigorously. Serve over ice in old-fashioned glass. Yield: 1 serving.

Mrs. Christa M. Corey, OWC
Incirlik, Turkey

FUZZ BUZZ

1 6-oz. can frozen pink lemonade
6 oz. vodka or rum
1 lg. unpeeled pitted peach, halved

Combine lemonade, vodka and peach in blender container; add enough crushed ice to almost fill blender. Blend at highest speed for 30 seconds or until ice is completely crushed. Serve in wine glasses. Yield: 4 servings.

Mrs. Richard A. Erickson, Staff Wives Rep., DLIWC
Ft. Ord, California

GREEK DELIGHT SOUR

1 6-oz. can frozen lemonade
1 1/2 lemonade cans whiskey
1/2 lemonade can water

Combine frozen lemonade, whiskey, water and 1 tray of ice in blender container; blend until smooth. Serve in frosted whiskey sour glasses; garnish with cherry and lemon slice. Yield: 7 servings.

Mrs. Patricia E. Schelhorn, Pres., OWC
Transportation Corps, Washington, D. C.

FROZEN PEACH DAIQUIRI

1 oz. frozen peaches
1 1/2 oz. light rum
1 tbsp. lemon juice
1 tbsp. lime juice

Combine all ingredients in blender container; add several ice cubes. Blend until smooth. Serve in wine glasses; garnish with thinly sliced lime or cherry. Yield: 1 serving.

Mrs. David Keers, Treas., OWC
Pt. Mugu, California

PISCO SOUR

3 jiggers Pisco
3 jiggers crushed ice
1 1/2 jiggers lime juice
Sugar to taste
4 or 5 drops of angostura bitters
1 egg white
1/8 tsp. cinnamon

Combine Pisco, ice, lime juice, sugar and bitters in blender container; blend well. Add egg white; blend briefly. Pour into glasses; sprinkle with cinnamon. Yield: 2 servings.

Mrs. Robert C. Seamans, Jr., Hon. Mem., OWC
Washington, D. C.

INSTANT FROZEN DAIQUIRI

I can frozen limeade
1 limeade can rum
1 limeade can water

Place frozen limeade in blender container; add rum, water and several ice cubes. Blend until mixed well. Pour into whiskey sour glasses; serve.

Mrs. Janet Spangler, Serv. Chm.
Edgewood Arsenal OWC
Aberdeen Proving Ground, Maryland

LEMONADE-RUM SLUSH

1 can frozen pink lemonade
1 lemonade can light rum

Combine lemonade and rum in 1-quart jar; fill jar with water to 1/4 inch from top. Fasten lid on jar. Place jar in freezer, turning occasionally until slushy. Spoon into wine glasses; garnish with lime slices and cherries. Serve with straws. Yield: 10-12 servings.

Mrs. David Keers, Treas., OWC
Pt. Mugu, California

HAWAIIAN PINK GIN

1 oz. red fruit punch concentrate
1 oz. grenadine
3 oz. pineapple luice
1 oz. cream
1 1/2 oz. gin
3 oz. ice

Combine all ingredients in blender container; blend well. Serve in whiskey sour glass.

Mrs. Margery Connor, OWC
USNS, Keflavik, Iceland

TEQUILA SOUR

1 1/2 oz. tequila
1 1/2 oz. orange juice
Juice of 1/2 lime
1 tsp. powdered sugar
1/8 tsp. grenadine
Lemon-lime carbonated drink

Combine tequila, orange juice, lime juice, sugar and grenadine. Fill highball glasses 2/3 full with crushed ice and carbonated drink. Pour 1 1/2 ounces tequila mixture into glasses. Yield: 2 servings.

Mrs. Sandy Hawkins, OWC
Lemoore NAS, California

GIN FIZZ

1 6-oz. can frozen lemonade concentrate
6 oz. gin
6 oz. half and half
3 egg whites

Place frozen lemonade concentrate, gin and half and half in blender container. Add egg whites; blend on high speed for very short time or until frothy.

Mrs. R. T. Murrian, Pres., OWC
RAF, Oxfordshire, England

ORANGE-MINT FIZZ

2 c. sugar
2 1/2 c. water
Juice and grated rind of 2 oranges
Juice and grated rind of 6 lemons
2 handfuls mint leaves, lightly crushed
Vodka or gin
Ginger ale or lemon-lime carbonated drink

Mix sugar and water; boil for about 10 minutes. Add fruit juices and grated rinds; pour over mint leaves. Cover tightly; let stand for 1 hour. Strain; cover. Keeps in refrigerator indefinitely. Fill tall glasses with crushed ice; pour in 1/3 cup orange mint, 1 jigger vodka and finish filling glass with ginger ale. Yield: 12 tall glasses.

Mrs. Gordon R. Flygare, W and M Chm., OWC
MAAG, Addis Ababa, Ethiopia

RAMOS FIZZ

Juice of 1/2 lemon
White of 1 egg
1 tbsp. powdered sugar
2 oz. gin
1 tbsp. sweet cream
1/2 tsp. orange flower water

Place all ingredients in blender with 3 ice cubes; blend at high speed. Pour into 8-ounce stemmed glass.

Mrs. Willard Barnett, Adv., OWC
Ellsworth AFB, South Dakota

RAMOS GIN FIZZ

1 1/2 oz. gin
3/4 oz. orange curacao
3/4 oz. sweet and sour mix
1 oz. half and half
1 egg
8 oz. crushed ice

Place all ingredients in blender container; blend. Yield: 1 serving.

Mrs. Margery Connor, OWC
NATO, Keflavik, Iceland

YELLOWBIRD

1 can frozen orange juice, thawed
10 oz. water
15 oz. pineapple juice
5 oz. rum
5 oz. creme de banana

Combine orange juice, water, pineapple juice, rum and creme de banana. Combine 1 part crushed ice and 2 parts rum mixture in blender container; blend and serve.

Mrs. Jo Ma MacMichael, ServLant OWC
Charleston Naval Base, Charleston, South Carolina

LIME SHRUB

1 1/2 c. sugar
2 1/2 c. water
1 qt. dark rum
1 c. fresh lime juice

Dissolve sugar in water. Add rum and lime juice; mix well. Bottle; let stand in cool place for at least 7 days before using. Serve iced and diluted with plain or carbonated water. May be served undiluted but is very potent.

Mrs. William J. Ryland, Pres., OWC
Fort Riley, Kansas

HOLIDAY ALE

1 qt. chilled apple juice
2 c. chilled cranberry juice
8 jiggers gin
2 c. chilled lemon soda
8 mint sprigs
8 lemon slices

Combine apple juice, cranberry juice, gin and lemon soda; pour over ice cubes in tall glasses. Garnish each glass with mint sprig and lemon slice. Yield: 8 servings.

Photograph for this recipe on page 22.

DOUBLE TANG COOLER

Juice of 1 fresh California lemon
2 to 3 tbsp. sugar or honey
1 c. cold water
1 jigger vodka
Lemonade ice cubes

Mix lemon juice and sugar until sugar is dissolved. Add water and vodka; pour over ice cubes in tall glasses. Yield: 1 serving.

GEORGIA BULLDOG

1 1/2 jiggers gin
3 tbsp. fresh orange juice
Ginger ale

Fill tall glass with crushed ice. Pour gin into glass; add orange juice. Fill glass with ginger ale.

Mrs. Douglas W. Curtis, Jr., VP, 570th Ladies Gp.
USAAG, Handorf, Germany

PURPLE PASSION

3 oz. grape wine
1 oz. vodka
Lemon-lime carbonated drink or sweet soda

Fill tall glass with crushed ice; pour in wine and vodka. Fill to top with carbonated drink.

Mrs. Edwin F. Miller, Welfare Chm., OWC
Fort Sheridan, Illinois

PINK KILLER

6 sprigs of fresh mint
1 jigger grenadine
2 jiggers limeade
2 jiggers orange juice
4 jiggers rum

Bruise mint in 2 very tall glasses; pack with shaved ice. Mix remaining ingredients in a pitcher and pour over ice. Garnish with fresh mint leaves; let stand to frost. Serve.

Capt. Carl L. Durst
University of Missouri Student, AFIT
Columbia, Missouri

EVA'S MINT JULEPS

Confectioners' sugar
4 sprigs of mint
1/2 tsp. sugar
Dash of water
3 oz. bourbon
Maraschino cherry with stem

Place mint julep cups in freezer to frost; ring top with confectioners' sugar. Crush mint with muddler; place in frosted mint julep cup. Add sugar and water. Pack cup with shaved ice; add bourbon. Garnish with additional sprigs of mint and maraschino cherry.

Mrs. Eva L. Kenison, Newsletter Ed., OWC
Edgewood Arsenal, Edgewood, Maryland

SANGAREES AND WINES

Wines and wine combinations have become increasingly
popular among Americans. If you have spent some
time trying selections available today, you are probably
among the wine enthusiasts.

We American wine drinkers are not as reserved as the British,
who always have a special time and place for drinking wine.
We enjoy wine chilled, at room temperature or over ice,
morning, noon and night, for any occasion.

Our following pages are brimming with ideas for wines
and sangarees (drinks made of wine or some other liquor,
sugar and spices). If you have never been able to find a wine
to your liking, you are soon to make a pleasant discovery.

SPANADA SANGRIA

1 can peaches
1 can crushed pineapple
1 gal. Spanada wine
1 lg. bottle ginger ale

Process peaches and pineapple in blender until no large chunks remain. Combine all ingredients in 6-quart pitcher or container; chill thoroughly. Serve in wine glasses. Yield: 30 servings.

Mrs. Stuart B. McCurdy, W and M Chm., OWC
MacDill AFB, Florida

CHARLESTON SANGAREE

1/2 c. water
1 c. sugar
1/4 tsp. cinnamon
1 lemon, sliced thin
1 orange, sliced thin
1 qt. red wine

Combine water, sugar and cinnamon in saucepan; bring to a boil. Boil for 5 minutes; cool thoroughly. Cover fruit slices with cooled syrup; chill for several hours or overnight. Place 1/2 cup syrup, part of the fruit, ice and wine in large pitcher; stir, mashing fruit slightly. Serve in wine glasses. Yield: 8-10 servings.

Mrs. Herbert W. Stewart, W and M Chm., OWC
Charleston AFB, South Carolina

EASY SANGRIA

1 qt. red wine
1 can lemon-lime carbonated drink
4 oz. white rum
Sugar to taste
Diced apple, orange and banana

Chill wine, lemon-lime drink and rum thoroughly. Combine all ingredients; serve over ice in highball glasses. Yield: 6 servings.

Mrs. Albert W. Costley, Jr., Corr. Sec., OWC
Moody AFB, Georgia

FESTIVE SANGRIA

2 oranges
1 fifth red wine
1 1/2 oz. brandy
2 limes, thinly sliced
1 peach, sliced
1/2 c. strawberries
Sugar to taste
1   7-oz. bottle club soda

Cut peel from each orange in a continuous strip; squeeze oranges, reserving juice. Combine wine, brandy, reserved orange juice and lime slices; chill for several hours. Combine peach slices, strawberries and sugar. Stir into wine mixture; let stand for 1 hour. Fasten orange strips over top of pitcher; let hang into pitcher. Pour wine mixture and soda in pitcher; pour over ice in tall glasses to serve. Yield: 4-6 servings.

Mrs. Howard E. Bethel, W and M Chm., OWC
Andrews AFB, Maryland

SANGRIA FOR A CROWD

1 qt. Burgundy
1 qt. lemon-lime carbonated drink
1 orange, sliced
1 lime, sliced
1 lemon, sliced
1 c. orange juice

Mix all ingredients together in large pitcher. Add ice and keep cold. Serve in wine glasses. Delicious with Mexican food. Yield: 16 servings.

Mrs. William A. Jack, Hon. Pres., OWC
Kelly AFB, Texas

SANGRIA TORREJON

1/2 bottle hearty Burgundy
Juice of 1 orange
Juice of 1 lemon
1/4 c. sugar
1/4 c. water
Orange, lemon and lime slices

Mix Burgundy, fruit juices, sugar and water together until sugar is dissolved; let stand for 1 hour or longer. Pour into glass pitcher; fill with ice. Serve in chilled glasses or punch cups; garnish with orange, lemon or lime slices. One-half cup pineapple, apple or cranberry juice may be substituted for orange and lemon juice. One or 2 jiggers apricot brandy may be added, if desired. Yield: 6 servings.

Mrs. Charles Langham, Parliamentarian, OWC
Hamilton AFB, California

SANGRIA SPECIAL

1 orange
1 fifth light dry red wine
1 ripe Elberta peach, peeled and sliced
6 slices lemon
1 1/2 oz. cognac
1 oz. triple sec
1 oz. maraschino
1 tbsp. (or more) sugar
6 oz. iced club soda

Cut entire peel from orange in a single strip, beginning at stem end and continuing until spiral reaches bottom. Pour wine into glass pitcher; add peach slices, lemon slices, cognac, triple sec, maraschino and sugar. Place orange peel carefully in pitcher, fastening top end of peel over rim. Let stand at room temperature for at least 1 hour. Add soda and 1 tray of ice cubes to pitcher; stir and serve in highball glasses. Yield: Six 6-oz. servings.

Mrs. Sandy Harborth, Hospitality Chm., OWC
Gunter AFB, Alabama

SANGRIA WITH PEACH BRANDY

1 bottle red wine
2 tsp. sugar
1/4 lg. bottle club soda
1 c. peach brandy
Lemon and orange slices

Combine red wine and sugar; cool thoroughly. Add soda, peach brandy and fruit slices; add ice to keep chilled. Serve in wine or brandy snifter immediately. Yield: 20 servings.

Mrs. Delmar D. Albers, Treas., Hosp., OWC
NAS, Memphis, Tennessee

AFTER SKI SPICED WINE

1 1/2 c. water
1/2 c. sugar
3 slices lemon rind
1 stick cinnamon
10 whole cloves
3 c. Burgundy

Combine water, sugar, lemon rind, cinnamon and cloves in saucepan; bring to a boil. Strain; add Burgundy. Serve in mugs. Yield: Ten 4-oz. servings.

Mrs. Karl O. Kuckhahn, Pres., OWC
Aberdeen Proving Ground, Maryland

ALASKAN CRANBERRY WINE

8 c. cranberries
1 gal. boiling water
9 c. sugar
1 oz. dry yeast

Crush cranberries in blender. Pour boiling water over cranberries; soak for 24 hours. Strain through jelly bag. Bring to boiling point; remove from heat. Add sugar; stir till dissolved. Cool to room temperature. Sprinkle yeast on top; stir. Cover; ferment for 14 days in warm place. Siphen into bottles; let sediment sink to bottom. Resiphon to clear bottles; process may take a month. Yield: 4 or 5 bottles.

Mrs. Delbert E. Smith, Parliamentarian, OWC
Elmendorf AFB, Anchorage, Alaska

ALASKAN GLUGG

12 cardamom seeds
20 whole cloves
6 sticks cinnamon
Peels of 4 tangerines
2 fifths brandy
1 fifth whiskey
1 lb. seeded muscat raisins
1/2 lb. blanched almonds
12 prunes

Place first 4 ingredients in a spice bag; simmer spice bag in 1 pint water in a large, heavy kettle for 20 to 30 minutes. Remove bag or leave in water as determined by personal preference. Add brandy, whiskey, raisins, almonds and prunes; heat for 15 minutes or to just below boiling point. Serve. If you want to serve with a flair, place 6 or 8 sugar cubes in a strainer and place above kettle. Pour warm brandy over sugar cubes and ignite. Ingredients in kettle may ignite due to volatility, so use caution. Yield: 42 servings.

Lt. David I. Scott
USCGAS, Annette, Alaska

EASY SWEDISH GLUGG

1 gal. port
3 c. raisins
Dried peel of 1 orange
3 to 5 sticks cinnamon
12 almonds
1/2 tsp. whole cloves
12 cardamom seeds
1 to 2 c. sugar
1 fifth whiskey

Combine port, raisins, orange peel, cinnamon sticks, almonds, cloves and cardamom seeds in saucepan. Bring to a boil; boil for 10 minutes. Add sugar to taste; stir until dissolved. Remove from heat; stir in whiskey. Return to heat; bring to a boil. Remove from heat; let stand for at least 12 hours. Strain port mixture; reheat to serve. Serve warm in punch cups. Yield: 15-20 servings.

Mrs. John R. Wright, Treas., OWC
USNAF, Sigonella, Sicily

GLUGG WITH VODKA

8 cinnamon sticks
8 whole cloves
15 cracked cardamom seeds
Dried peel of 1 orange
1/2 box raisins
1/4 c. blanched almonds
1 qt. pale dry sherry
1 qt. port
1 qt. 100-proof vodka
1/4 c. sugar

Tie cinnamon sticks, cloves, cardamom seeds and orange peel in cheesecloth bag. Tie raisins and almonds in second cheesecloth bag. Place both bags in large saucepan; cover with water. Simmer for 20 minutes. Remove bags; squeeze dry. Place raisins and almonds in jar; let cool. Cover; refrigerate until ready to use. Discard first cheesecloth bag. Pour wines and vodka into seasoned water; heat to steam-rising stage. Ignite; sprinkle on sugar and let burn for 1 second. Cover; remove from heat. Bottle and seal

wine mixture. Heat glugg to serve. Place several raisins and almonds in punch cups with handles; pour in warm glugg. Yield: 30 servings.

Susan Ruth Brand, Key Caller, OWC
USN Amphibious Base, Virginia Beach, Virginia

NORTH DAKOTA SWEDISH GLUGG

2 fifths claret or port
10 whole cardamom seeds
5 whole cloves
1 1/2 sticks cinnamon
5 strips orange peel
1 c. blanched almonds
1 c. raisins
1/2 lb. lump sugar
1 fifth brandy, aquavit or vodka

Empty claret into saucepan. Tie spices in square of cheesecloth. Add spice bag, orange peel, almonds cnd raisins. Cover; heat slowly to boiling point. Remove spice bag and orange peel. Serve in heated glugg pot or deep chafing dish. Place sugar on small metal grill; place over hot glugg. Pour brandy over sugar; set aflame. Burn until sugar is almost melted and flame dies. Place remaining sugar in glugg. Serve hot in punch cups with several raisins or almonds in each cup. Yield: 25 servings.

Mrs. Richard A. Miller, 2nd VP, OWC
Kelley Barracks, Stuttgart, Germany

SWEDISH HOLIDAY GLUGG

4 qt. port
1 fifth blended whiskey
3 or 4 slivers lemon peel
12 dried prunes
1/2 c. raisins
1/4 c. shelled almonds
18 opened cardamom seeds
10 to 12 whole allspice
10 to 12 whole cloves
3 or 4 sticks cinnamon
1 c. sugar

Combine all ingredients in large pan. Cover; bring to a boil. Remove from heat; let stand, covered, overnight. Strain, reserving raisins and almonds for future use. Bottle and seal. May be served hot or cold as a liqueur.

Mrs. Nathan Jack Hansen, Family Services Adv., OWC
Chanute AFB, Illinois

JIM'S GLUH WEIN

1 qt. dry red wine
4 tbsp. sugar
5 whole cloves
8 cinnamon sticks
8 lemon slices

Heat wine, sugar and cloves in heavy saucepan; do not boil. Strain off cloves. Serve in small mugs; garnish with a cinnamon stick and thin slice of lemon. Prosit! Yield: 8 servings.

Capt. Henry James Zabinski
Sembach Air Base, Germany

SPICY GLUH WEIN

3 qt. water
1 1/2 c. sugar
12 whole cloves
1/2 orange, cut in wedges
3 cinnamon sticks
2 wedges lime
1 gal. red Burgundy

Combine water and sugar in a large saucepan. Stick the cloves in the orange wedges, then add with the cinnamon sticks and lime wedges to the syrup. Boil for 15 minutes. Add Burgundy; bring to just under boiling point. Serve, adding slices of lime studded with cloves, if desired. Yield: 20 servings.

Capt. Richard H. Frantz
Seymour Johnson AFB, North Carolina

HOT MULLED BURGUNDY

1 1/2 c. boiling water
1/2 c. sugar
1/2 lemon, sliced
3 sticks cinnamon
3 whole cloves
1 lg. bottle California Burgundy or claret
Nutmeg

Combine boiling water, sugar, lemon, cinnamon and cloves; stir until sugar dissolves. Add Burgundy; simmer for 20 to 30 minutes. Do not boil. Strain; serve hot with sprinkling of nutmeg. May be made well in advance and reheated when ready to serve. Yield: 12 servings.

Mrs. R. T. Murrian, Pres., OWC
RAF, Oxfordshire, England

HOT MULLED WINE

1 c. sugar
1/2 c. water
2 sticks cinnamon
1/2 lemon, sliced
2 doz. cloves
4 c. hot lemon, orange or pineapple juice
1 qt. (or more) red wine
Lemon and pineapple slices

Combine first 5 ingredients in saucepan; boil for 5 minutes or until syrupy. Strain syrup; add to hot lemon juice. Reduce amount of sugar if very sweet fruit juice is used. Heat wine, but do not boil. Combine lemon mixture and wine; keep hot in double boiler. Serve very hot in punch cups with slices of lemon and pineapple. Yield: 12-16 servings.

Mrs. J. B. McIlhenny, Past Co-Chm. Gp. VI, OWC
Camp Lejeune, North Carolina

HOT RASPBERRY SPICED WINE

1 fifth dry white wine
1 3-oz. package raspberry gelatin
1 tbsp. lemon juice
2 sm. bay leaves
1 stick cinnamon
Dash of salt

Combine all ingredients; bring to a simmer. Serve in heatproof glasses. Yield: About 6 servings.

Mrs. Frederick J. Kirch, Past Pres., OWC
NAD, Hawthorne, Nevada

HOT SPICED WINE

4 c. cranapple juice
1/2 gal. port
1/4 c. sugar
9 or 10 whole cloves
5 or 6 cardamom seeds
6 or 7 cinnamon sticks

Combine juice, 2 cups port, sugar, cloves, cardamom seeds and half the cinnamon sticks in a medium saucepan; simmer for 10 minutes. Add remaining port and cinnamon sticks. Let stand over low heat until ready to serve. Serve hot. Good for apres ski, also at a Christmas open house!

Capt. William P. Rembacz
Hahn Air Base, Germany

MAFFETT'S HOT WINE

1 bottle red wine
3 pt. cranberry juice
1 c. water
1/2 c. sugar
3 sticks cinnamon or 1 tsp. ground
   cinnamon
Dash of nutmeg
Dash of cloves
Orange and lemon slices (opt.)

Combine all ingredients except fruit slices in heavy saucepan; heat thoroughly. Float fruit slices in hot wine. Serve in mugs on a cold afternoon and deal the cards. May be stored in refrigerator and reheated. Yield: 10 servings.

Mrs. Charles T. Bell, OWC
Seymour Johnson AFB, North Carolina

SPICY MULLED WINE

1/2 gal. vin rose wine
4 slices unpeeled orange
3 pinches of whole cloves
4 cinnamon sticks
1 tbsp. lemon extract
1 to 3 c. sugar

Combine all ingredients in large kettle. Heat; do not boil. Remove from heat; cool. Place in non-metallic containers; let stand for at least 2 days before using. Reheat before serving; do not boil. Yield: About 12 servings.

Mrs. Frederick J. Kirch, Past Pres., OWC
NAD, Hawthorne, Nevada

BRIDGE MIXER

3/4 c. apple juice or cider per serving
Cinnamon sticks
1/4 c. rose wine per serving

Heat apple juice and 3 or 4 cinnamon sticks in saucepan. Add wine; heat just to a simmer, but do not boil. Preheat mugs with boiling water. Pour wine mixture into mugs and add a fresh cinnamon stick. Serve at once.

Mrs. Richard M. Drennan, Pres., OWC
Francis E. Warren AFB, Wyoming

PARTY GLUGG

Rind of 2 oranges
2 bottles claret
10 whole cloves
2 sticks cinnamon, broken
2 c. golden raisins
15 crushed cardamom seeds
1 bottle brandy
1/2 box lump sugar
1 bottle port
1 bottle bourbon

Break orange peel into small pieces. Pour 1 bottle claret into 6-quart kettle; add orange peel, cloves, cinnamon, raisins and cardamom seeds. Cover tightly; simmer for 10 minutes. Add brandy and remaining bottle of claret. Place sugar in a large strainer; set aside. Bring claret mixture to a quick boil. Remove from heat. Ignite claret mixture; pour over sugar into another kettle until sugar is dissolved. Add port; let stand, covered, until cooled. Stir in bourbon, then pour in large container and seal. Let stand for at least 2 weeks. Strain glugg; heat thoroughly, but do not boil. Pour into wine glasses or punch cups to serve. Yield: 30 servings.

Mrs. Jan Narken, Red Gp. Gourmet Chm., OWC
Wright Patterson AFB, Ohio

SCHUSSWINE

8 oz. Lake Country Red dinner wine
Juice of 1 1/2 lemons
2 tsp. sugar
1 tbsp. angostura aromatic bitters
4 oz. water

Mix all ingredients; heat through. Serve hot in mugs.

COCKTAILS

Cocktails are often the most popular area of entertaining. They are noted for relaxing us, easing the tension, "breaking the ice" and perking up our appetites, but we certainly don't mean to insinuate their purpose is solely medicinal. They are not just a tranquilizer; they are also an exciting and delicious area of beverages.

The realm of cocktail making seems to grow yearly. Creative hosts and hostesses, like the ones who authored our following cocktail recipes, are constantly coming up with new ideas. Select some of these delicious, refreshing beverages for your next party.

BOLL WEEVIL

1/4 c. apricot brandy
1/4 c. creme de cacao
3/4 c. vanilla ice cream

Place all ingredients in blender container; blend until smooth. Serve in chilled cocktail glasses. Yield: 2 servings.

Lt. Col. Phil Serrin
Pentagon, Washington, D. C.

BULLSHOT

Juice of 1/4 lime
Dash of Worcestershire sauce
1 drop of hot sauce
1 jigger vodka
2/3 c. consomme
Pepper and salt to taste

Combine all ingredients; serve in brandy snifter over ice. Yield: 1 serving.

Mrs. William L. Rhule, Mag. Chm., OWC
Grissom AFB, Indiana

CHI-CHI DELIGHT

2 oz. vodka
2 oz. pineapple juice
1 to 1 1/2 oz. coconut syrup
Juice of 1/2 lemon

Blend all ingredients with ice; serve over crushed ice. Garnish with spear of fresh pineapple and maraschino cherry.

Mrs. Freeman A. Grant, Jr., Cookbook Chm., OWC
NAS, Barbers Point, Hawaii

CALIFORNIA CHI-CHI

6 oz. vodka
4 tbsp. coconut syurp
12 oz. pineapple juice

Place all ingredients in blender filled with crushed ice; blend. Serve in cocktail glasses; garnish each with pineapple spear, cherry and mint sprig. Yield: 4 servings.

Mrs. Ian Birnie, W and M Chm., OWC
Castle AFB, Merced, California

R AND R CHI-CHI

2 2-oz. jiggers coconut syrup
2 2-oz. jiggers pineapple juice
1 2-oz. jigger light rum

Dash of triple sec
1 c. crushed ice
1 long spear fresh pineapple

Place first 5 ingredients in shaker in order listed; shake till cool. Pour into wide-mouth stem glass; garnish with pineapple.

Mrs. John Doglione, Pres., OWC
Travis AFB, Vacaville, California

APPLE-CHAMPAGNE COCKTAIL

1 qt. chilled apple juice
1 qt. chilled champagne
16 maraschino cherries
16 twists of lemon peel

Combine apple juice and champagne; pour into champagne glasses. Place cherry and twist of lemon peel in each glass. Yield: Sixteen 1/2-cup servings.

CHAMPAGNE COCKTAIL

1 lump sugar
1 or 2 drops of angostura bitters
1 1/2 tsp. brandy
Champagne
Spiral rind of 1/2 lemon

Place sugar in champagne glass; sprinkle with angostura bitters. Add brandy; fill glass with champagne. Add lemon rind and serve immediately. Yield: 1 serving.

Mrs. Charles A. Bell, OWC
Maxwell AFB, Alabama

EASY FROZEN DAIQUIRI

1 6-oz. can frozen limeade concentrate
6 oz. light rum
Ice cubes

Combine frozen limeade concentrate and rum in blender; fill blender with ice cubes. Blend until ingredients are well mixed and ice is completely crushed. Yield: 3-4 servings.

Mrs. Sam S. Ryburn, Jr., Sec., OWC
San Vito Air Station, Brindisi, Italy

FREEZER DAIQUIRI

1 can lemonade concentrate
10 oz. light rum
20 ice cubes
10 to 12 maraschino cherries with stems

Combine lemonade and rum in blender container; blend well. Add ice cubes gradually. After 4 to 5 cubes have been blended into mixture, pour half the mixture into freezer container. Blend remaining cubes with mixture in blender. May be frozen until ready to serve. Stir well. Serve in cocktail glasses garnished with cherries. Yield: 10-12 servings.

Mrs. Fred E. Robbins, OWC
Ft. MacArthur, California

FROZEN CHERRY DAIQUIRIS

1 sm. can frozen lemonade
2 tsp. sugar
1 maraschino cherry
1 tsp. cherry juice
Few drops of red food coloring
3/4 c. light rum
1 to 1 1/2 trays ice cubes, crushed

Combine all ingredients in blender container. Blend until ice is like slush. Pour into container and cover; store in freezer until ready for use. Keeps for 2 weeks. Stir before serving. Limeade may be substituted for lemonade, using green food coloring. Yield: 1 quart.

Mrs. James H. Hindmarsh, OWC
Montauk AFS, New York

FROZEN PARTY STRAWBERRY DAIQUIRIS

1 6-oz. can frozen lemonade
1 pkg. frozen strawberries
6 oz. rum

Combine lemonade, strawberries and rum in blender container; blend, adding crushed ice gradually, until mixture is smooth and of desired thickness. Serve in cocktail glasses. Raspberries or peaches may be substituted for strawberries. Yield: Eight 4-oz. servings.

Mrs. Stephen M. Horn
Asst Treas., Youth Coord., OWC
Tachikawa AFB, Japan

HAWAIIAN DAIQUIRI

3 oz. frozen limeade concentrate
4 oz. light rum
2 oz. grenadine
1/2 c. crushed pineapple

Place all ingredients in blender container with 2 cups ice cubes; blend at low speed until ice cubes are crushed. Blend at high speed for 1 to 2 minutes. For variety, half a banana may be substituted for pineapple. Serve in cocktail glasses. Yield: 4 servings.

Mrs. Ray E. Huebner, Sp. Act. Chm., OWC
Ft. Monmouth, New Jersey

MAKE-AHEAD STRAWBERRY DAIQUIRIS

1 6-oz. can frozen limeade
1 6-oz. limeade can light rum
1/2 16-oz. package frozen whole
  strawberries
1 c. cracked ice

Combine all ingredients in blender container; blend until smooth. May store unused mixture in freezer. May be frozen in plastic containers until served. Yield: 6-8 servings.

Mrs. Larry Henry, Pres., OWC
Roeblinnen Germany

LIGHT STRAWBERRY DAIQUIRI

1   10 1/2-oz. pkg. frozen strawberries
1   6-oz. can frozen limeade
1   6-oz. can white rum

Combine strawberries, limeade, rum, 6 ounces water with 1/2 tray of ice cubes in blender container. Blend thoroughly until smooth and all ice is crushed. Serve in champagne glasses. Yield: 8 servings.

Mrs. Peter J. Luther, Asst. Treas., O and CWC
Camp Darby, Leghorn, Italy

LIME FROZEN DAIQUIRI

6 oz. frozen lime juice
6 oz. rum
1 bottle maraschino cherries

Combine lime juice and rum in a blender; blend for 5 seconds. Add crushed ice to blender, allowing 1 1/2 inches free space from ice to top of blender. Blend for 10 seconds. Serve in long-stemmed glasses, garnished with maraschino cherries. Yield: 4-6 servings.

Mrs. Douglas W. Curtis, Jr., VP, 570th Ladies Gp.
USAAG, Handorf, Germany

PINK STRAWBERRY DAIQUIRI

1 sm. can frozen pink lemonade
1/2 pkg. frozen strawberries
6 oz. brandy
6 oz. rum

Combine lemonade, strawberries, brandy and rum in blender container; fill to top with crushed ice. Blend until smooth and all ice is crushed. Serve immediately in champagne glasses. Yield: 8 servings.

Mrs. George W. Cherry, Corr. Sec., OWC
Langley AFB, Virginia

PERFECT DAIQUIRI

1   6-oz. can frozen limeade concentrate
6 oz. rum

1 tbsp. confectioners' sugar
Ice

Combine limeade and rum in blender container; add confectioners' sugar. Blend well, adding 1 tray of ice gradually until mixture thickens. May be stored in freezer until ready to serve. Serve in champagne glasses. Yield: 6 servings.

Mrs. Pat Pickett, Corr. Sec., Cookbook Chm., OWC
Lemoore NAS, California

ONE-TWO-THREE DAIQUIRI

1   6-oz. juice can rum
2   6-oz. cans frozen concentrated lime juice
3   6-oz. juice cans water

Combine all ingredients in container; cover. Blend well. Store in freezer until slushy. Pour into chilled cocktail glasses; serve immediately. Whiskey may be substituted for rum and lemonade for lime juice to make a One-Two-Three Whiskey Sour. Yield: 9 servings.

Mrs. Robert M. Anttila, OWC
Norfolk Naval Station, Virginia

QUICK FROZEN DAIQUIRI

1 sm. can frozen limeade
1 sm. can rum
Ice cubes

Combine limeade and rum in blender container. Blend well, adding ice cubes, one at a time, until desired thickness is reached. Serve in champagne glasses. Yield: 6 servings.

Mrs. Betty Johnston
Thrift Shop Chm., Wiesbaden Area OWC
Lindsey Air Station, Wiesbaden, Germany

SHERBET SURPRISE

5 oz. light rum
2 packets daiquiri mix
1 pt. sherbet

Combine rum and daiquiri mix in heavy-duty blender; mix briefly. Add sherbet; blend until smooth. Fill remainder of blender container with crushed ice; blend until smooth, stirring so all pieces of ice are blended. Yield: 16 servings.

Mrs. Richard Dunbar, Ombudsman, OWC
Long Beach Naval Shipyard, Long Beach, California

SMOOTH FROZEN DAIQUIRI

Cracked ice
1 6-oz. can frozen limeade
6 oz. white rum
1 to 2 tsp. sugar (opt.)

Fill blender with cracked ice, add limeade, rum and sugar. Blend at medium to high speed for 1 minute. May be stored in freezer until ready to serve. Serve in cocktail glasses. Yield: 4 servings.

Mrs. John F. Schneider, Pres., OWC
Ft. Campbell, Kentucky

LEMON-STRAWBERRY DAIQUIRI

8 oz. frozen strawberries, thawed
Juice of 2 lemons
1/2 c. light rum
10 ice cubes

Combine strawberries, lemon juice and rum in blender container; add ice gradually. Blend until thickened and ice is crushed. Serve in daiquiri or champagne glasses. Yield: 6 servings.

Mrs. Christie F. Treat, Newsletter Ed., OWC
Daley Barracks, Bad Kissingen, Germany

DRILLER'S DELIGHT

1 oz. lemon juice
1 tsp. sugar
1 oz. gin or vodka
1 egg
Splash of orange juice
Splash of cream or half and half
Dash of orange flower water

Mix all ingredients well in blender with cracked ice; serve immediately.

Lt. Walt Cunningham
USN Dental, Taipei, Taiwan

EXOTIC MOKIHANA

3/4 oz. grenadine
3/4 oz. orange curacao
1 oz. light rum
1 oz. dark rum
2 oz. lemon juice
1 1/2 oz. pineapple juice
151-proof rum

Pour grenadine, curacao, light rum, dark rum, lemon juice and pineapple juice over crushed ice in double old-fashioned glass. Garnish with pineapple finger, lemon wheel or cherry. Top off glass with 151-proof rum. Yield: 1 serving.

Mrs. Sandra Swofford, OWC
Ansbach, Germany

FROZEN BLUE HAWAII

1 c. rum
2 c. Tahiti Joe's Blue Hawaii mix
1/2 c. crushed pineapple
1/4 c. sugar

Combine rum, mix, pineapple, sugar and 1 tray of ice in blender container; blend until mixture is slushy. Pour into clear cocktail glasses; garnish with maraschino cherries. Yield: 8 servings.

Judith S. Barrett, OWC
Wheeler AFB, Hawaii

HELEN'S SOMETHING PINK

1 6-oz. can frozen pink lemonade
1 6-oz. lemonade can gin
1 6-oz. lemonade can milk
1 egg

Place pink lemonade in blender container; add gin, milk and egg. Blend until frothy. Pour into large wine glasses or whiskey sour glasses; serve immediately. Yield: 4 servings.

Mrs. John Doglione, Pres., OWC
Travis AFB, California

HENRY WALLSLAMMER

1 1/2 jiggers gin
1/2 jigger dark rum
Orange juice
Galliano to taste

Combine gin and rum in tall glass over ice; add orange juice. Float Galliano on top; stir gently. Yield: 1 serving.

Capt. Bob Brunsman, Chief, Career Control Sect.
Hahn AFB, Germany

HONOLULU SIPPER

2 oz. bourbon
Pineapple juice

1 pineapple spear
1 slice lime

Place cracked ice in tall glass; add bourbon. Fill with pineapple juice; garnish with pineapple spear and lime slice. Serve with straw. Yield: 1 serving.

Bobbi Dozzo, Ed., OWC
Westover AFB, Massachusetts

JOE'S MARTINIS

16 oz. gin
4 oz. dry vermouth
1 1/2 to 2 oz. water
2 juniper berries

Combine all ingredients; pour into 1-quart bottle. Place in freezer compartment of refrigerator for at least 4 hours or until icy. Yield: 8-10 servings.

Mrs. William J. Ryland, Pres., OWC
Fort Riley, Kansas

JOHN'S MARGARITA

4 oz. tequila
2 oz. Cointreau or triple sec
1 oz. Rose's lime juice
1 oz. lemon juice

Mix all ingredients in shaker with several ice cubes. Pour mixture into salt-rimmed cocktail glass, discarding ice cubes. Yield: 2 servings.

Mrs. John R. Wright, Treas., Sigonella OWC
USNAF, Sigonella, Sicily

MAI TAI COOLER

1 oz. light rum
1 oz. dark rum
2 oz. orange or pineapple juice
1 1/2 oz. Mai Tai mix
1 splash orgeat syrup
1 splash orange curacao
1 splash grenadine syrup
1 pineapple spear
1 orange slice
1 cherry
1/2 oz. 151-proof rum

Combine all ingredients except fruits and 151-proof rum in Mai Tai glass; add crushed ice to fill glass to within 1 1/2 inches from top.

Mix well. Add pineapple spear, orange slice and cherry. Add more crushed ice to fill glass to within 1/4-inch from top. Do not mix. Pour 151-proof rum on top. Use straw and sip slowly from bottom of glass.

Mrs. Robert M. Anttila, Supply Corps OWC
Norfolk Naval Station, Norfolk, Virginia

MAI TAI SUPERB

1 oz. lemon juice
1 oz. pineapple juice
1 oz. passion fruit nectar
1 oz. orgeat syrup
1/2 oz. orange curacao
1 oz. dark rum
1 1/2 oz. light rum

Mix all ingredients; serve over crushed ice. Yield: 1 serving.

Mrs. Margery Connor, OWC
NATO, Keflavik, Iceland

TROPICAL MAI TAI

1 1/2 oz. light rum
1 1/2 oz. dark rum
1 oz. orgeat syrup
1/2 oz. lemon juice
1/2 oz. lime juice
1/2 oz. orange curacao
1/2 oz. 151-proof rum

Fill 15-ounce glass with ice; add light rum, dark rum, syrup, juices and curacao. Float 151-proof rum on top. Garnish with cherry and pineapple slice. Yield: 1 serving.

Cmdr. Charles W. Lord, SC, USN
Ships Parts Control Center
Mechanicsburg, Pennsylvania

VIP MAI TAI

3 oz. medium rum
1 tsp. orgeat syrup
1 tsp. orange curacao
Fresh pineapple stick

Fill double old-fashioned glass with crushed ice. Add rum and orgeat syrup; stir. Float curacao on top. Add fresh pineapple stick stirrer.

Mrs. Lorraine Cummins, Awa Lau Wahine Wives Club
Honolulu, Hawaii

MISAWA MAZE

1 1/2 to 2 jiggers vodka
1/2 tsp. Scotch whisky
Tonic water

Pour vodka into highball glass. Add Scotch whisky and ice; fill glass with tonic water. Stir very gently; sip slowly.

Mrs. Joyce Stephens, Pres., OWC
Misawa AFB, Japan

MISSIONARY'S DOWNFALL

1 oz. light Puerto Rican rum
1/2 oz. peach liqueur
1/2 oz. fresh lime juice
1/2 oz. honey
2 oz. fresh or canned pineapple chunks
Mint leaves to taste

Combine all ingredients in blender container with cracked ice; blend well. Serve in cocktail glasses; garnish with additional mint leaves. Yield: 1 serving.

Mrs. Ralph P. Swofford, III, OWC
Ansbach, Germany

HAWAIIAN COCKTAIL

1 c. pineapple juice
1/2 c. orange juice
1/4 c. lemon juice
1 qt. ginger ale
6 to 8 jiggers vodka

Combine juices; chill. Add ginger ale and vodka just before serving. Garnish with lemon slices or pineapple spears, if desired; serve immediately.

NEGRONI COCKTAIL

1 oz. gin
1 oz. dry Compari
1 oz. sweet fortified vermouth
1/2 fresh orange slice

Combine gin, Compari, vermouth and crushed ice in blender; blend until smooth. Serve in chilled stemmed cocktail glass. Garnish with orange. Yield: 1 serving.

Mrs. John C. Donahue, Hon. Pres., OWC
Naval Weapons Station, Concord, California

MIODUSKI LUAU

1/2 c. rum or bourbon
1 3-oz. can frozen pineapple punch or
*   lemonade*
2 tbsp. orange juice concentrate
1 ripe banana
2 tsp. maraschino cherry juice

Combine all ingredients in blender container; blend until smooth. Add crushed ice gradually, blending to consistency of soft sherbet. Yield: 4 servings.

Capt. Henry X. Mioduski, II
Goodfellow AFB, San Angelo, Texas

PARADISE COCKTAIL

2 oz. gin
2 oz. apricot brandy
6 oz. orange juice

Combine gin, brandy and orange juice in blender container; add 1 tray of ice. Blend well. Serve in champagne glasses. Yield: 4 servings.

Bobbi Dozzo, Ed., OWC
Westover AFB, Massachusetts

ORANGE AU GO-GO

2 tsp. grenadine
1 jigger orange juice
Juice of 2 limes
2 jiggers light rum
1 c. crushed ice

Combine all ingredients in blender container. Blend for about 2 minutes or to desired consistency. Serve in cocktail glasses. Yield: 2 servings.

Mrs. Lawrence Fay, Bazaar Chm., NOWC
Charleston Naval Base, Charleston, South Carolina

PEACH SEVENTY-FIVE

1 sm. box frozen peaches
6 oz. brandy
6 oz. rum
1 sm. can frozen lemonade

Combine peaches, brandy, rum, lemonade and cracked ice in blender; blend until frothy. Serve in champagne glasses; garnish with mint. Yield: 8 servings.

Mrs. George W. Cherry, Corr. Sec., OWC
Langley AFB, Hampton, Virginia

PINA COLADA

1 tbsp. light corn syrup
1 tsp. Rose's lime juice
1 1/2 jiggers light rum
1 1/2 jiggers canned coconut milk
Dash of cream
9 chunks pineapple
1 tbsp. pineapple juice

Combine corn syrup, lime juice, rum, coconut milk, cream and 5 to 7 ice cubes in blender container. Blend until almost slushy. Add pineapple and pineapple juice to mixture in blender; blend until pineapple is coarsely shredded. Pour into punch cups; serve. Yield: 2 servings.

Mrs. William C. Angermar, Pres., Bad Kissingen OWC
Bad Kissingen, Germany

PINK PUSSYCAT

3/4 oz. unsweetened grapefruit juice
3/4 oz. cranberry juice
1 1/2 oz. gin or vodka

1 1/2 tsp. sugar
Juice of 1/4 lime

Combine all ingredients in shaker over cracked ice. Shake well. Serve in old-fashioned glass. Yield: 2 servings.

Mrs. Paul F. Cottrell, Pres., OWC
Seymour Johnson AFB, North Carolina

RED ROCKET

1 jigger bourbon
5 oz. cranberry juice

Fill highball glass with ice cubes; add bourbon. Fill glass with cranberry juice. Yield: 1 serving.

Mrs. R. Y. McBurney, Hon. Adv., OWC
Shaw AFB, South Carolina

TEST PILOT

1 oz. 151-proof rum
3/4 oz. dark Puerto Rican rum
3/4 oz. dark Jamaican rum
3/4 oz. honey
3/4 oz. orange juice
1/4 oz. fresh lime juice
2 dashes of angostura bitters
2 dashes of grenadine

Combine all ingredients in blender container with cracked ice; blend well. Serve in double old-fashioned glass. Garnish with pineapple stick, lime slice and cherry. Yield: 1 serving.

Mrs. Ralph P. Swofford, III, OWC
Ansbach, Germany

TWENTY-FOUR HOUR DELIGHT

Juice of 1 doz. lemons
1/2 doz. lemon rinds
1 fifth bourbon
1 1/3 c. sugar
3 c. carbonated water

Pour lemon juice into glass container; add lemon rinds, bourbon and sugar. Place in refrigerator for 24 hours, stirring frequently to dissolve sugar. Remove rinds; squeeze out all liquid. Add carbonated water; serve in cocktail glasses. Yield: 24 servings.

Mrs. John Quesinberry, 1st VP, OWC
March AFB, California

PUNCHES

Making and serving punch seems to be the ladies' area, done
mostly at female gatherings. This is an appropriate way to
serve punch, of course, but it's rather unfortunate that
punch isn't served for many other occasions too. A good
punch has all the attributes of any mixed drink and often
more. Punch can be made in and served from one large
container, which often makes hosting much easier.
But aside from convenience, punch often has more eye
appeal than ordinary drinks. What could be more appetizing
than fresh fruit slices and pink chunks of ice floating in
a delectable liquid.

Punch doesn't always have to be served from a cut glass
punch bowl. Guests won't mind if you serve it from
pitchers or even gallon jugs on picnic tables, especially
if the punch you serve is from one of our following recipes.

BIG CRANBERRY SLUSH

1 qt. cranberry juice
2 cans frozen limeade
1 c. vodka

Blend all ingredients together in large bowl; freeze to slush stage. Place in blender container; blend until smooth. Serve in wine glasses. Yield: 12 servings.

Mrs. Vivian C. Redfield, OWC
Chanute AFB, Illinois

BOURBON-TEA PUNCH

1 c. sugar
1 1/2 c. lemon juice
2 fifths bourbon
1 qt. strong tea, chilled
2 lg. bottles club soda, chilled

Dissolve sugar in lemon juice, stirring well; add bourbon and tea. Pour over block of ice in punch bowl; stir in club soda. Garnish with fruit slices, if desired. Yield: 45 servings.

Mrs. Pat Pickett, Cookbook Chm., OWC
NAS, Lemoore, California

BRANDY-CHAMPAGNE PUNCH

1 c. sugar
1/2 c. lemon juice
3 oz. brandy
3 oz. orange curacao
1 lg. bottle club soda
3 bottles champagne

Combine sugar and lemon juice with 1/2 cup water; stir until sugar is dissolved. Pour sugar mixture over block of ice in punch bowl; add brandy and curacao. Stir in soda and champagne just before serving. Yield: 36 servings.

Mrs. Pat Pickett, Cookbook Chm., OWC
NAS, Lemoore, California

BUDDHA PUNCH

Ice ring
1 qt. Rhine wine
1 c. orange juice
1 c. lemon juice
3 oz. orange curacao
3 oz. rum
Angostura bitters to taste
1 qt. carbonated water
1 qt. champagne

Freeze water in mold to make ice ring. Combine Rhine wine, orange juice, lemon juice, curacao, rum and bitters in punch bowl. Add carbonated water and champagne just before serving. Float ice ring in punch; garnish with slices of oranges and lemon. Serve in punch cups. Yield: 10 servings.

Mrs. Elizabeth B. Swan, OWC
Ft. McClellan, Alabama

CAVALRY PUNCH

1/2 c. lemon juice
3 lemons, sliced
1/2 c. curacao
2 c. Tokay wine or port
1 qt. rum
1 qt. brandy
1 can pineapple chunks
2 c. strong tea
1 cinnamon stick
Dash of nutmeg
1 1/2 c. sugar
4 qt. champagne, chilled

Mix all ingredients except champagne; chill for 24 hours to age properly. Add champagne just before serving. This was served to the Officers and Ladies of the 9th U. S. Cavalry, Fort Robinson, Nebraska at a Regimental Ball on 10 June, 1893. Yield: 30 servings.

Maj. William J. Ryland
Fort Riley, Kansas

ANNIVERSARY CHAMPAGNE PUNCH

1 bottle champagne
1/2 c. sugar
1 c. fresh lemon juice
2 c. apple juice
2 c. orange juice
2 12-oz. cans lemon-lime carbonated drink

Chill champagne for at least 4 hours. Combine sugar and fruit juices; stir until sugar is dissolved. Chill well. Add champagne and carbonated drink just before serving. Yield: 25 punch cups.

Mrs. Sherill Allen, OWC
Athenai Airport, Athens, Greece

BRIGHT CHAMPAGNE PUNCH

1/2 gal. sauterne
1 qt. ginger ale
1 qt. club soda
Squeeze of lemon
1 1/2 bottles champagne

Combine sauterne, ginger ale, club soda and lemon juice; mix well. Pour over ice in large punch bowl. Add champagne; serve immediately. Yield: 75 punch cups.

Mrs. Nancy Teri Suehs, NOWC
NAVSTA ADAK, Alaska

BUBBLY CHAMPAGNE PUNCH

1 bottle sauterne
1 bottle dry champagne
1 bottle sparkling water
2 jiggers curacao
2 jiggers brandy
2 jiggers sugar

Chill sauterne, champagne and sparkling water. Place curacao, brandy and sugar in punch bowl; stir well. Add sauterne, champagne and sparkling water; serve. May be prepared as needed so effervescence won't be lost.

Mrs. Thomas M. Parker, OWC
Bainbridge Naval Tng. Ctr., Bainbridge, Maryland

CHAMPAGNE COOL AID

4 oz. triple sec
8 oz. brandy
1 bottle sauterne
1/4 bottle soda water
2 bottles champagne

Allow ice to cool punch bowl. Add all ingredients to punch bowl in order listed; add maraschino cherry juice for holiday coloring, if desired. Yield: 15 servings.

Col. Worth M. Speed
Richards-Gebaur AFB, Grandview, Missouri

CHRISTMAS CHAMPAGNE PUNCH

1 jar cherries
1 fifth champagne
1 fifth sauterne
2 sm. bottles club soda
1 orange, sliced thin
1 lemon, sliced thin

Place cherries, cherry juice and water in mold; freeze for 24 hours. Mix champagne and sauterne in punch bowl; stir in club soda. Add ice mold and orange and lemon slices.

Mrs. Richard M. Doucet, Rec. Sec., OWC
Grissom AFB, Indiana

CHRISTMAS CHEER

1 fifth champagne
1 qt. cranberry juice
1/2 qt. soda water
Lemon or lime slices

Pour champagne, cranberry juice and soda water over ice block in punch bowl; float lemon slices in punch. Yield: 8 servings.

Mrs. Thomas L. Waters, Pres., OWC
Ft. Hood, Texas

COMFORTING CHAMPAGNE PUNCH

2 qt. champagne
1 fifth Southern Comfort
1 qt. sparkling water
Dash of angostura bitters
3/4 c. lemon or lime juice
Ice ring

Mix first 5 ingredients; pour over ice ring in punch bowl. May be garnished with fruits or fruits may be frozen in ice ring.

Mrs. Robert Boughn, Hon. Pres., OWC
Fort MacArthur, California

ROSY CHAMPAGNE BRIDAL PUNCH

1/2 c. sugar
2 c. water
1 1-pt. 2-oz. can pineapple juice
1 1-qt. bottle cranberry juice cocktail
1 6-oz. can frozen lemonade concentrate
1 fifth champagne
Lemon slice twists
Clusters of seedless grapes

Mix sugar and water in saucepan; heat until sugar is dissolved, stirring constantly. Cool. Combine with juices and lemonade concentrate;

chill. Pour over block of ice in punch bowl. Pour in champagne just before serving; garnish with lemon slice twists and clusters of grapes. Yield: 24 punch cups.

Mrs. Richard M. Doucet, Rec. Sec., OWC
Grissom AFB, Indiana

PINK CHAMPAGNE PUNCH

1 qt. fresh or frozen strawberries
1/2 c. sugar
3 oz. brandy
1 bottle sauterne
2 qt. pink champagne, chilled
1 bottle sparkling water, chilled

Cover strawberries with sugar. Add brandy and sauterne; let stand for 1 hour. Add ice; stir. Add pink champagne and sparkling water. Yield: 15 servings.

Mrs. Malcolm L. Landess, Adv., OWC
Castle AFB, California

PINEAPPLE-CHAMPAGNE PUNCH

Juice of 1 doz. lemons
3 qt. ice water
4 c. sugar
1 whole pineapple, pureed in blender
1 qt. dry sauterne
1 qt. champagne

Mix lemon juice and ice water. Mix sugar and pineapple; stir into lemon mixture. Pour in sauterne and champagne just before serving; may be garnished with sliced strawberries. Yield: 30 punch cups.

Mrs. Herbert W. Stewart, W and M Chm., OWC
Charleston AFB, South Carolina

LEMON-CHAMPAGNE PUNCH

1 12-oz. can frozen lemonade
1 46-oz. can unsweetened pineapple
*   juice*
1 bottle Rhine wine
Ice mold
2 bottles inexpensive champagne
1 10-oz. package frozen whole
*   strawberries, thawed*

Mix lemonade, pineapple juice and wine in punch bowl; add ice mold. Add champagne and

strawberries just before serving. Yield: 50 punch cups.

Mrs. Patricia A. Thisted, Pub. Rel. Chm., OWC
McGuire AFB, New Jersey

EASY CHAMPAGNE PUNCH

1/4 gal. lime or raspberry sherbet
1 qt. ginger ale
1 qt. champagne

Spoon sherbet into punch bowl. Pour ginger ale and champagne over sherbet. Yield: 16 punch cups.

Mrs. Gwen Jenks, POW-MIA Rep., OWC
Williams AFB, Arizona

BANANA-STRAWBERRY PUNCH

1 box. fresh strawberries
5 bananas, peeled
1/3 c. sugar
1 qt. extra dry champagne or ginger ale,
*   chilled*
1 pt. pineapple sherbet (opt.)

Wash and cap strawberries. Blend 4 bananas with strawberries and sugar with electric mixer or in blender. Pour into punch bowl; add champagne. Top with mounds of sherbet. Slice remaining banana; add to punch. Garnish with several whole or halved strawberries. Yield: 10-12 punch cup servings.

TROPICAL CHAMPAGNE PUNCH

1/4 c. sugar
3 tbsp. lemon juice
2 c. pineapple juice
2 c. sauterne, chilled
1 bottle champagne

Combine sugar, lemon juice, pineapple juice and sauterne; chill thoroughly. Place ice in 4 to 6 pilsner glasses; divide punch equally among glasses. Fill each glass to brim with champagne just before serving. Yield: 18-20 servings.

Mrs. H. H. Henderson, Pres., OWC
JUSMMAT, Ankara, Turkey

ZESTY CHAMPAGNE PUNCH

1/4 c. white corn syrup
1/4 c. Cointreau
1/4 c. brandy
2 fifths champagne
1 qt. club soda
1 fifth sauterne

Combine corn syrup, Cointreau and brandy; mix well. Pour into punch bowl; add champagne, soda and sauterne. Add ice; serve. Yield: 40 punch cups.

Mrs. R. E. Fredrick, OWC
NAS, Barbers Point, Hawaii

CHERRY-BOURBON PUNCH

1 fifth bourbon, chilled
1 12-oz. can orange juice concentrate
1 12-oz. can lemonade concentrate
2/3 c. maraschino cherry juice
3 28-oz. bottles club soda, chilled

Combine bourbon, orange juice, lemonade and cherry juice in large punch bowl; stir until thoroughly blended. Stir in soda just to mix. An ice ring with sliced lemons or oranges may be floated in punch, if desired. Serve in Tom Collins glasses. Yield: 16-20 servings.

Mrs. Charles F. Bernhardt, Jr., Publ. Chm., OWC
Webb AFB, Texas

TANGY CHI-CHI PUNCH

1 oz. vodka
Sweet and sour mix to taste

1 to 2 tbsp. coconut syrup
Milk
Pineapple juice
Pineapple wedge
Cherry

Combine vodka, sweet and sour mix, coconut syrup and small amount of milk in Mai Tai glass; stir well. Add crushed ice and enough pineapple juice to fill glass; stir. Garnish with pineapple wedge and cherry on pick. Yield: 1 serving.

Mrs. Raymond K. Seip, Reservations Chm., OWC
Wheeler AFB, Hawaii

CHAMPAGNE BRUNCH PUNCH

2 fifths extra dry or pink champagne
1 qt. orange sherbet

Chill champagne. Allow sherbet to stand at room temperature for 30 to 40 minutes or until quite soft. Place sherbet in punch bowl. Add champagne; stir lightly. Raspberry, lemon or pineapple sherbet may be substituted for orange sherbet. Yield: 25 punch cups.

Mrs. Freeman A. Grant, Jr., Cookbook Chm., OWC
NAS, Barbers Point, Hawaii

MOCHA CHOCOLATE FLUFF

1/2 c. strong coffee
2 1/2 10-oz. chocolate bars
5 or 6 ice cubes
1 pt. chocolate ice cream
1 c. bourbon

Combine coffee and 2 chocolate bars in blender container; blend until smooth. Add ice cubes, one at a time, blending well. Add ice cream and bourbon; blend until smooth. Shave remaining chocolate bar; garnish each glass with shavings. Yield: 4 servings.

Mrs. James N. Posey, W and M Chm., OWC
Ellsworth AFB, South Dakota

COFFEE PUNCH

2 trays coffee ice cubes
1 qt. vanilla ice cream
Rum to taste

Crush 1 tray ice cubes; blend in ice cream 30 minutes before serving. Crush remaining ice cubes; add to ice cream mixture just before serving. Stir in rum. Serve in coffee mugs. Yield: 8 servings.

Mrs. I. Lorraine Cummins, Awa Lau Wahine Wives Club
Pearl Harbor, Honolulu, Hawaii

VODKA CHI-CHI PUNCH

8 oz. pineapple juice
2 oz. coconut syrup
1 1/2 oz. vodka
1/2 oz. gin
1/2 oz. lemon juice

Combine all ingredients in cocktail shaker; shake with crushed ice. Serve in tall glass; garnish with fresh pineapple spear and cherry. Yield: 1 serving.

Mrs. Thomas L. Waters, Pres., OWC
Ft. Hood, Texas

CRANBERRY-COLD DUCK PUNCH

2 bottles cold duck
1 qt. cranberry juice
1 28-oz. bottle club soda

Chill all ingredients; pour over a block of ice in punch bowl. Serve in punch cups. Yield: 29 servings.

Mrs. Edwin R. Cliatt, Welfare Treas., OWC
F. E. Warren AFB, Wyoming

FRESH CITRUS FRUIT PUNCH

1 qt. water
1 1/4 c. sugar
1 c. fresh lemon juice
Lemon peels to taste
1 1/2 c. fresh grapefruit juice
3 c. fresh orange juice
2/3 c. fresh lime juice
2 12-oz. bottles ginger ale
2 bottles sauterne

Combine water, sugar and lemon juice. Bring to boiling point; boil for 2 minutes. Add lemon peels; let stand for 2 minutes. Remove peels; discard. Cool syrup. Add remaining ingredients; pour into punch bowl over ice. Garnish with fresh orange, lemon and lime slices and fresh mint. Yield: 5 quarts.

CHRISTMAS PUNCH

2 qt. cranberry juice
2 qt. pineapple juice
1/2 c. sugar
1 qt. vodka
2 qt. ginger ale
Orange and lemon slices

Combine cranberry juice, pineapple juice and sugar in punch bowl; add vodka, ginger ale, orange and lemon slices. Add enough ice to chill well. Serve in punch cups. Yield: 56 servings.

Mrs. Karl O. Kuckhahn, Pres., OWC
Aberdeen Proving Ground, Maryland

COLD DUCK-SAUTERNE PUNCH

Strawberries
Peach slices
1/2 fifth brandy
3 bottles sauterne
1 lg. bottle club soda
3 bottles cold duck

Prepare ice ring using strawberries and peaches. Pour brandy and sauterne over block of ice in punch bowl. Stir in club soda and cold duck just before serving. Float ice ring in punch. Serve in champagne glass. Yield: 6 servings.

Mrs. J. A. Simmons, Cookbook Chm., OWC
Camp Lejeune Marine Corps Base, North Carolina

DAIQUIRI PARTY PUNCH

1 6-oz. can frozen limeade
1 can frozen daiquiri mix
2 1-qt. bottles lemon-lime carbonated
    beverage
1 1-pt. bottle club soda
1/2 fifth rum

Combine all ingredients in order listed; blend thoroughly. Chill well; serve over ice. Float lime slices on top, if desired. Serve in punch cups. Yield: 24 servings.

Mrs. Jane Bentley, Sp. Act. Chm., OWC
McChord AFB, Washington

EASY DAIQUIRI PUNCH

3 lg. bottles Tom Collins mix
3 6-oz. bottles ginger ale
2 cans frozen daiquiri mix or 1 bottle
    daiquiri mix
1 pt. light rum

Combine all ingredients; chill thoroughly. Pour over ice ring. Serve in punch cups. Yield: 27 servings.

Mrs. Michael Kennedy, Corr. Sec., OWC
Homestead AFB, Florida

COOL SMOOTHIE

2 fifths Catawba white wine
1 qt. club soda
1 qt. pale ginger ale
1 fifth bourbon

Combine all ingredients in order listed in punch bowl; blend well. Garnish with ice mold. Serve in punch cups. Yield: 25 servings.

Mrs. Patricia E. Schelhorn, Pres.
Transportation Corps Wives Club
Washington, D. C.

CURACAO-BRANDY PUNCH

2 c. lemon juice
1 1/2 c. orange juice
1 1/2 c. sugar
2 c. orange curacao
3 oz. grenadine
2 fifths brandy
2 lg. bottles club soda, chilled

Combine lemon juice, orange juice and sugar; stir until sugar is dissolved. Add curacao, grenadine and brandy; mix well. Pour over block of ice in punch bowl. Stir in club soda just before serving. Yield: 45 servings.

Mrs. Pat Pickett, Cookbook Chm., OWC
NAS, Lemoore, California

POTENT DAIQUIRI PUNCH

2 1/2 c. white rum
1/2 c. Cointreau
1 c. dry vermouth
2 cans frozen daiquiri mix
3 tbsp. sugar
3 1/2 c. club soda

Combine first 5 ingredients in punch bowl; add ice. Add soda; mix thoroughly. Frozen limeade may be substituted for daiquiri mix, if desired. Serve in punch cups. Yield: 20 servings.

Mrs. Janet Long LaGrassa, Publ. Chm., OWC
Hawkins Barracks, Oberammergau, Germany

EASY SHERRY PUNCH

5 fifths dry sherry
7 cans frozen lemonade, thawed
1 bottle Tom Collins mix

Combine 1 fifth sherry and 2 cans frozen lemonade. Pour into ring mold; garnish with desired fruit slices. Freeze overnight. Combine remaining sherry, remaining lemonade and Tom Collins mix in punch bowl. Float ice ring in punch. Serve in punch cups.

Mrs. R. S. Siefken, 1st VP, OWC
Laughlin AFB, Texas

FESTIVE EGGNOG

12 eggs, separated
1 c. sugar
1/2 c. brandy
1/4 c. peach brandy
1 1/2 c. whiskey
1 1/2 qt. milk
1 1/4 tsp. nutmeg

Beat egg yolks until thick and lemon colored; add sugar gradually. Add brandy drop by drop, beating constantly; add peach brandy and whiskey in same manner. Refrigerate overnight. Stir in milk and nutmeg. Beat egg whites until stiff; fold into eggnog. Yield: 16 punch cups.

Mrs. Sharon Simko, March Lady Ed., OWC
March AFB, California

OVERNIGHT EGGNOG

1 doz. eggs, separated
Pinch of soda
6 oz. rum or brandy
2 lb. sugar
1 qt. milk
1 qt. whipping cream
2 fifths Canadian Club or bourbon
Nutmeg to taste

Beat egg yolks well; beat egg whites until soft peaks form. Fold egg yolks into egg whites; fold in soda. Add rum and sugar; beat until stiff. Add milk, whipping cream and Canadian Club;

mix well. Refrigerate overnight. Stir just before serving; sprinkle with nutmeg. Yield: 2 gallons.

Maj. Tommy G. Harrison
Offutt AFB. Nebraska

HAPPY HOLIDAY EGGNOG

12 egg yolks
1 c. sugar
1 qt. milk
18 oz. bourbon
6 oz. rum
1 qt. heavy cream, stiffly beaten
Nutmeg

Beat egg yolks until light; beat in sugar until mixture is thick. Stir in milk; stir in bourbon and rum slowly. Chill for several hours. Pour into punch bowl; fold in cream. Sprinkle with nutmeg. Serve in punch cups. Yield: 24 servings.

Mrs. W. J. Yamber, OWC
St. Petersburg, Florida

PARTY EGGNOG

3 c. milk
1 c. light cream
Sugar
2 eggs, separated
Dash of salt
1 tsp. vanilla
2 cinnamon sticks
Whiskey or rum to taste
1/2 c. heavy cream, whipped
Grated nutmeg

Combine milk and light cream in top of double boiler; heat until scalded. Beat 1/3 cup sugar with egg yolks and salt; stir in milk mixture slowly. Return to top of double boiler; cook over hot water, stirring constantly, until mixture coats spoon. Cool; add vanilla and cinnamon sticks. Beat egg whites until foamy; beat until soft peaks form, adding 3 tablespoons sugar gradually. Fold into custard, mixing thoroughly; chill for 3 to 4 hours. Pour into punch bowl; add whiskey. Fold 1 1/2 teaspoons sugar into whipped cream. Place dollops of whipped cream on eggnog; sprinkle with nutmeg. Yield: 8 punch cups.

Mrs. George L. Ramsey, Pres., O and CWC
Wiley Kasern, Neu Ulm, Germany

QUANTITY EGGNOG

10 lg. eggs, separated
6 tbsp. sugar
1 fifth bourbon
1 qt. milk
3 oz. brandy
1 pt. heavy cream, whipped
Nutmeg

Beat egg yolks until lemon colored, adding sugar gradually. Add bourbon, then milk. Add brandy; fold in whipped cream. Beat egg whites until very stiff; fold into eggnog. Chill. Serve in punch cups; sprinkle with nutmeg.

Mrs. Pat Pickett, Cookbook Chm., OWC
NAS, Lemoore, California

RICH HOLIDAY EGGNOG

6 eggs, separated
3/4 c. sugar
2 c. heavy cream
2 c. milk
1 1/2 c. light rum, brandy or bourbon
2 tbsp. dark rum
Nutmeg

Beat egg yolks until thick and lemon colored. Add 1/2 cup sugar; beat until sugar is dissolved. Add cream and milk; stir in rum slowly. Refrigerate for 4 hours, allowing rum to cook eggs. Beat egg whites until stiff, adding remaining sugar gradually; fold into eggnog. Sprinkle lightly with nutmeg. Yield: 12 punch cups.

Mrs. Margery Connor, OWC
NATO, Keflavik, Iceland

FESTIVE PUNCH

2 c. sugar
1 qt. pineapple juice
1 6-oz. jar maraschino cherries
1 qt. tea
Juice and rind of 2 oranges
Juice of 6 lemons
1 qt. gin
1 qt. bourbon
1 qt. club soda

Combine sugar, pineapple juice, cherries, tea, orange juice and rind, lemon juice and 1 quart water; mix well. Stir in gin and bourbon; add soda. Pour over block of ice. When punch is well chilled, remove ice. Serve in punch cups or old-fashioned glasses. Mixture freezes well; do not add soda until ready to serve. Yield: 20 servings.

Mrs. Alvan C. Gillem, III, Hon. Pres., OWC
Maxwell AFB, Alabama

SNOWY EGGNOG

5 eggs, separated
10 tbsp. sugar
7 c. half and half
3/4 c. cognac
Grated nutmeg

Beat egg yolks with 5 tablespoons of sugar until light. Stir in half and half and cognac; blend well. Chill for several hours. Pour into chilled punch bowl. Beat egg whites until frothy. Add remaining sugar gradually, beating until stiff peaks form; fold 2/3 of the meringue into eggnog. Spoon remaining meringue on top; sprinkle with nutmeg. Yield: 25 punch cups.

Mrs. Eva L. Kenison, Newsletter Ed., OWC
Edgewood Arsenal, Edgewood, Maryland

DIFFERENT EGGNOG

3 eggs, separated
1 pkg. vanilla pudding and pie filling mix
1/2 c. sugar
1 tsp. vanilla
1/2 c. peach brandy
1 c. whipping cream, whipped
Nutmeg

Beat egg yolks lightly; stir in pudding mix and sugar. Bring to a boil over medium heat, stirring constantly; cool. Beat egg whites until stiff; fold egg whites, vanilla and brandy into pudding mixture. Chill. Pour into punch bowl. Serve in punch cups; top each serving with whipped cream and dash of nutmeg. Yield: 12 servings.

Mrs. Stuart B. McCurdy, W and M Chm., OWC
MacDill AFB, Florida

COLONIAL AMERICAN EGGNOG

12 egg yolks
1 c. sugar
1 pt. milk
1 qt. light rum

1 pt. heavy cream, whipped
Nutmeg

Beat egg yolks until light. Add sugar; beat until thick. Stir in milk and rum; chill for 3 hours. Fold in whipped cream; chill for 1 hour. Sprinkle with nutmeg before serving. Yield: 20 punch cups.

Mrs. Barbara S. Johnson, W and M Chm., OWC
Ft. MacArthur, California

FIELD ARTILLERY PUNCH

1 c. sugar
Juice of 6 lemons
2 tbsp. bitters
2 qt. claret
1 qt. sherry
1 qt. rye whiskey
1 qt. brandy
1 qt. champagne or club soda

Mix all ingredients except champagne together. Store in refrigerator for several days to blend. Pour mixture over ice in punch bowl; add champagne. Serve in punch cups or glasses. Bourbon or Scotch whisky may be substituted for rye whiskey, if desired. Yield: 30 servings.

Col. Arthur V. Corley
Ft. Huachuca, Arizona

FINN'S FAKE FARKLEBERRY PUNCH

1 c. lemon juice
2 c. orange juice
2 c. apple juice
1 c. vodka
1 c. sugar
1 qt. champagne

Place lemon juice, orange juice, apple juice and vodka in a mixing bowl. Add sugar; stir until sugar dissolves. Add champagne just before serving; stir gently. Create a large cube of ice with a milk carton or gelatin mold to float in punch bowl. Chill all ingredients, then the ice will not melt fast enough to dilute punch.

Lt. Cmdr. James R. Finn
Naval Construction Bn. Ctr.
Port Hueneme, California

ALABAMA FISH HOUSE PUNCH

3/4 lb. sugar
1 qt. fresh lemon juice
1 qt. sparkling water

2 qt. Jamaica rum
1 qt. brandy
4 oz. peach brandy

Dissolve sugar in small amount of water. Combine sugar mixture and remaining ingredients in large punch bowl. Add 10-pound cake of ice. Let stand for 2 hours before serving; stir occasionally. Serve in punch cups. Yield: 20-25 servings.

Mrs. Leslie L. Fredericks, OWC
Gunter AFB, Montgomery, Alabama

JACK'S FISH HOUSE PUNCH

1 c. simple syrup
1 c. lime juice
1 1/2 bottles rum
1 bottle brandy
1 c. peach brandy
3 qt. champagne

Combine first 5 ingredients in punch bowl. Add champagne and desired amount of ice just before serving. Serve in punch cups. Yield: 50 servings.

Mrs. Nathan Jack Hansen, Family Services Adv., OWC
Chanute AFB, Illinois

FLORIDA BOURBON PUNCH

2 6-oz. cans frozen lemonade
1 fifth bourbon
2 qt. Tom Collins mix
1 qt. soda

Thaw lemonade; place in a punch bowl. Add remaining ingredients and enough ice to chill. Serve in punch cups. Yield: 1 gallon.

Mrs. Donald B. Koch, VT-3 OWC
Whiting Field, Pensacola, Florida

HONOLULU PUNCH

1/2 slice pineapple
1/2 oz. lemon juice
Dash of rock candy syrup
1 1/2 oz. light rum

Combine all ingredients with 3 small scoops crushed ice in blender container; blend well. Strain into sherbet glass. Serve with cut straw. Yield: 1 serving.

Mrs. Leslie L. Fredericks, OWC
Gunter AFB, Montgomery, Alabama

FROZEN JUICE PUNCH

1 can frozen grape juice
2 cans frozen orange juice
1 can frozen lemonade
1 can frozen limeade
2 qt. ginger ale
Gin to taste
Sugar to taste

Combine all ingredients in punch bowl with 2 quarts water; mix well. Serve in highball glasses or punch cups. Yield: 30 servings.

Vivian C. Redfield, OWC
Chanute AFB, Illinois

HOPKINS SPECIAL

1 lg. can mixed fruit punch
1 lg. can pineapple juice
2 c. strawberries
1/2 lg. can crushed pineapple
1 fifth mixed rum and brandy
3 qt. ginger ale

Combine mixed fruit punch and pineapple juice; freeze overnight. Combine strawberries, pineapple and rum and brandy in plastic container. Place fruit punch mixture in punch bowl; add rum mixture. Stir in ginger ale. Serve in punch cups. Yield: 20 servings.

Mrs. James T. Boddie, Pres., OWC
Randolph AFB, Texas

APPLE CIDER PUNCH

4 qt. apple cider or juice
1/2 c. (firmly packed) brown sugar
24 whole cloves
16 whole allspice
8 2-in. cinnamon sticks
2 whole nutmegs, cracked
1 to 2 c. golden rum

Combine all ingredients except rum in large saucepan; bring to a boil. Reduce heat; simmer for 15 minutes. Remove from heat; cool. Refrigerate for several hours. Strain; add rum. Reheat. Serve in punch bowl; garnish with lemon or orange peel. May be served cold. Yield: Twenty-four 6-ounce servings.

Gwen Jenks, POW-MIA Rep., OWC
Williams AFB, Arizona

HOLIDAY HOT PUNCH

4 oranges
Whole cloves
1 qt. rum
Sugar to taste
1/2 gal. sweet cider
Nutmeg and cinnamon to taste

Stud oranges with cloves; place in baking pan. Bake at 350 degrees for 30 minutes. Place oranges in stainless steel or aluminum punch bowl; pour rum and sugar over oranges. Ignite rum; add cider slowly to extinguish flame. Stir in cinnamon and nutmeg; serve hot in punch cups. Yield: 30 servings.

Mrs. George Snead, Jr., Hon. VP, O and CWC
Ft. Huachuca, Arizona

HOT CHRISTMAS WASSAIL

24 1-in. sticks cinnamon
64 cloves
4 tsp. whole allspice
24 c. apple juice or cider
8 c. cranberry juice cocktail
1 c. sugar
4 tsp. aromatic bitters
3 oranges, studded with cloves
1 qt. rum

Tie cinnamon, cloves and allspice in cheesecloth bag. Pour apple juice and cranberry juice cocktail into 40-cup electric coffee pot; add sugar and bitters. Place basket in pot; place spice bag and oranges in basket. Percolate through cycle on medium strength setting. Remove basket; add rum. Serve hot in punch bowl. Yield: Forty 1-cup servings.

Mrs. Henry H. Mauz, Jr., Pres., NOWC
USNB, Charleston, South Carolina

VITTE TOS

Juice of 6 lemons
Juice of 6 oranges
1 lb. honey
3 cinnamon sticks
1 tsp. carraway seed
1 tsp. whole nutmeg
1 tsp. whole cloves
Bourbon or blended whiskey

Combine all ingredients except bourbon in saucepan; bring to a boil. Boil for 5 to 10 minutes. Strain; add equal amount of bourbon. Serve immediately. May be placed in thermal container for football game warmer-upper. Yield: 15 servings.

Mrs. M. H. Herman, NWC
Philadelphia Naval Hosp., Philadelphia, Pennsylvania

WASSAIL BOWL

3/4 c. boiling water
2 tbsp. tea
1 bottle Madeira
1 c. sugar
3 eggs, separated
1/2 c. brandy
3 warm baked apples

Pour water over tea; steep for 5 minutes. Combine Madeira and sugar in saucepan; heat, stirring, until sugar dissolves. Pour tea through strainer into hot Madeira mixture; keep warm. Beat egg whites until stiff but not dry; turn into punch bowl. Beat egg yolks until thick and pale yellow; fold into egg whites. Stir Madeira mixture into eggs gradually. Heat brandy; add to punch. Float apples in Wassail Bowl before serving. Yield: About 2 quarts.

WINTER NIGHT BREW

12 whole cloves
4 cinnamon sticks
2 tsp. whole allspice
1 gal. apple cider
1/2 to 1 c. (packed) brown sugar
1 2/3 c. whiskey

Tie spices in cloth bag. Mix cider and brown sugar in large pan or kettle; place bag of spices in cider mixture. Simmer for 20 minutes. Add whiskey; remove spice bag. Serve hot in punch cups. Yield: 32 servings.

Mrs. Ray E. Huebner, Activities Chm., OWC
Ft. Monmouth, New Jersey

HOT MULLED WINE PUNCH

1 1/2 c. boiling water
1/2 c. sugar
1/2 lemon, sliced
3 sticks cinnamon
3 whole cloves
1 lg. bottle California Burgundy
   or claret
Nutmeg

Combine water, sugar, lemon, cinnamon and cloves; stir until sugar dissolves. Add Burgundy; simmer for 20 minutes. Do not boil. Strain; serve hot in punch cups with sprinkling of nutmeg. May be made in advance and reheated. Yield: 12 servings.

Mrs. W. J. Wagner, Hostess, OWC
US Naval Hosp., Camp Lejeune, North Carolina

HOT RUM-CIDER

3 qt. apple cider or juice
4 cinnamon sticks
Dash of nutmeg
1 pt. rum

Mix cider, cinnamon and nutmeg; heat until steaming. Remove from heat; add rum. Place in punch bowl; serve immediately in punch cups. Yield: 20 servings.

Mrs. John B. Gamber, Memshp. Chm., OWC
Sembach Air Base, Germany

LA VENTA PUNCH

3 parts rum
2 parts Chianti
1 part lime juice
1 part simple syrup

Combine all ingredients; blend well. Store in refrigerator for at least 2 weeks before serving. Serve in punch cups.

Mrs. Charles E. Conser, Property Chm., OWC
Aberdeen Proving Ground, Aberdeen, Maryland

NEVER AGAIN PUNCH

3 bottles white rum
1 bottle dark rum

2 bottles sauterne
2 bottles champagne or soda
2 46-oz. cans pineapple juice
1 oz. bitters

Chill all ingredients well; combine in punch bowl. Serve in punch cups. Yield: 30 servings.

Mrs. Albert W. Costley, Jr., Corr. Sec., OWC
Moody AFB, Georgia

PINK OPEN HOUSE PUNCH

1 fifth Southern Comfort
3 qt. lemon-lime carbonated beverage
6 oz. fresh lemon juice
1 6-oz. can frozen orange juice
1 6-oz. can frozen pink lemonade
Few drops of red food coloring

Freeze water in mold to make ice ring. Chill Southern Comfort, carbonated beverage and lemon juice. Combine Southern Comfort, lemon juice and frozen juices, stirring to thaw juices. Add carbonated beverage and food coloring. Float ice ring in punch; garnish with lemon and orange slices. Serve in punch cups. Yield: 32 servings.

Joyce Mitchell, Co-Chm., Gp. VI, OWC
Camp Lejeune Marine Base
Jacksonville, North Carolina

ORANGE DELIGHT

1 c. fresh orange juice
2 tsp. sugar
4 tsp. malted milk powder
2 jiggers vodka

Combine all ingredients in blender container with half tray ice cubes. Blend well until mixture forms a slush. Serve in highball glasses. Yield: 2 servings.

Mrs. Peter J. Luther, Asst. Treas., O and CWC
Camp Darby, Italy

PARTY-STARTER PUNCH

6 sliced oranges
6 sliced lemons
4 17-oz. cans chunk pineapple, drained
4 med. packages frozen sliced strawberries,
   thawed
1 bottle cognac

2 bottles sauterne, chilled
4 bottles champagne, chilled

Combine fruits and cognac; let soak for 24 hours. Chill. Mix sauterne and champagne; pour over cognac mixture. Pour over block of ice in punch bowl. Yield: 48 servings.

Maj. Frank M. Stewart
Fort Lee, Virginia

PEACH SLUSH

1/2 overripe peach
1 tsp. (heaping) sugar
2 jiggers whiskey
Crushed ice

Mash peach with sugar. Add whiskey; stir well. Fill large glass with crushed ice; add peach mixture. Yield: 1 serving.

Mrs. Joel M. Couch, Pres., OWC
Bolling AFB, Washington, D. C.

PROMOTION PUNCH

2 qt. sauterne
1 qt. cognac
4 qt. champagne
2 qt. carbonated water

Mix sauterne and cognac; pour over ice in punch bowl. Add champagne and carbonated water. Serve immediately. Do not mix punch long in advance, but have plenty of ingredients available. Ice may be in a block or ring mold, as desired. Serve in punch cups. Yield: 100 servings.

Lt. Col. F. Lee Early, Jr.
Ft. Campbell, Kentucky

RASPBERRY PUNCH

1 6-oz. can frozen lemonade
2 pkg. frozen raspberries
1 fifth rose wine
1 pt. raspberry sherbet

Prepare lemonade according to can directions; thaw raspberries partially. Combine lemonade and raspberries with wine in punch bowl. Allow sherbet to soften slightly; float on punch. Stir slightly. Serve in punch cups. Yield: 8-10 servings.

Mrs. Nancy Bethel, W and M Co-Chm., OWC
Andrews AFB, Washington, D. C.

QUIET PUNCH

1 qt. sauterne
1 pt. cognac
2 qt. champagne
1 qt. sparkling water
Cherry ice ring

Pour the sauterne and cognac into punch bowl; add champagne and sparkling water. Float frozen cherry ring on top.

Lt. Col. Oliver J. Bussen
Defense Depot, Ogden, Utah

ROMAN BOWL PUNCH

2 c. diced pineapple
1/2 c. sugar syrup
1 fifth light rum
1 fifth dark rum
1 1/2 c. unsweetened pineapple juice
1 1/3 c. peach brandy
1/2 c. lemon juice
1/2 c. orange juice
2 fifths champagne

Place pineapple in punch bowl with sugar syrup; add remaining ingredients except champagne. Add block of ice; stir in champagne. One pint sliced, fresh strawberries may be added, if desired. Sugar syrup is made by boiling equal amounts of sugar and water. Yield: 40 punch cups.

Mrs. Jane M. Flach, Luncheon Chm., OWC
COMSUBPAC, Pearl Harbor, Hawaii

RUDOLPH THE RED NOSE REINDEER PUNCH

1 qt. cranberry juice
2 c. orange juice
Juice of 4 lemons
1/2 c. sugar
2 fifths light rum
4 oz. cognac
Few drops of red food coloring
1 qt. ginger ale, chilled
Fresh orange and lemon slices

Combine first 7 ingredients; chill. Place block of ice or ice mold in punch bowl. Pour in chilled mixture; add ginger ale and sliced fruit. Serve in punch cups. Yield: 30 servings.

Mrs. R. H. Steckler, 1st VP, OWC
Hamilton AFB, California

JAX SPECIAL

2 c. sugar
2 qt. dry gin
2 lg. cans pineapple chunks, drained
3 bottles chilled champagne
2 28-oz. bottles chilled club soda
Ice mold

Combine sugar and gin in large container; stir well. Cover tightly; chill for at least 12 hours. Shake often. Pour gin mixture and pineapple into punch bowl; add champagne and club soda. Stir gently; add ice mold. Serve immediately in punch cups. Yield: 35-40 servings.

Mrs. John G. Vaaler, W and M Chm., OWC
Ft. Sam Houston, San Antonio, Texas

SMOOTH OPEN HOUSE PUNCH

2 1/2 c. Southern Comfort
6 oz. fresh lemon juice
1 ˚6-oz. can frozen orange juice, thawed
2 6-oz. cans frozen lemonade, thawed
2 1/4 qt. lemon-lime carbonated beverage

Chill all ingredients. Combine Southern Comfort, lemon juice, orange juice and lemonade in punch bowl. Add carbonated beverage and desired amount of ice just before serving. Garnish with orange and lemon slices. Serve in punch cups. Yield: 25 servings.

Mrs. L. D. Freymuller, Treas., OWC
St. Louis, Missouri
Mrs. Bruce Burrows, Soc. Chm., OWC
Camp New Amsterdam, Holland

MOLASSES-RUM TODDY

1 18-oz. can unsweetened pineapple
  juice
1/4 c. Grandma's West Indies Molasses
3/4 c. rum
Juice of 1 lime or lemon
4 to 6 cinnamon sticks

Pour pineapple juice into saucepan; blend in molasses. Stir in rum and lime juice; heat to serving temperature. Pour into mugs; add 1 cinnamon stick to each serving. Yield: 4-6 servings.

THREE FRUIT-RUM PUNCH

1/4 c. sugar
1/4 c. water
1 qt. chilled apple juice
1 can frozen orange concentrate
1/4 c. lemon juice
8 jiggers rum

Combine sugar and water; bring to a boil, stirring until sugar is dissolved. Chill. Combine apple juice, orange concentrate, lemon juice, rum and sugar syrup; beat well to blend. Pour into punch bowl over block of ice; garnish with thin orange slices. Serve in punch cups. Yield: 6 servings.

Photograph for this recipe on page 23.

KEMOO'S PINE TAI

1 oz. light rum
1 oz. dark rum
2 oz. pineapple juice
2 oz. orange juice
1 oz. lemon juice
1/2 oz. grenadine

Place all ingredients in container; add cracked ice. Cover; shake well. Serve in mug or punch cup. Garnish with pineapple spear, mint sprig, cherry and a slice of orange, if desired. Yield: 1 serving.

Mrs. Myrna N. Lee, Publ. Chm., OWC
White Sands Missile Range, New Mexico

MAI TAI PUNCH

3 oz. light rum
3 oz. dark rum
1 oz. grenadine
1 1/2 oz. lemon juice
1 oz. Orgeat syrup
1 oz. triple sec
10 pz. pineapple juice
Crushed ice

Mix first 7 ingredients in order listed; serve over ice in Mai Tai glasses. May be topped with additional rum, if desired. Yield: 4 servings.

Mrs. Raymond K. Seip, Reservations Chm., OWC
Wheeler AFB, Hawaii

LADIES' AFTERNOON RUM PUNCH

Pineapple juice
3 bottles light rum
2 bottles sauterne
2 qt. ginger ale

Freeze ice ring of pineapple juice and water. Chill two 46-ounce cans pineapple juice and remaining ingredients; combine in punch bowl. Add ice ring just before serving. Serve in punch cups or goblets. Yield: 50 servings.

Mrs. Richard P. Geer, Pres., OWC
Lackland AFB, San Antonio, Texas

PLANTER'S PUNCH

1 qt. orange juice
2 c. lemon juice
5 sliced bananas
1 fresh pineapple, sliced or chopped
5 bottles dry white wine
1 1-lb. box brown sugar
3 qt. light rum
1 pt. dark rum
1 pt. creme de banane

Combine fruit juices, bananas, pineapple and wine in crock with sugar. Let stand, covered, overnight. Add rum and creme de banane; let stand for 12 hours longer. Strain into punch bowl over ice. Sugar syrup or additional lemon juice may be added to taste. Serve in punch cups. Yield: 30 servings.

Barbara S. Johnson, W and M Chm., OWC
Ft. MacArthur, California

PUERTO RICAN RUM PUNCH

2 c. sugar
6 c. pineapple juice
1/2 c. lime juice
5 c. white rum

Dissolve sugar in 2 cups pineapple juice in saucepan over low heat. Remove from heat; mix with remaining pineapple juice, lime juice and rum. Blend well; place in freezer containers. Freeze until ready to serve. Serve in daiquiri or sherbet glasses. Yield: 20 servings.

Mrs. William E. Heck, Jr., Pres., OWC
Picatinny Arsenal, New Jersey

PINK PARTY PUNCH

4 12-oz. packages sliced frozen
    strawberries
1/2 c. sugar
4 fifths rose wine
4 6-oz. cans frozen lemonade
2 qt. club soda

Thaw strawberries; combine strawberries, sugar and 1 fifth rose wine in large container. Cover; let stand for 1 hour. Strain wine mixture; pour back into container, reserving strawberries. Add lemonade, stirring to thaw; chill. Freeze strawberries in water in ice ring. Chill remaining rose wine and soda. Add wine and soda to punch; pour into punch bowl. Float strawberry ring in punch. Serve in punch cups.

Mrs. Joseph H. Meyer, Pres., OWC
White Sands Missile Range, New Mexico

RECEPTION PUNCH

Juice of 9 doz. lemons
4 lg. fresh pineapples, cut in chunks
7 c. sugar
3 1/2 qt. white wine
3 1/2 qt. good champagne
1/2 pt. curacao
10 bx. fresh strawberries, cleaned

Combine lemon juice, pineapple chunks and sugar. Add remaining ingredients just before serving; pour over large pieces of ice. Eight number 2 cans chunk pineapple may be substituted for fresh pineapples; frozen strawberries may be used. Yield: 11 gallons.

Mrs. Alvan C. Gillem, Hon. Pres., OWC
Maxwell AFB, Montgomery, Alabama
Mrs. Frank Knapp, Adv., OWC
Offutt AFB, Nebraska

PUNCH FOR A BUNCH

1 qt. light rum
1 lg. can pineapple juice
1 lg. grapefruit juice
2 lg. cans frozen orange juice concentrate
1 lg. can frozen lemonade concentrate
1 lg. bottle club soda
1 lg. bottle ginger ale

Mix rum, pineapple juice, grapefruit juice, orange juice and lemonade. Pour over block of ice in punch bowl. Add club soda and ginger ale just before serving. Serve in punch cups. Yield: 20-40 servings.

Mrs. Henry H. Mauz, Jr., Pres., OWC
US Navy Base, Charleston, South Carolina

FRUITED WHISKEY PUNCH

3/4 c. lemon juice
3 c. orange juice
2 1/4 c. pineapple juice
2 fifths of whiskey
2 qt. ginger ale
Sugar to taste

Pour fruit juices and whiskey over ice in punch bowl. Stir in ginger ale and sugar until sugar is dissolved. Garnish with orange, lemon and pineapple slices and maraschino cherries. Serve in punch cups. Yield: 45 4-oz. servings.

Mrs. Joseph H. Meyer, Pres., OWC
White Sands Missile Range, New Mexico

STRAWBERRY PUNCH

1 6-oz. can frozen orange juice
1 6-oz. can frozen lemonade
1 lg. package frozen whole strawberries
1 46-oz. can pineapple Juice
1 46-oz. can mixed fruit punch
1 qt. ginger ale
1/2 fifth gin or vodka
1 pt. mint sherbet

Thaw frozen juices and strawberries. Combine all ingredients except sherbet in punch bowl. Drop sherbet by spoonfuls into punch. Serve in punch cups. Yield: 24 servings.

Mrs. Josiah A. Wallace, Hon. Pres., OWC
Ft. McClellan, Alabama

STAGGERING STRAWBERRIES

1 qt. fresh strawberries
1 qt. apricot brandy or cognac
2 qt. champagne
1 qt. club soda
1 qt. apple juice

1 qt. vodka or bourbon
2 oranges

Soak strawberries in apricot brandy for 24 to 36 hours. Chill large punch bowl; add strawberries and brandy, champagne, club soda, apple juice and vodka. Slice oranges thinly; float on punch. Serve in punch cups. Yield: 25-30 servings.

Dr. David R. Stoop
Naval Aerospace Medical Inst.
NAS, Pensacola, Florida

SPECIAL ANNIVERSARY PUNCH

1 12-oz. package frozen strawberries
2 tsp. grated lime rind
Juice of 1 lime
1 bottle sauterne, chilled
1 bottle sparkling Burgundy, chilled
1 bottle dry champagne, chilled

Combine strawberries, lime rind and lime juice in saucepan; mix well. Simmer for 10 minutes; force through food mill or sieve. Cool. Pour fruit mixture over ice in punch bowl. Add sauterne, sparkling Burgundy and champagne just before serving. Garnish with whole strawberries and lime slices, if desired. Serve in punch cups. Yield: 25 servings.

Mrs. Frank X. Hoff, Sr. Hostess, Rifle Range, OWC
Marine Corps Base, Camp Lejeune, North Carolina

WINE PUNCH

5 bottles German Rhine wine
1/2 c. sugar
2 lb. frozen strawberries
1 qt. champagne or sparkling water
1 c. rum

Mix 3/4 bottle wine and sugar. Add strawberries; soak for 5 hours. Add remaining wine, champagne and rum; chill thoroughly. Pour into punch bowl; garnish with ice ring. Yield: 20 servings.

Mrs. Michael Kennedy, Corr. Sec., OWC
Homestead AFB, Florida

THANKSGIVING PUNCH

4 oz. lemon juice
2 oz. sugar

8 oz. cranberry juice
8 oz. orange juice
8 oz. strong tea
1 fifth rum
12 whole cloves
Lemon slices

Combine lemon juice, sugar, cranberry juice, orange juice and tea in punch bowl. Stir in rum, cloves and enough ice cubes to chill. Garnish with lemon slices; serve in punch cups. Yield: 15 servings.

Mrs. W. J. Yamber, OWC
St. Petersburg, Florida

SUMMER PATIO PUNCH

1 6-oz. can frozen tangerine juice
2 sm. cans mandarin oranges, drained
2 lg. cans frozen lemonade, thawed
1 c. sugar
1 qt. pineapple juice
1 No. 2 1/2 can crushed pineapple
1 sm. bottle maraschino cherries, halved
1 qt. lemon-lime carbonated beverage
1 bottle light white wine
Sprigs of mint

Prepare tangerine juice according to package directions; fill small mold. Freeze. Combine oranges, lemonade, sugar, pineapple juice, pineapple and cherries. Chill for several hours. Pour into punch bowl; add carbonated beverage and wine. Float frozen ring in punch; garnish with mint sprigs. Serve in punch cups. Yield: 50 servings.

Mrs. Keith E. Phillips, OWC
US Military Training Mission, Saudi Arabia

WHISKEY SOUR PUNCH

1 qt. lemon juice
1 qt. orange juice
1 qt. bourbon
4 c. sugar
3 qt. club soda

Combine lemon juice, orange juice, bourbon and sugar. Stir well. Pour into large punch bowl. Add soda. May float large ice rings in punch bowl to chill, if desired. Yield: 50 servings.

Mrs. Willard Barnett, Adv., OWC
Ellsworth AFB, South Dakota

DRINKS WITHOUT SPIRITS

The drinks in this section are ideal for occasions when you don't feel it is quite proper to serve liquor: for teenage parties, for Sunday brunches or afternoon parties. Or maybe you and your friends prefer drinks without liquor. These refreshing, non-alcoholic drinks lend themselves to numerous occasions, and they are equally good as a "no special occasion" drink.

We cannot possibly pretend that for drinks to be good tasting, they must be made with liquor. All of us know that isn't true, and we prove it with our following "Drinks without Spirits" recipes.

BANANA SLUSH

2 c. sugar
3 to 4 med. bananas
1 1/2 c. orange juice
1/4 c. lemon juice
1 46-oz. can pineapple juice
2 qt. ginger ale

Combine sugar with 3 cups water in saucepan; bring to a boil. Reduce heat; simmer for 20 minutes or until sugar is dissolved and mixture forms thin syrup. Mash bananas well. Combine syrup, bananas, orange juice, lemon juice and pineapple juice; mix well. Freeze until firm. Place mixture in punch bowl; add ginger ale. Stir to a slush. Serve immediately in punch cups. Yield: 25-30 servings.

Mrs. J. T. Boddie, Pres., OWC
Randolph AFB, Texas

BRIDE'S PUNCH

2 6-oz. cans frozen orange juice
1 6-oz. can frozen lemonade concentrate
1 12-oz. can apricot nectar
2 c. pineapple juice
2 1/2 c. chilled ginger ale
1 10 1/2-oz. package sliced strawberries
Frozen fruit ring

Mix orange juice, lemonade, apricot nectar, pineapple juice and 7 cups water; chill well. Pour orange juice mixture into punch bowl; add ginger ale, mixing well. Float strawberries and frozen fruit ring. Serve in punch cups. Yield: 30 4-oz. servings.

Mrs. Sandy Harborth, Hosp. Chm., OWC
Gunter AFB, Montgomery, Alabama

CHRISTMAS WASSAIL

6 tea bags
1/4 tsp. allspice
1/4 tsp. cinnamon
1/4 tsp. nutmeg
3/4 c. sugar
1 1-pt. bottle cranberry juice cocktail
1 1/2 c. water

1/2 c. orange juice
1/3 c. lemon juice

Combine 2 1/2 cups boiling water and tea bags; steep for 5 minutes. Remove tea bags; add spices and sugar, stirring to dissolve. Add remaining ingredients; heat to boiling point. Serve in tea cups. May use candy canes as stirrers, if desired. Yield: 8-10 servings.

Mrs. Kieth G. Wilson, Parliamentarian, OWC
Aviano Air Base, Italy

CHERRY FIRE PUNCH

1 9 oz. frozen orange juice concentrate
1 c. pineapple juice
1/3 c. lemon juice
1 10-oz. package frozen sweet cherries
1 7-oz. bottle quinine water

Combine 5 cups water, orange juice concentrate, pineapple and lemon juices; stir until well blended. Chill until ready to serve. Thaw fruit according to package directions; add to punch mixture. Stir in quinine water and ice cubes. Serve immediately in punch cup. Yield: 16 servings.

Mrs. Janet Long LaGrassa, Publ. Chm., OWC
Hawkins Barracks, Oberammergau, Germany

COFFEE FRAPPE

2 tbsp. instant coffee
2 1-in. pieces stick cinnamon
3 c. hot water
Few drops of bitters
Sugar to taste
1/4 c. whipping cream
2 tsp. confectioners' sugar
Crushed ice
Grated orange rind

Combine coffee and cinnamon sticks in bowl; add hot water and bitters. Sweeten with sugar; cool. Beat cream and sugar in small bowl until stiff. Pour coffee mixture over crushed ice in stemmed cocktail glasses, discarding cinnamon sticks. Top each glass with generous spoonful of cream mixture; sprinkle with orange rind. Yield: 4 servings.

Mrs. Stuart B. McCurdy, W and M Chm., OWC
MacDill AFB, Florida

COFFEE PUNCH

Large ice ring
16 tsp. (heaping) instant coffee
1 qt. hot water
1/2 c. sugar
1 1/2 c. milk
1/2 gal. vanilla ice cream
Whipped cream

Freeze water in large mold to make ice ring. Combine coffee and hot water; add sugar and milk. Break ice cream into chunks; place in punch bowl. Pour coffee mixture over ice cream; add ice ring. Dot with whipped cream. Serve in punch cups. Yield: 35 servings.

Helga E. Kelly, W and M Chm., OWC
Ft. Hancock, New Jersey

CRANBERRY PUNCH

2 c. cranberries
3 c. water
1 c. sugar
1/2 c. orange juice
1 tbsp. lemon juice
2 c. ginger ale, chilled

Cook cranberries in water for 10 minutes; force through sieve. Add sugar; return to heat. Bring just to a boil. Add orange juice and lemon juice; stir well. Chill. Pour into punch bowl; add ginger ale and desired amount of ice. Serve in punch cups.

Mrs. James P. Smith, Jr., OWC
Naval Hosp., Portsmouth, New Hampshire

CRANBERRY SHRUB

3 qt. cranberry juice
1 qt. sparkling water
1 qt. lime sherbet

Chill cranberry juice and sparkling water. Pour into punch bowl. Add sherbet by spoonfuls. Serve in punch cups. Yield: 32 servings.

Jane M. Flach, Luncheon Chm., NOWC
COMSUBPAC, Pearl Harbor, Hawaii

PINEAPPLE FRAPPE

1 1-lb. 4-oz. can crushed pineapple
1 c. canned pineapple juice
16 ice cubes

Place all ingredients in electric blender; blend at high speed until smooth. Yield: 6 servings.

PINEAPPLE-MELON COOLER

1 sm. cantaloupe
1 1-lb. 4-oz. can crushed pineapple
12 ice cubes
Sparkling water, chilled

Peel and seed cantaloupe; cut into chunks. Place cantaloupe, pineapple and ice cubes in electric blender; blend at high speed until smooth. Fill serving glasses 2/3 full. Fill glasses with sparkling water; stir. Yield: 6 servings.

PINEAPPLE-BERRY FROST

1 1-lb. 4-oz. can crushed pineapple
1 c. sliced strawberries
12 ice cubes
Vanilla ice cream

Place pineapple, strawberries and ice cubes in electric blender; blend at high speed until smooth. Pour into serving glasses; top each glass with scoop of ice cream. Yield: 6 servings.

DEE'S WEDDING PUNCH

4 c. sugar
Juice of 12 lemons

Grated lemon rind
8 qt. ginger ale
8 46-oz. cans pineapple juice

Combine sugar, 6 cups water, lemon juice and small amount of grated rind in saucepan. Boil until syrupy; cool. Place chunks of ice in punch bowl. Pour 1 quart ginger ale and 1 can pineapple juice into punch bowl; add 1/8 of the lemon syrup. Add remaining ingredients in same proportion as needed. Garnish with mint and fruit slices, if desired.

Mrs. Henry Earle Goff, Corr. Sec., OWC
Offutt AFB, Nebraska

FRUIT FIZZ

1/2 c. lemon juice
1 c. orange juice
3/4 c. sugar
1 c. strawberries, halved
1 pt. ginger ale

Do not strain lemon and orange juice. Mix juices. Add sugar; shake or beat thoroughly. Add strawberries and ginger ale; serve with an ice cube. Yield: 6 cups.

Mrs. James Ramsden, OWC
Ft. McClellan, Alabama

FRUIT PUNCH ROYALE

4 c. sugar
8 tea bags
1 pt. canned fruit punch syrup
1 pt. canned raspberry syrup
1 12-oz. can frozen lemonade
2 12-oz. cans frozen orange juice
1 46-oz. can pineapple juice
3 lg. bottles ginger ale
1 lg. bottle lemon-lime carbonated drink

Combine sugar with 2 cups water; bring to a boil. Boil for 5 minutes; remove from heat. Cool. Steep tea bags in 2 cups boiling water. Cool. Combine sugar syrup with tea in large container; add fruit punch and raspberry syrups, lemonade, orange juice, pineapple juice and 3 gallons water. Add ginger ale and lemon-lime drink. Pour over ice in punch bowls; serve immediately in punch cups. Yield: 200 servings.

Patricia A. Thirsted, Pub. Rel. Chm., OWC
McGuire AFB, New Jersey

HOT APPLE CIDER

1 c. sugar
6 whole cloves
2 sticks cinnamon
3 whole allspice
1 tsp. ground ginger
2 c. orange juice
1/2 c. lemon juice
5 c. apple cider

Combine sugar, cloves, cinnamon, allspice and ginger and 2 cups water in saucepan; bring to a boil. Boil for 10 minutes; remove from heat. Let stand for 1 hour; strain. Combine sugar mixture with orange juice, lemon juice and cider; bring to a boil. Serve immediately in punch cups or mugs. Yield: 12 servings.

Mrs. John Korkosz, Hosp. Chm., OWC
Loring AFB, Maine

HOT VEGETABLE JUICE CUP

1 46-oz. can cocktail vegetable juice
1 10 1/2-oz. can beef consomme
1 tbsp. Worcestershire sauce
2 tbsp. soy sauce
Hot sauce to taste

Combine all ingredients in large saucepan; bring just to a boil. Serve hot in punch cups. Yield: 8 servings.

Mrs. William W. Lewis, Past Pres., OWC
Tempelhof Air Base, Berlin, Germany

PERCOLATOR PUNCH

1 c. brown sugar
4 1/2 tsp. whole cloves
4 sticks cinnamon, broken
1 tsp. salt
2 46-oz. cans pineapple juice
1 1/2 qt. cranberry juice

Combine sugar, spices and salt in basket of 30-cup coffee pot. Combine 4 1/2 cups water with pineapple and cranberry juices in pot. Perk through cycle. Serve in cups. Yield: 30-40 servings.

Mrs. John C. Gazlay, Pres., OWC
Fort Polk, Louisiana

DELICATELY SPICED TEA

2 c. orange-flavored instant breakfast
  drink
1 1/2 c. instant tea
2 c. sugar
1 4-oz. package instant lemonade
1/4 tsp. cinnamon
1/2 tsp. ground cloves

Combine all ingredients; mix well. Store in air-tight jar. Add 2 teaspoons mixture to 1 cup boiling water; stir until mixture is dissolved. Add butter and rum to taste for hot toddy.

Mrs. Elizabeth B. Swan, OWC
Ft. McClellan, Alabama

EVERYBODY'S FAVORITE RUSSIAN TEA

2 1/2 c. orange-flavored instant
  breakfast drink
1/2 c. instant tea
1 1/2 c. sugar
1 tsp. ground cloves
1 tsp. cinnamon

Combine all ingredients; mix well. Store in airtight jar. Place 2 teaspoons tea mixture in cup; fill with boiling water. Stir until tea mixture is dissolved. Yield: 25 servings.

Mrs. Richard A. Miller, 2nd VP, OWC
Kelley Barracks, Stuttgart, Germany

LOW-CALORIE SPICED TEA

1 c. instant low-calorie tea with lemon
1 c. orange-flavored instant breakfast
  drink
1/2 tbsp. ground cloves
1 tbsp. cinnamon

Combine all ingredients; blend thoroughly. Place 1 teaspoon tea mixture in cup; add boiling water. Stir until tea mixture is dissolved.

Mrs. E. T. Westfall, Hon. Chm., NOWC
Portsmouth Naval Shipyard
Portsmouth, New Hampshire

ORANGE-SPICED TEA

2 c. orange-flavored instant breakfast
  drink

1 pkg. lemonade mix
1/2 c. instant tea
2 tsp. cinnamon
1 tsp. ground cloves
2 c. sugar

Combine all ingredients; mix well. Store in air-tight container. Place 1 1/2 to 2 teaspoons mix in cup; add boiling water. Stir until mix is dissolved.

Mrs. Freeman A. Grant, Jr., Cookbook Chm., OWC
NAS, Barbers Point, Hawaii

TANGY RUSSIAN TEA

1 2-oz. jar orange-flavored instant
  breakfast drink
1 pkg. lemonade mix
1 1/4 c. sugar
1/2 tsp. ground cloves
1 tbsp. cinnamon
1/2 c. instant tea

Combine all ingredients; mix well. Store mix in airtight jar. Place 2 heaping teaspoons mix in 1 cup boiling water; stir until mix is dissolved. Yield: 20 servings.

Mrs. Myrna N. Lee, Publ. Chm., OWC
White Sands Missile Range, New Mexico

LO-CAL BERRY SHAKE

8 oz. skim milk
1/2 c. unsweetened frozen berries
Artificial sweetener to taste
1/2 tsp. vanilla
3 crushed ice cubes

Combine all ingredients in blender container; blend until smooth. Serve immediately. Yield: 1 serving.

Mrs. R. S. Hughes, Treas., NOWC
Portsmouth Naval Shipyard, New Hampshire

BRANDIED FRUIT MILK SHAKE

1/3 c. Brandied Fruit
1 pt. vanilla ice cream
2 to 3 c. milk

Combine all ingredients in blender container; blend until smooth. Milk may be added, if desired.

Brandied Fruit

1 c. canned drained pineapple chunks
1 c. sliced drained peaches
1 8-oz. jar maraschino cherries
1 pkg. yeast
1 1/2 c. sugar

Place fruits in 6-cup apothecary jar with loose-fitting cover. Add yeast and sugar; stir well until sugar is dissolved. Let stand, covered, at room temperature for 2 weeks. Every 2 weeks add 1 cup of drained and sliced fruit and 1 cup sugar. Alternate fruit. Do not allow contents to measure less than 2 cups. May be served on ice cream or parfaits, if desired.

Mrs. Timothy L. Thomas, Gourmet Chm., OWC
Wright-Patterson AFB, Ohio

ORANGE EGGNOG

6 eggs, separated
1 1/2 c. orange juice
1/4 c. sugar
3 to 4 c. milk
Grated orange rind

Combine beaten egg yolks, orange juice and 1 teaspoon sugar; beat well. Beat egg whites until soft peaks form; add remaining sugar gradually, beating until stiff peaks form. Fold egg white mixture into egg yolk mixture, reserving 1 cup egg white mixture. Spoon eggnog into tall glasses about 1/2 full. Fill glasses to within 1 inch from top with milk. Spoon reserved egg white mixture into top of each glass. Sprinkle with orange rind. Yield: 6 servings.

Mrs. Charles F. Bernhardt, Jr., Publ. Chm., OWC
Webb AFB, Texas

MINTED LEMON ALE

10 to 12 sprigs of fresh mint
1 c. fresh lemon juice
1/2 c. sugar
1 qt. chilled ginger ale

Remove leaves from sprigs of fresh mint. Pour lemon juice, sugar and 1/2 cup water over mint leaves. Let stand for 30 minutes. Add ginger ale and enough ice to chill. Serve in old-fashioned glasses. Yield: 10-14 servings.

Mrs. George C. Hubbard, Corr. Sec., OWC
Patrick AFB, Florida

MINT DRINK

2 c. sugar
1 c. chopped fresh mint
Juice and chopped rind of 4 lemons
Crushed ice
Ginger ale

Combine sugar and 1 quart water in saucepan; boil for 10 minutes. Place mint, lemon juice and chopped lemon rinds in bowl; pour hot sugar syrup over mint mixture. Let stand overnight; strain. Place in covered container; chill. Combine 1/3 crushed ice, 1/3 mint syrup and 1/3 ginger ale in tall glasses. Yield: 10 servings.

Mrs. R. H. Steckler, 1st VP, OWC
Hamilton AFB, California

RECEPTION PUNCH

4 c. sugar
2 c. fresh lemon juice
1 qt. fresh orange juice
2 c. fresh lime juice
1 1-pt. 12-oz. bottle ginger ale

Combine sugar with 1 quart water and 1/4 cup lemon juice. Bring to boiling point; boil for 3 minutes. Cool. Add orange juice; add 3 quarts cold water, remaining lemon juice and lime juice. Pour into punch bowl over ice; add ginger ale. Garnish with lemon slices studded with cloves. Yield: About 6 quarts.

CHRISTMAS PUNCH

1 qt. canned unsweetened pineapple juice
1 qt. vanilla ice cream
1 qt. lemon sherbet
1 qt. pale dry ginger ale, chilled
Grated nutmeg (opt.)

Chill pineapple juice overnight. Combine ice cream and sherbet in large bowl; allow to soften. Add pineapple juice, beating with rotary beater until frothy. Pour into punch bowl; stir in ginger ale. Serve in punch cups immediately. Sprinkle with nutmeg if desired. Yield: 4 quarts.

Mrs. H. L. Wilkerson, Hon. Pres., OWC
Camp LeJeune, North Carolina

GOLDEN SHERBET PUNCH

2 c. sugar
1 1/2 c. fresh mint
3/4 c. lemon juice
1   12-oz. can apricot nectar
1   6-oz. can frozen limeade concentrate
1   6-oz. can frozen orange juice
   concentrate
1   6-oz. can pineapple juice concentrate
2 qt. ginger ale, chilled
1 qt. lemon sherbet

Combine sugar and mint with 2 cups boiling water. Allow to cool; strain. Add lemon juice, apricot nectar, limeade, orange juice, and pine-apple juice concentrate; mix well. Chill thoroughly. Add ginger ale and lemon sherbet just before serving. Garnish with sprigs of mint. Serve in punch cups. Yield: 20-25 servings.

Mrs. Charles N. Reed, Corr. Sec., OWC
Great Lakes Naval Hosp., Great Lakes, Illinois

SHERBET PUNCH

Sherbet
Ginger ale, chilled

Place sherbet in punch bowl; add ginger ale until of desired consistency. Serve immediately in punch cups.

Mrs. Sherill Allen, OWC
Athenai Airport, Greece

DAPPLE APPLE FLIP

6 individual tea bags
1 can frozen apple juice

2 tbsp. lemon juice
Sugar

Place tea bags in teapot; pour 3 cups boiling water over tea bags. Brew for 3 to 5 minutes. Pour into large pitcher; let stand at room temperature until cool. Stir in frozen apple juice until thawed; add 4 cups cold water and lemon juice. Sweeten to taste with sugar. Pour over ice cubes in tall glasses. Garnish with lemon wedges. Yield: 8 servings.

Mrs. Stuart B. McCurdy, W and M Chm., OWC
MacDill AFB, Florida

FRUIT PUNCH FOR WEDDINGS

1 c. sugar
2 cans frozen orange juice
1 lg. can apricot juice
1 lg. can pineapple juice
1 c. lemon juice
2 qt. ginger ale
1 qt. tea

Combine sugar and 2 cups water in saucepan; boil until syrupy. Chill all ingredients well. Pour into punch bowl; serve immediately in punch cups. Yield: 46 servings.

Mrs. Thomas M. Parker, OWC
Bainbridge Naval Training Center, Maryland

HOSPITALITY TEA PUNCH

3 c. boiling water
5 orange and spice-flavored tea bags
1   6-oz. can frozen grape juice
3/4 c. lemon juice
2 c. orange juice
4 c. cold water
1 c. sugar
Ice
Lemon slices
1   12-oz. bottle ginger ale, chilled

Pour boiling water over tea bags in teapot. Cover; steep for 5 minutes. Discard tea bags; cool tea. Combine tea, grape juice, lemon juice, orange juice, cold water and sugar in large punch bowl, stirring to dissolve sugar. Add ice just before serving; garnish with lemon slices. Stir in ginger ale. Serve in punch cups. Yield: 3 quarts.

Mrs. John C. Gazay, Pres., OWC
Fort Polk, Louisiana

PINEAPPLE-LIME PUNCH

2 1/2 c. chilled canned pineapple juice
1 pt. lime sherbet
1 pt. vanilla ice cream
1 12-oz. bottle chilled sparkling water

Combine pineapple juice, sherbet and half the ice cream in large bowl; beat until smooth. Add sparkling water. Spoon remaining ice cream into punch. Serve in punch cups immediately. Yield: 14 servings.

Mrs. Paul D. Martin, Treas., OWC
Ellsworth AFB, South Dakota

SUMMERTIME COOLER

3 pkg. lime powdered drink mix
3 qt. ginger ale
2 qt. lime sherbet

Mix powdered drink mix according to package directions. Add ginger ale; stir slightly. Float lime sherbet in punch, allowing it to melt slightly. Serve in punch cups. Yield: 30 servings.

Mrs. J. A. Simmons, Cookbook Chm., OWC
Camp Lejeune Marine Corps Base, North Carolina

SIPPING NECTAR

1 6-oz. can frozen orange juice
1 5-oz. can frozen lemonade
1 12-oz. can apricot nectar
1 12-oz. can pineapple juice
1 lg. bottle ginger ale, chilled

Thaw frozen juices. Combine orange juice, apricot nectar, pineapple juice and lemonade in 2-quart container; chill well. Pour punch into medium bowl; add ginger ale. Serve immediately in punch cups. Yield: 12 servings.

Mrs. Robert W. Kesteloot, Memshp. Chm., NOWC
Naval Station, San Diego, California

SPARKLING GARNET PUNCH

1 2 to 3-lb. bunch seedless grapes
3 qt. cranberry juice
1/4 c. sugar
8 whole allspice
3 sm. cinnamon sticks
5 16-oz. bottles club soda
3 drops of almond extract

Wash grapes carefully; freeze in 1 bunch on cookie sheet overnight. Combine cranberry juice, sugar, allspice and cinnamon in large saucepan; bring to a boil. Reduce heat; simmer for 10 minutes. Cool; strain, discarding spices. Chill overnight. Place frozen grapes in punch bowl; add remaining ingredients, stirring to blend well. Serve in punch cups. Three to four bottles champagne may be substituted for club soda.

Mrs. David C. Robinson, Pres., OWC
Illesheim, Germany

THREE-FRUIT PUNCH

2 6-oz. cans frozen orange juice
2 6-oz. cans frozen lemon juice
6 c. water
1 46-oz. can pineapple juice
1 c. sugar
2 12-oz. bottles ginger ale, chilled

Thaw frozen juices; add water and pineapple juice. Stir in sugar. Ladle into wide-topped freezer containers, leaving 1-inch space. Cover tightly; freeze. Partially thaw fruit juice mixture at room temperature for about 4 hours; place in punch bowl. Stir with fork to break up ice chunks; add ginger ale. Serve in punch cups. Yield: 25 servings.

Mrs. R. Y. McBurney, Hon. Adv., OWC
Shaw AFB, South Carolina

TOMATO-CONSOMME PUNCH

1 1-qt. 4-oz. can tomato juice
2 cans consomme
2 12-oz. cans cocktail vegetable juice
Juice of 2 lemons
White pepper
Worcestershire sauce
1 thinly sliced lemon

Mix first 4 ingredients together; season to taste with pepper and Worcestershire sauce. Chill. Add lemon slices and enough ice cubes to chill just before serving. Serve in punch cups. Yield: 10 servings.

Helga E. Kelly, W and M Chm., OWC
Fort Hancock, New Jersey

GOLDEN SPARKLER PUNCH

1   46-oz. can apricot juice
2   6-oz. cans frozen orange juice
1   6-oz. can frozen lemon juice
1   1 pt. 2-oz. can pineapple juice
6   7-oz. bottles lemon-lime carbonated
    beverage

Combine all ingredients; chill well. Pour into
punch bowl; add desired amount of ice. Serve
in punch cups. Yield: 32 servings.

Jane Bentley, Sp. Activities, OWC
McChord AFB, Washington

HOT CHOCOLATE MIX

1   16-oz. can instant chocolate drink mix
1   11-oz. jar non-dairy coffee creamer
1   8-qt. carton instant nonfat dry milk
1/2 lb. confectioners' sugar

Combine all ingredients in large container; mix
thoroughly. Combine 1/2 cup mix with 1 cup
boiling water; stir well. Add vanilla, if desired.
Garnish with whipped cream or marshmallows.
Mix will keep indefinitely.

Mrs. William C. Angerman, Pres., OWC
Daley Barracks, Bad Kissingen, Germany

EVER-READY SPICE TEA

1 sm. package lemonade mix
2 c. orange-flavored instant breakfast
   drink
2 1/2 c. sugar
1 c. instant tea
1 tsp. ground cloves
2 tsp. cinnamon

Combine all ingredients; mix thoroughly. Store
mix in airtight jar. Place 1 heaping teaspoon
mix into 1 cup boiling water; stir until mix is
dissolved. Yield: 50 servings.

Mrs. Edwin F. Miller, Welfare Chm., OWC
Ft. Sheridan, Illinois

INSTANT SPICED TEA

1 1/2 c. orange-flavored instant
   breakfast drink
3/4 c. instant tea
1 pkg. dry lemonade mix
1 1/2 c. sugar

1 tsp. cinnamon
1/2 tsp. ground cloves

Combine all ingredients; blend thoroughly.
Store in glass jar with airtight lid. Place 2 heaping teaspoons tea mixture in cup; add boiling
water, stirring until mixture is dissolved.

Mrs. James J. Bothe, OWC
U. S. Naval Facility, Eleuthera, Bahamas

REGAL RUSSIAN TEA

2 c. sugar
2 c. orange-flavored instant breakfast
   drink
1/2 c. instant lemon-flavored tea
1 1/2 tsp. cinnamon
3/4 tsp. ground cloves

Combine all ingredients; mix thoroughly. Store
in airtight jar. Place 2 teaspoons of mix in each
cup; add boiling water. Stir until mix is dissolved. Yield: 50 servings.

Mrs. Henry Earle Goff, Corr. Sec., OWC
Offutt AFB, Nebraska

CRANBERRY NOG

1 c. cranberry juice cocktail
1 tsp. lemon juice
1 egg
1 c. milk

Chill all ingredients; pour into blender container. Blend until frothy. Serve in punch cups;
garnish with dollops of whipped cream and
with nutmeg. Yield: 2 servings.

Mrs. Lawrence Fay, Bazaar Chm., NOWC
Charleston Naval Base, South Carolina

ORANGE-APPLE PUNCH

1 qt. apple juice
1 oz. red cinnamon candies
1   18-oz. jar orange-flavored instant
    breakfast drink
1   46-oz. can orange drink
3   12-oz. cans ginger ale
1 fresh orange, sliced

Heat apple juice; add cinnamon candies and
breakfast drink, stirring until dissolved. Remove
from heat; cool. Stir in orange drink. Add
ginger ale just before serving. Serve over
crushed ice. Float oranges slices in punch bowl.

Serve in old-fashioned glasses. Yield: 18-24 servings.

Mrs. George C. Hubbard, Corr. Sec., OWC
Patrick AFB, Florida

ALMOST ORANGE JULIUS

1 c. fresh orange juice
1/2 c. instant nonfat dry milk
1 1/2 tbsp. sugar
1/8 tsp. vanilla
1/2 c. shaved ice

Combine all ingredients in blender container; blend at high speed until frothy. Serve immediately in tall glass. Yield: 1 serving.

Mrs. James C. Pantling, Jr., Past Pres., NCS OWC
NAVCOMMSTA, Guam

PINEAPPLE-ORANGE REFRESHER

Pineapple juice
1/2 c. sugar
6 12-oz. cans lemon-lime carbonated drink
1/2 c. lemon juice
2 6-oz. cans frozen orange juice
1 sliced lemon
1 sliced orange

Mix equal parts of pineapple juice and water together in ring mold; freeze. Combine sugar and 1 cup water; stir until dissolved. Add 2 46-ounce cans pineapple juice, carbonated drink and lemon juice. Prepare frozen orange juice according to can directions; add to punch. Pour into punch bowl. Float ice ring on punch; garnish with orange and lemon slices. Serve in punch cups. Yield: 36 servings.

Mrs. Richard P. Geer, Pres., OWC
Lackland AFB, Texas

QUANTICO NAVY RELIEF PUNCH

4 med. ripe bananas
1 sm. can frozen grapefruit juice,
    thawed
3 sm. cans frozen orange juice, thawed
1 46-oz. can pineapple juice
1 c. sugar
2 1/2 qt. water
2 qt. lemon-lime carbonated beverage

Mash bananas; beat with electric mixer until smooth and fluffy or liquify in blender. Add remaining ingredients except carbonated beverage. Mix well. Refrigerate overnight. Add carbonated beverage just before serving; stir

slightly. May freeze strawberries in ice ring and float ring on punch, if desired. Yield: 8 quarts.

Mrs. J. A. Simmons, Cookbook Chm., OWC
Camp Lejeune, North Carolina

SPARKY PUNCH

2 cans frozen orange juice
2 cans frozen lemonade
1/2 lg. can pineapple juice
1 bottle lemon-lime carbonated beverage

Combine orange juice, lemonade and pineapple juice; mix well. Add 2 quarts water. Pour into punch bowl. Stir in lemon-lime beverage and ice. Serve immediately in punch cups.

Nancy Teri Suehs, NOWC
NAVSTA ADAK, Alaska

RED PUNCH

1 lg. package raspberry powdered drink
    mix
1 46-oz. can pineapple juice
Ginger ale to taste

Combine powdered drink mix with 2 cups water; stir in pineapple juice. Pour over ice in punch bowl; add ginger ale. Ice cubes of pineapple juice mixture may be used, if desired. Serve in punch cups. Yield: 12 servings.

Mrs. John F. Schneider, Pres., OWC
Ft. Campbell, Kentucky

SATTLER PUNCH

1 c. sugar
1 6-oz. can frozen lemonade
1 6-oz. can frozen orange juice
1 6-oz. can frozen limeade or daiquiri
    mix
2 lg. cans pineapple juice
1 qt. ginger ale
1 qt. club soda
Ice ring
Fresh mint sprigs

Dissolve sugar in 1 cup hot water; combine with lemonade, orange juice, limeade and pineapple juice in punch bowl. Add ginger ale and club soda just before serving. Float ice ring; garnish with mint sprigs. Serve immediately in punch cups. Yield: 24 servings.

Mrs. Betty A. Sattler, Decorations Chm., OWC
Amphibious Base, Little Creek, Norfolk, Virginia

THE MAKING OF KENTUCKY BOURBON

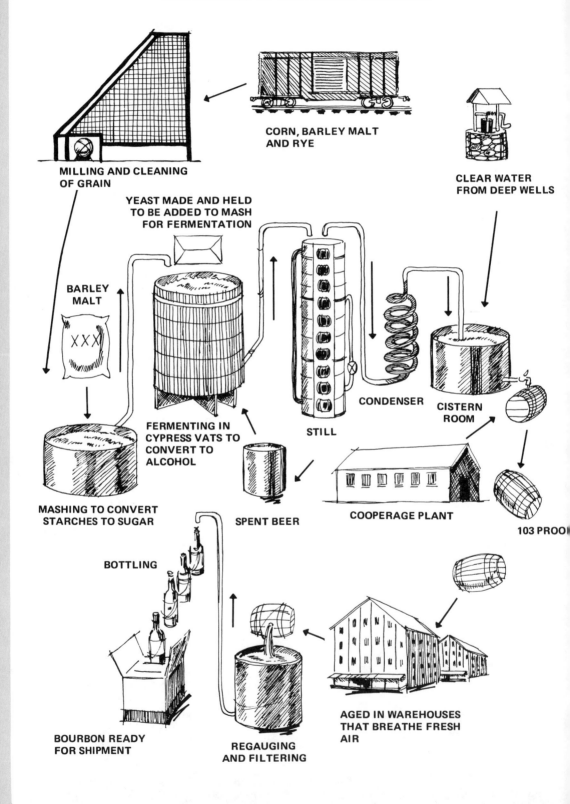

CORN, BARLEY MALT AND RYE

MILLING AND CLEANING OF GRAIN

CLEAR WATER FROM DEEP WELLS

YEAST MADE AND HELD TO BE ADDED TO MASH FOR FERMENTATION

BARLEY MALT

XXX

FERMENTING IN CYPRESS VATS TO CONVERT TO ALCOHOL

CONDENSER

CISTERN ROOM

STILL

MASHING TO CONVERT STARCHES TO SUGAR

SPENT BEER

COOPERAGE PLANT

103 PROOF

BOTTLING

BOURBON READY FOR SHIPMENT

REGAUGING AND FILTERING

AGED IN WAREHOUSES THAT BREATHE FRESH AIR

DRINK /INDEX

COLOR PHOTO EXPLANATION

This edition in the Recipes on Parade series contains hundreds of successful party plans from members of Officers' Wives' Clubs. Beautiful full-color photographs, chosen by the editors of Favorite Recipes Press, feature a variety of menu ideas. Located throughout the volume, the photographs — along with their accompanying recipes — offer food suggestions designed for entertaining guests.

PLANNING A PARTY

Planning a successful party is truly an art. Careful planning helps make sure that nothing is left to chance. Give yourself enough time to plan every detail so that you won't be madly throwing things together at the last minute. If you don't, your fatigue will make you the wet blanket of your own party.

One of the details which goes into careful preparation is deciding on the type of party you wish to have. This should be your first step after you've decided to have a party. Needless to say, you're having this party because you want to, for aside from a few parties held for business reasons, people rarely have parties except for the pleasure they and their guests derive from them. Deciding on the type and theme of party will help you in organizing it. If you decide on a Mexican fiesta, you will then have basic ideas for the decorations and menu settled in your mind.

The type of party you give will usually depend on your life style, the size of your home and your budget. But don't necessarily let these things limit you, for dances can be held in small houses as well as in mansions. One young couple living in a five room bungalow decided to give a dance with ten couples invited. They emptied their dining room of furniture and turned it into the dancing area, set the refreshment table up in the hall and used the living room for conversation. The guests all had a marvelous time and did not feel in the least cramped.

The next step in preparing your party is deciding on the time and place. A graduation tea, small buffet dinner for friends, or evening bridge party are perfect for midweek. But, if you work or if most of your friends work, you might want to plan a large party like a dance or a cocktail party for a weekend night.

If you are planning a party with a co-hostess, get together with her and decide where you want to have it. For parties outside your home, for instance, in a school community center or country club, be sure to reserve the room you wish to use two to three weeks in advance.

Planning your guest list should be your next step. Your guests are one of the important details in planning a good party, because guests make the party. Choose compatible people — especially for a small party such as an informal sit-down dinner. Again the type of party you choose to have will be an important factor in planning your guest list. There are three main choices when planning a guest list. Either mix old friends who know each other well, people who are not acquainted, but who you feel will enjoy each other, or a combination of the two. The last makes for the best mixture at parties, for your friends will appreciate meeting new people and the added spark that they bring to your group will liven your party.

Now that you've decided on the type of party you wish to have, the day, the time, and the guest list, you can begin planning the other details needed to make this party successful. If you're planning an elegant seated dinner with twenty-five guests, you may want to look into a catering service or extra kitchen help. These services should be contacted at least two or three weeks before your party, and should be checked with a week prior to your party date to make certain there will be no last minute slip-ups.

Your next detail in planning a party should be the menu. One of the advantages to having a theme for your party is that it gives you a guide for planning your menu. Party food can range from a full catered dinner to a few simple hors d'oeuvres and drinks. Food does not have to be the most important aspect of a party, so plan what will fit your budget and cooking abilities.

After planning your menu, you should decide on the type of decorations you wish to use. Again, theme parties will help you in this. If you're using a zodiac theme for a dinner party, you could make the place cards in the shape of each guest's zodiac sign, carrying this idea throughout the rest of your decorations. Elaborate decorations are not necessary. Advance preparation will allow time to create various and delightful types of decorations. Fresh flowers and candles always look lovely at dinners or bridal showers. And for children's parties, any cute home-made decorations following the theme will appeal to the young guests.

A good idea for economizing is to shop for decorations when stores are having sales, such as after Christmas or Halloween. Then store your bargains for next year's party. When school is out for the summer, construction paper, felt-tipped pens and pencils are often less expensive. If you have access to a wholesale house, this is a perfect place to get your supplies at a sizable discount.

Also take advantage of your garden or the garden of your friends for flowers and greens. Or, if you live near the country, look for leaves, Spanish moss and other natural decorations to create the perfect mood for your party. Many city dwellers will not have access to these, so if you wish to have flowers, contact your local florist in plenty of time so he can be sure to have the type and arrangement you wish.

Now we come to the most important detail for a successful party, the guests and the manner in which you invite them. Your invitations should be issued at least two to three weeks in advance. Whether your invitations are written or spoken, they should accomplish two things:

they should inform your guests that you desire their company at your party in the warmest and most sincere way possible, and they should clearly give your guests all the pertinent information as to date, time, dress, and so on.

There is nothing worse than arriving at a party in slacks when everyone else is in long skirts and cocktail dresses. To keep this dilemma from occurring at your party, be sure to specify the desired apparel. In this modern world, almost anything goes as far as dress is concerned. But guests should be told what the expected mode of dress will be. Be sure to let your guests know if you're planning any sort of special activity like swimming, or be specific if you want your guests to wear costumes. For a formal occasion, specify either "black tie" or "white tie" on the invitation.

An invitation for a children's party should not only include the time the party begins, but also the time you expect it to end. This will insure that your party is not too long for little people's attention spans. And it will let the mothers know exactly when they are to pick up their children. It is often a good idea to indicate in your invitation to adult parties the time you expect the party to end. This will give your guests who might have baby-sitters an idea of when they will get home, and will also ward off guests who tend to stay late into the night.

Written or printed invitations are especially nice and can set your mood for the party in advance. Some of the most delightful invitations are the handmade ones. These can reflect the theme of the party, adding to the festive air and helping create the party mood, just as engraved invitations indicate to your guests that a party is formal. Handmade invitations allow your immagination to run free.

Whether you extend a written or a telephoned invitation to an informal party is entirely up to you. A written one does make sure the guests have all the necessary information concerning the party, but this can also be accomplished over the phone. The only time a written invitation is entirely necessary is for a formal dinner, banquet, ball, debut and so on. These are usually written in the third person and responded to in like manner.

If you're planning a bridesmaids' luncheon, a formal anniversary dinner or a wedding brunch, the table setting is a most important detail. It should carry out the theme of your party. Choose cloths, flowers and place cards that reflect your party's format. A table covering can be anything from a lovely antique damask cloth to an India print bedspread, just as long as the party mood is carried through.

The kind of silver and china you use will also reflect the party mood. If you're planning an outdoor party, straw table mats and colorful paper plates are great and make cleaning up afterwards so easy. Centerpieces can range from flowers and candles to miniature handmade Maypoles or rocket ships. Your table reflects your personality, so use your imagination and don't feel stifled by traditional rules. If you think that your good crystal and silver look appropriate with your multi-colored everyday china or even your stainless steel steak platters, or other combinations of table settings seem to help set the mood for your party, don't hesitate to use them.

When you use place cards, let them reflect your party theme. They could be cut in the shape of ships for a bon voyage party. Or for a party

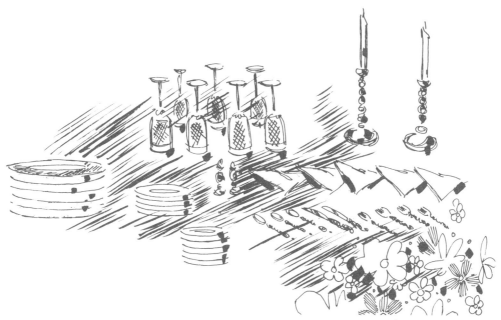

with a French theme, you could make miniature menus with a person's name on the front and your dinner menu inside.

When you first plan to have your party, check your linen and other table supplies to make certain you have all you need for the type party you want to give. This advance preparation will enable you to borrow or rent anything extra you may need. Several days before your party, wash all the dishes and polish the silver to be used. Then, on the day of your party, all you'll have to do is wipe off the glasses and set your table.

Place cards are a marvelous way to get people who don't know each other acquainted, or to seat an extrovert next to an introvert. It is always nice to have an equal number of men and women at your parties, especially at sit-down dinners, where the old rule of boy-girl, boy-girl applies. Your seating arrangement should again reflect the mood and spirit of your party.

If you allow yourself two to three weeks for planning your party, you will have plenty of time to arrange all the needed details to make your party a success. All the last minute things like cleaning your house, decorating and buying perishables can be accomplished in the days just before your party. Those last days will be exciting instead of hectic because your advance planning will have everything under control.

THE SIZE OF YOUR PARTY

The size of your party, of course, depends on how many guests you wish to invite. Take into account how many you can comfortably manage in the space available. It is no pleasure to be elbow-to-elbow in a small room — wall-to-wall people will assure only spilling of drinks and stepped-on toes. If you wish to give a cocktail party for a larger number of people than your living room will accommodate, consider setting up the bar in the hallway and urging guests toward the patio; or opening the entire house or apartment to your guests with snacks and hors d'oeuvres in every room. Still another solution, perhaps the most practical, is to split your guest list, entertaining on two nights rather than one.

Secondly, out of consideration for your friends and in an effort to assure them of a pleasant evening, invite people who are likely to enjoy one another's company. And never ask anyone you dislike — although you may have become obligated to such a person. It is better to *remain* so than to blight the party atmosphere. It is a mistake to attempt to fulfill all social obligations at once with a single huge bash — randomly tossing people together in an effort to invite everyone to whom you "owe" an invitation.

A dinner party is a better choice when you wish to entertain a dozen or fewer people whom you know well, unless there are plans for the group to go on to, for example, the theatre. Ordinarily this sized gathering at a cocktail party tends to split into a huddle of men on one side of the room and a clique of women on the other, and it is then difficult to get people circulating without being obtrusive. Thus a dinner party keeps the group integrated.

A final consideration when making up your guest list is to include several outgoing personalities — Life-of-the-party people can often rescue a slow evening. Also, ask a few people from varying age groups. Don't be afraid to ask older or younger people whose interests are compatible with those of yourself or your guests.

Invitations should be issued well enough in advance of the event to assure that the majority of invitees will be able to attend. Two weeks is in most cases adequate notice. However, for a formal wedding or debut, four to six weeks is recommended — especially if there are to be out-of-town guests.

Sometimes it is more convenient to telephone invitations if fewer than twenty guests are invited. This not only saves a lot of desk work, but enables you to know right away how many guests to expect. Of course, when you are fortunate enough to know the number of guests attending, you eliminate the risks of running out of food or drink, or over-spending for items not needed.

Sooner or later, all of us face the responsibility of entertaining a large group, too large for household facilities. We must then choose a suitable party area.

First, choose an area that you are familiar with. A private club is usually your best choice. It isn't open to the public, yet it is usually large enough to accommodate any size group. Always make sure you notify your club in ample time for arrangements to be made. Some private clubs can be rented even by non-members, so check all possibilities.

Hotels often have large party rooms for rent. Grand ballrooms and presidential suites frequently hold over a thousand people. Small party rooms are very comfortable for groups of fifty to a hundred.

If the type of party you've planned lends itself well to the outdoors, consider a popular picnic site, camping area or public park. Outdoor parties relieve any worry of space, and small and large groups alike usually enjoy the free-spirited atmosphere of being outside.

To eliminate burdens of too much expense or too much time consuming work in giving large parties, hostesses frequently combine their efforts. With the combined talents of several hostesses, parties can be a fantastic center of entertainment and good food, or if not conducted properly, an extreme bore and "comedy of errors". When you are asked to participate in giving a party and you wish to accept, do so with the understanding that you will devote as much help as is expected of you. If you ask friends or neighbors to join you in giving a party, make sure you ask only those you can trust to hold up their end of the bargain.

Co-hostesses should be congenial toward each other with a mutual interest in entertaining. The ideal combination would include someone artistic to arrange centerpieces and other decorations, someone talented in planning menus and preparing appropriate food for the occasion, someone who is willing to issue invitations and keep an account of how many guests are expected, someone who will supply entertainment like games for bridal parties and music for dancing parties, and any other hostesses who are needed.

All the hostesses should have the spirit of the party, work closely together and make sure their efforts are in unity with each other. Incidentally, steer clear of possible co-workers who lose their temper easily or get their feelings hurt frequently. After all, you are planning a *party*, not an international issue for the U.N.

Again, planning is the all important key to giving and enjoying a successful party. Planning every detail in advance will enable you to feel as though you are creating an exciting event, not laboring in effort to get through the "chore" of entertaining. Parties should be just as much fun for the hostess as they are for the guests.

STOCKING A BAR

Liquor is usually an expected item at most parties, and of course, the cocktail party revolves almost entirely around the bar. Therefore, it is always important to determine as near as possible how much you will need.

There are a number of things you must take into consideration when buying liquor. You, yourself, know what your guests enjoy most, so stock up on whatever is popular with your social circle. Liquor prices, sizes of containers and availability vary in different areas of the country. You may find the following equivalents helpful:

1 jigger	*= 1 1/2 ounces*		*1 fifth*	*= 25.6 ounces*
8 ounces	*= 1 cup*			*(12 to 16 servings)*
1 pint	*= 16 ounces*		*1 quart*	*= 32 ounces*
	(8 to 10 servings)			*(16 to 20 servings)*

Fortunately, you never have to worry about buying too much liquor. It keeps, and there will always be another party eventually.

Next, make sure you have enough mixers on hand: soft drinks, tonic water, soda water, juices and a pitcher of ice water. Store ice cubes in a plastic bag in the freezer before the party so you will have plenty. Have all the accompanying fruits on hand: lemon and lime wedges, orange slices, cherries and olives, etc.

In the whirl of planning mixed drinks, don't forget your non-drinkers. Be especially certain you provide them with their favorite fruit juice or soft drink.

Always have a pot of hot coffee ready near the end of the evening. Drivers, among others, sometimes like to make their last one coffee.

WINES AND SPIRITS

For the wine novice, the blur of bottles on a shelf offers a complete case of confusion. What wine goes with what food? What is a "good" year? Am I really getting a bargain or is this wine "dead"? The choice of wine is so complex that hundreds of wine experts have written reams of material on French wines. To lesson the confusion somewhat, we shall deal with the grossly underrated American wines.

J.B. Priestly, a contemporary English novelist and critic, summed up the feeling of Americans toward their own wines thusly, "You Americans have the loveliest wines in the world, but you don't realize it. You call them *domestic* wines, and that's enough to start trouble anywhere."

Unfortunately he was right. A great many Americans are vaguely knowledgeable about wines in general, but unknowledgeable about American wines in particular. That is very much like the New Yorker who bragged he had seen the world, but (sad to say) he had never seen the Empire State Building or the Statue of Liberty.

Each wine making area of the United States produces a distinctive wine. Wines of the mild California climate come from *vitis vinifera* vines, which originally came from Europe. In the northern states where there are rugged winters, the hardy native or hybrid vines, produce the best wines. These vines, like the Catawba or Concord, impart a "foxy" taste in the wine which is less noticeable in sparkling and sherry-type wines. (For this reason, the Finger Lakes area is noted for champagne and sparkling Burgundies.) It is not possible to compare the wines of these two sections, as the tastes are so completely different.

IN THE BEGINNING . . .

The *vitis vinifera* vines were introduced to California in 1769 (if we are to believe legend) when the Franciscan Friars came to the California coast from Mexico. These Spanish monks brought with them European vines which produced the mission wine used for sacramental purposes. California's rich soil, climate and abundant sunshine proved to be uncommonly suitable, and a red wine superior to that produced in Mexico or Spain was born.

With the discovery of gold in 1848, and the resulting explosion of the population from a few hundred to hundreds of thousands, the future of the wine industry of California was assured. The massive migration brought to California the Easterners, whose native wines has a spicy or "foxy" tang, and European immigrants, who were accustomed to their daily glasses of classic European wine.

Consequently, the infant California wine industry, started by a French-man and a Hungarian, had a conveniently located mass market of wine drinkers. In the tent cities of the Gold Rush, quite a few of the false-front saloons served harsh whiskey, hot beer and domestic wines which were already quite excellent. However, domestic wines were already being underrated. The old maxim, "if it's imported, it must be better" was already undermining the American wine industry.

Working separately, a Frenchman from Bordeaux, Jean Louise Vignes and a Hungarian, Count Agoston Hazasthy introduced hundreds of varieties of classic French and German vines. Both men were convinced that they could coax from the earth some of the best wines the world had ever known. Everything was working in favor of the young wine industry; the climate was always mild and stable, the location was excellent, and later, many of the immigrants who did not find gold, found jobs in the wine cellars. There was also an abundance of Chinese labor to care for the vineyards, which were kept well manicured.

The wine industry was progressing very favorably in California thanks to a man who made numerous important contributions to California's viniculture. Count Agoston Hazaszthy distributed over 200,000 vines to growers at his own expense. For nearly 50 years the California wine producers bottled and aged some of the finest wines in the world. But when the country was launched into the ruinous experiment of Prohibition, viniculture suffered a severe blow.

As far as the drinking public is concerned, the United States wine industry has spent many years in trying to re-educate a country who became accustomed to drinking "hootch", bath-tub gin and home-made "scotch". For those coming back to the United States from European vacations, drinking wine in Europe proved to be a very pleasurable experience. But many returned thinking the best wines were French.

When it comes time to select a bottle of imported wine, most become bogged down in vintage years, labels and foreign phrases. However, the California wine industry has done everything possible to make selecting wine easy. It does not confuse the novice with technicalities or phrases understandable only to another wine producer. In the United States, wines are named by three methods: generics, varietals and trade names.

"Generics" were names brought over with the immigrants in the 19th Century. Some of these names, like Chablis and Sherry are still in use today.

There has been a growing tendency since the late 1940's to name wines after their predominating grape variety; for example, Riesling or Chardonnay. These are collectively called "varietals".

Thirdly, some of the wineries use family or trade names of their own coinage: for example Ripple and Mogen David.

The producers themselves market most of their wines (as compared to the European way which is to sell the grapes to a producer who will blend them). The producer puts his name on the label and that of the shipper or distributor. Other information, such as alcholic content, must be on the label and is regulated by laws.

Until recently, the United States wine industry did not date their wines as the producers do in Europe. The reason for this is that the California weather is not a main factor in the growing or harvesting of the grapes as it is in Europe. The climate for wine producing in California is the best in the world and, therefore, there is never really a "bad" year. For example, in France, the vintage years for red Bordeaux (during the 1960's) were '61, '62, '64 (St. Emilion, Pomerol, Graves only), and '66. Thus, in 1961, the red Bordeaux was rated superb while the '63 and '65 were very poor. The '64 was considered great and the '66 excellent. 1968 was considered unexceptional, while 1969 was considered "promising". California wines do vary; however, it is usually noticeable only to the wine connoisseur.

When wine is dated in the United States, it is done to protect customers against a wine that is too old. Occasionally the date of bottling, if not marked on the label, will be imprinted on the bottom of the bottle.

A bottle of California wine may be drunk as soon as it is bought, or it may be "laid down" in a wine cellar where it will age and improve successfully up to 15 years. White California wines are meant to be drunk while they are young. However, they may be stored without fear of spoilage for six to seven years.

Since California generally names its wines by the predominating grape used, it is best for the novice to have a working knowledge of the type of varieties used.

CALIFORNIA WHITE WINES

One group of varietal wines offer themselves as light, fresh-flavored types which are best when drunk young with the mildly subtle flavor of poultry or shellfish: *Emerald Riesling, Gewurztraminer, Green Hungarian, Grey Riesling, Johannisberg* or *White Riesling* and *Sylvaner*. Of these six wines, only occasional bottlings of *Johannisberg* and *Gewurztraminer* are expected to age. Each of these has shown ability to remain fresh for five years, sound for ten. In California, *Johannisberg Riesling* makes a rich fruity, even robust wine.

A second group of fuller-bodied varietal white wines includes: *Semillon, Chardonnay* (or *Pinot Chardonnay*), *Sauvignon Blanc*, and *Chenin Blanc*. A Napa Valley or Sonoma bottling of Chardonnay or Sauvignon Blanc wine will gain with age up to six or seven years. For the wine enthusiast who wants to "lay down" in his wine cellar several bottles of intensely flavored white wines for aging, these two are highly recommended.

CALIFORNIA RED WINES

The California Red wines are very light and quite fruity tasting. These include: *Gamay, Grignolino, Pinot St. George, Ruby Cabernet* and *Zinfandel*. Fresh and appealing, these wines are highly suited to informal dining. A light chilling during summer months brings out the freshness and enhances them. *Zinfandel* deserves a special note of recognition as it is the most widely planted of all red-wine grapes in California. Incredibly adaptable, the *Zinfandel* (a mystery vine unique to California) produces relatively good wines in each of the five climate zones of California. It is at its best in the Napa and Sonoma areas where it produces a highly distinctive red wine capable of aging for ten years and is often described as raspberry-like.

Barbera, Cabernet Sauvignon, Petite Sirah and *Pinot Noir* are four other of the robust varietal reds of California. The French call the *Pinot Noir* the "noblest vine of all" as it has a highly characteristic flavor. Most of California Pinot Noir's reach peak flavor within five years while a few have needed ten years and an exceptionally few, twenty.

Cabernet Sauvignon, the celebrated vine which produces the great clarets of Bordeaux, can always be expected to age twenty years with some grace. This wine is highly tannic; when young it is strongly marked by the instantly recognizable flavor of its grape and acquires a subtleness through long aging.

Burgundies are the most popular of California's generic reds and are usually dry with a pronounced fruitiness. *Mountain Reds* are quite similar to the *Burgundies*, while *Chianti* is quite tart and *Vino Rossos* are sweet.

CALIFORNIA ROSES
A great majority of California's roses are generics, although a few are made as varietals. The grape giving the best results is the *Grenache,* unexcelled in the vin rose of Germany's Rhone Valley.

WINE AND WINE SERVING
Much to the amazement of tourists who visit California wineries, most produce a great many varieties of wine. The practice of producing several types of wines was started after the Prohibition era when competition was keen. For this reason their famed vineyards offer a wide range for every taste, every occasion. Most people prefer drier wines

with dinner, and sweeter wines at dessert or after dinner. The wine producers say that personal preferences should determine selection. If you prefer champagne, then by all means serve it throughout the meal!

WHICH WINE WITH WHICH FOOD?
Selecting the right wine often intrigues, but more often intimidates. Many a hostess has been driven to iced tea to avoid appearing "unknowledgeable" in serving wine. One rule of thumb which is generally correct is *white wine with white meat* and *red wine with red meat*. There are, of course, some notable exceptions. One exception is that any dish cooked in red wine (fish, for example) should be accompanied with red wine.

One way to "never go wrong" is to remember *the richer the food, the fuller flavored the wine*. For example, red or white, light or full wines are served with all poultry; the selection of the wine depending on the preparation of the dish. A good claret sets off roast chicken or turkey very well; chicken in a rich sauce calls for a white burgundy and chilled rose is good with cold chicken.

TWO WINES AT A MEAL
There are certain traditional guidelines that may be followed if two wines are being served during the course of a meal. They are: *white before red; dry before sweet; light before full; young before old*.

Discussed separately, these rules appear quite logical. *White before red; dry before sweet*: the white wine, which is dry, would appear to be quite bland or bitter and very disappointing if served after the richness of the red wine. One exception is the sweet white dessert wines which are correctly served at the end of the meal. *Light before full; young before old* generally applies to serving two types of the same red or white wine. A good bottle of aged red wine accompanied with some flavorful cheeses makes an excellent after dinner course, especially if a lighter young red wine was served with the main course. Certainly there is nothing fancy about serving two wines with one meal; it is a simple way to add an extra note of elegance to a meal and let the guest know that he is well-thought of. If only two or three people are dining, they may find that two half bottles of different wines are more enjoyable than a full bottle of one wine.

ADD A GOURMET TOUCH — COOKING WITH WINES

When used in cooking, wine provides a special goodness to the food by accenting the natural savor of the food . . . at the same time adding its own inviting fragrance and flavor. The only secret in cooking successfully with wine is to use a quality wine, as the alcohol evaporates during the cooking, leaving only the actual flavor of the wine. A fine wine with rich body and aroma will insure a distinct, delicate flavor.

	Food	Amount of Wine	Type of Wine
Soup	Cream soups	1 T. per cup	Sauterne or Sherry
	Meat and Vegetable Soups	1 T. per cup	Burgundy or Sherry
Sauces	Brown	1 T. per cup	Sherry or Burgundy
	Cheese	1 T. per cup	Sherry or Sauterne
	Cream	1 T. per cup	Sherry or Sauterne
	Dessert	1 T. per cup	Port or Muscatel
	Tomato	1 T. per cup	Sherry or Burgundy
Meats	Ham, baked	2 c. for basting	Port or Muscatel
	Liver, braised	¼ c. per pound	Burgundy or Sauterne
	Pot Roast	¼ c. per pound	Burgundy
	Gravy for Roasts	2 T. per cup	Burgundy or Sherry
	Stew, Beef	¼ c. per pound	Burgundy
	Stew, Lamb or Veal	¼ c. per pound	Sauterne
	Tongue, boiled	½ c. per pound	Burgundy
Fish	Baked, Broiled or Poached	½ c. per pound	Sauterne
Poultry and Game	Chicken	¼ c. per pound	Sauterne or Burgundy
	Gravy for roasted or fried Chicken or Turkey	2 T. per cup	Sauterne, Burgundy or Sherry
	Duck, roasted	¼ c. per pound	Burgundy
	Pheasant	¼ c. per pound	Sauterne, Burgundy or Sherry
	Venison	¼ c. per pound	Burgundy
Fruit (Fresh, Canned, Frozen)	In syrup or juice (Fruit cups, compotes, etc.)	2 T. per cup over fruit or in syrup or juice	Port, Muscatel, Sherry, Rose, Sauterne, Burgundy
	Drained	At the table, pour over fruits without dilution	Champagne or other Sparkling Wine

WINE BUYING GUIDE

Every hostess has known the moment of uncertainty when it comes time to buy enough wine to serve her guests. The following is a guide that will give you approximate amounts based on 3- to 3½ ounce servings for dinner wines and champagne. Amounts for appetizer and dessert wines are based on 2 to 2½ ounce servings.

If you must buy a large quantity of beverages for a large gathering, plan on at least three servings for each guest. One case of twelve (4/5 quart) bottles will yield about 100 glasses, or will provide 3 - 4 servings for 25 to 30 guests.

Size of Bottle	Ounces	Appetizer and Dessert Wines	Dinner Wines and Champagne
Split (2/5 pt.)	6.4	2 servings	2 servings
Tenth (4/5 pt.)	12.8	4 servings	4 - 6 servings
Pint	16.0	5 servings	5 - 7 servings
Fifth	25.6	8 servings	8 - 12 servings
Quart (4/5 qt.)	32.0	10 servings	10 - 14 servings
Magnum	52.0	16 servings	16 - 20 servings
½ Gallon	64.0	20 servings	20 - 30 servings
Gallon	128.0	40 servings	40 - 60 servings

WINE SELECTION GUIDE — THE FIVE CLASSES OF WINES

APPETIZER AND DESSERT WINES

APPETIZER WINES

Aperitif or appetizer wines are commonly drunk before meals or served with the soup course, as they are usually dry. They may be chilled, poured over ice or served at room temperature (60 to 65 degrees). Sherry and Vermouth are both dry, and best when served with appetizers. Port, while usually thought of as a dessert wine, can be served as an appetizer wine with cheese and nuts. (Most hostesses prefer to serve white Port, instead of red, as an aperitif.)

DESSERT WINES

Dessert wines should be poured after dinner with the dessert or served later. They are all sweet, rich wines that are particularly good with desserts, fruit, nuts, cheeses, cakes and pastries. Serve at room temperature. Dessert wines are: Rare Tawny and Tinta Port, Muscatel, Tokay, Sweet Champagne, Cream Sherry, Sweet Sherry, Sauterne, Marsala and Malaga.

SPARKLING WINES

Ranging from extremely dry to very sweet, from pale gold to deep red, these festive wines are appropriate at any time. They go well with food or by themselves. Sparkling wines are best when well chilled. Champagnes are classified by their sweetness: *Natural* - very dry; *Brut* - dry; *Extra Dry* - with just a hint of sweetness; *Dry* - medium sweet; *Sec* - noticeably sweet; *Demi-Sec* - very sweet. Pink Champagne is a sparkling rose; Sparkling Burgundy is a red wine and Sparkling Muscat is a Muscat wine which has artificial carbonation added.

SPECIAL NATURAL WINES

The introduction of "pop" wines, and the overwhelming acceptance by young Americans has been an immeasurable boon to the California wine industry. Pop wines are blended white wines and concentrated flavoring which are allowed to ferment. What makes these wines so popular is that artificial carbonation is added to the wines during the bottling process. Since there is no need for these wines to age, they are lower in cost. A typical bottle of "pop" wine costs between 60 cents to $1.00 as compared to a bottle of three-year-old California white varietal dinner wine at $3.50, or a ten-year-old vintage French Burgundy for about $20.00.

DINNER WINES

WHITE WINES

Pleasantly dry or with just a hint of sweetness, white wines are pale golden or slightly gold-green in color. They are at their best when served chilled with fish, seafood, poultry, cheese, lamb, veal, omelets and pork (except ham). The grapes used to make these wines are primarily Johannisburg Riesling, Grey Riesling, Traminer and Sylvaner. Other varietals which produce a richer, fuller-flavored white are Pinot Chardonnay, Folle Blanche, Pinot Blanc and Dry Semillon. Generic names of some of the white wines are: Rhine, Chablis, Sauterne, Light Muscat, Sauterne, Riesling, and White Chianti.

ROSE WINES

These are light, fruity wines, occasionally dry, quite often slightly sweet. The color ranges from a cheerful pink to a deep rose. Rose wines are best served slightly chilled, and are delicious anytime, with or without food.

RED WINES

Red wines are drunk either fresh and fruity or after they have aged to a rich robustness. Fresh young red wines are dry and aromatic, and light to medium in body. Serve at room temperature with steaks, roasts, game, cheese or casseroles. Zinfandel and Ruby Cabernet are the two principle grapes used. Rich red wines, which have been aged, have a distinctive flavor and appealing ruby color.

SERVING CHEESE

No matter how diverse customs are, most nations of the world will agree on one thing: cheese is delicious! Of course, as you travel from north to south, east to west, you'll run into considerable controversy on just which cheese is the best. Every country has its favorite and takes a great deal of pride in their domestically produced cheese. In France, the preferred cheese (and understandably so) is Roquefort. In England, it's Cheddar; Holland, Gouda; Germany, Muenster; and Switzerland, Gruyere.

Because the United States is a "melting pot" of many nationalities, Americans can remain neutral and enjoy the whole spectrum of cheese

— and many are our own contributions. Today, the United States is the largest producer of all types of cheese. These include Brick, Colby, Cream, Liederkranz and Monterey, which orginated in America. Some types, such as English Cheddar, have become so domesticated that they are often referred to as "American" processed cheese.

The dining usages of cheese are as varied as the food itself. On the following pages is a list of cheeses, where they originated, and the primary usages.

CHEESE	COUNTRY OF ORIGIN	CONSISTENCY & TEXTURE	COLOR & SHAPE
Asiago	Italy	Hard to hard grating; granular, tiny gas holes	Light yellow; cylindrical
Bel Paese	Italy	Soft; smooth, waxy body	Slightly grey surface; creamy yellow interior; small wheels
Bleu Blue	France United States	Semisoft, visible veins of mold, pasty, sometimes crumbly	Creamy white, marbled with blue-green mold; cylindrical or pre-packaged packs
Brick	United States (Wisconsin)	Semisoft, tiny gas holes smooth, waxy body	Light yellow to orange; yellow brown surface when aged; brick shaped
Brie	France	Soft; thin edible crust, russet brown surface, creamy interior	Creamy yellow interior; medium and small wheels
Caciocavallo	Italy	Hard, compact, flaky	Light tan surface, light colored interior shaped like a beet and bound with cord
Cheddar Processed	England United States	Hard, smooth, firm body	Creamy yellow to orange; varied shapes, with rind and rindless
Colby	United States	Hard type but more open in texture than Cheddar	Light yellow to orange; cylindrical
Cottage	Uncertain	Soft, moist, delicate curds of varying sizes	White, sold in pre-packaged containers
Cream	United States (New York)	Smooth, soft, buttery	White, foil wrapped in rectangular portions
Edam	North Holland	Hard type, but softer than Cheddar; more open mealy body	Creamy yellow with red wax coat; cannonball shape

CHEESE	COUNTRY OF ORIGIN	CONSISTENCY & TEXTURE	COLOR & SHAPE
Gjetost	Norway	Hard, buttery	Golden brown, cubical
Gouda	South Holland	Semi-hard, similar in texture to Edam	Creamy yellow, red wax coated; round and flat
Gruyere	Switzerland	Hard; tiny gas holes	Light yellow; flat wheels
Liederkranz Brand	United States (New York)	Soft with robust flavor	Creamy yellow interior; russet surface, foil-wrapped
Limburger	Belgium	Soft; smooth waxy body	Creamy white, rectangular
Monterey (Jack)	United States (California)	Semisoft; smooth	Creamy white wheels
Mozzarella	Italy	Semisoft, plastic	White to light yellow; slices and rectangles
Muenster	Germany	Semisoft, smooth and mild	Yellow tan or white surface, creamy white interior
Parmesan	Italy	Hard grating, brittle	Light yellow, cylindrical
Provolone	Italy	Hard, compact, flaky	Golden yellow; yellowish-white interior
Ricotta	Italy	Soft; grainy or dry	White; packaged fresh or dry
Roquefort	France	Semisoft; visible veins of mold, crumbly	White; marbled with blue-green mold; cylindrical
Stilton	England	Semisoft; visible veins of mold, crumbly	White; marbled with blue-green mold; cylindrical
Swiss	Switzerland	Hard; smooth, with large gas holes or eyes	Rindless blocks and large wheels with rinds

FLAVOR	RIPENING PERIOD	MODE OF SERVING AND USES
Piquant, sharp in aged cheeses	2-6 months table use; 12 months grating	Seasoning, table use, processing
Mild to moderately robust	6 to 12 weeks	Table use, dessert
Piquant, spicy	2 months minimum, to 9 months for pronounced flavor	Desserts, salads, canapes, dips, table use

FLAVOR	RIPENING PERIOD	MODE OF SERVING AND USES
Mild	2 weeks or longer	Sandwiches, salads, table use
Mild to pungent	4 to 8 weeks	Dessert, table use
Sharp	3 months minimum 12 months for grating	Seasoning, table use
Mild to sharp	2 to 12 months or longer	Dessert, sandwiches, table use
Mild	1 to 3 months	Table use, sandwiches, cooked foods
Mild, slightly acid	Unripened	Salads, dips, cooked foods, table use
Mild, slightly acid	Unripened	Salads, sandwiches, table use, cooked foods
Mild, nut-like	2 months or longer	Cheese trays, table use, dessert
Sweetish, caramel	4 to 8 months	As is, on crackers, dessert
Mild, nutlike	2 to 6 months	As is, on crackers, with fresh fruit, dessert
Nutlike, sweetish	3 months minimum	As is, dessert, cheese trays, processing
Robust, aromatic	1 to 2 months	As is, table use, processing
Robust, highly aromatic	1 to 2 months	Sandwiches, on crackers
Mild	2 to 6 weeks, table use 6 to 9 months, grating	As is, sandwiches
Mild, delicate	Unripened	As is, pizza, cooked foods
Mild to mellow, between Brick and Limburger	2 to 8 weeks	As is, in sandwiches, table use
Sharp, piquant	14 months minimum to 24 months or longer	As is, as seasoning (grated)
Mild to sharp, usually smoked	2 to 12 months	As is, cooked foods
Bland, semisweet	2 to 3 months	As is, in cooked foods, seasoning
Sharp, spicy, piquant	2 months minimum to 5 months or longer	As is, dessert, salads, on crackers
Piquant, spicy but milder than Roquefort	2 to 6 months or longer	As is, dessert, cooked foods
Sweetish, nutlike	2 months minimum to 9 months or longer	As is, in sandwiches, salads

FONDUE

The word "fondue" comes from the French word "fondre", meaning to melt. The original fondue was developed in Switzerland during the 18th Century. The Swiss baked bread and made cheese during the summer and fall months. This supply had to last through the long winter until the next summer. Needless to say, before the next summer the bread and cheese became very hard. Some enterprising Swiss woman hit upon the idea of melting the cheese and dipping bread chunks in it. The result: the first fondue.

FONDUE VARIETY

The classic fondue is, of course, cheese. The basic cheese fondue is made with two types of Swiss cheeses: Emmenthaler, a mild cheese, and the stronger Gruyere. The very mildest fondue is made wholly of Emmenthaler while the very strongest is made entirely of Gruyere.

Cheese for a fondue should be diced or shredded but never grated. Grating will make the cheese lump. Toss your bits of cheese with the amount of flour called for in the recipe, usually a couple of tablespoons. Be certain to use the cheese specified in your recipe, for only particular kinds of cheese can be used to prepare fondue.

To heighten flavor, rub the fondue pot lightly with half a garlic clove, then add the required amount of wine. The kind of wine you choose is important. It should be a light, dry, sparkling white wine. The Swiss prefer Neuchatel, but Rhine, Reisling, or Chablis will do as well. The wine is heated until bubbles form around the edges and on the bottom of the pot. Then add the cheese, a handful at a time, stirring constantly with a wooden spoon. When all the cheese has been added, flavor with Kirsch or brandy, if desired, and nutmeg and ground pepper.

Your guests scoop up the cheese mixture with speared pieces of crusty French or Italian bread. Each piece must have a crust so that the cheese will cling to it. The prize of the evening is the cheese crust left on the bottom of the pot; traditionally, this goes to the person who has not dropped his bread in the pot.

Fondue Bourguignonne consists of pieces of meat or seafood speared on a fork and cooked in a pot of hot cooking oil. Some cooks prefer to use a mixture of peanut oil and butter, while others use coconut oil, salad oil or olive oil. The latter oil will smoke quickly and so it is not preferred for fondues.

The meat chosen for fondue Bourguingnonne is most frequently beef — tenderloin, sirloin, or porterhouse are the preferred cuts although other cuts may be used if they are first tenderized. Veal is apt to be tough unless you use tenderloin. If you use pork, be sure to caution your guests that it must be thoroughly cooked. Allow five to seven ounces of meat per person.

Seafood may also be used. The most popular seafood fondue is shrimp; allow about two pounds of raw, shelled shrimp for four people. For other seafoods, including fish, allow the same proportions.

Each place setting should have the meat or seafood that is to be fondued, served in individual bowls. For a pleasant color note, try lining each bowl with greens before filling with pieces of meat or seafood. The individual place setting should include a salad fork and a dinner fork as well as each person's fondue fork. The fondue fork is only for cooking in oil; the prongs will become too hot to eat with. You'll also want at least one dinner plate per person.

Don't forget at least four to six sauces. The best ones for meat fondue are bearnaise, chili, bottled steak sauce, horseradish, barbecue, and Cumberland. Use the same basic list for seafood fondues, substituting lemon butter and tartar sauce for the steak sauces.

EQUIPMENT

There are three types of fondue pots. Two are earthenware and the other is metal. Cheese fondue is traditionally prepared in a caquelon, a round heavy pottery dish with a wide mouth and a heavy handle such as the one shown in the illustration above.

A smaller version of this same dish is used to prepare dessert fondues. The third type of fondue pot is a metal pot that is wider at the bottom than at the top. It is deeper than the earthenware pot. This fondue pot is used to prepare fondue Bourguignonne and vegetable fondues that require hot oil. The metal can bear the 360-degree heat needed to keep the oil hot, without cracking as would an earthenware pot. The pot's shape will help keep oil from spattering as foods are fondued. The very best metal pots are enameled steel with an extra-heavy bottom. These pots come in a wide range of brilliant colors. Other metal fondue pots may be made of stainless steel, copper, or sterling silver.

The heat source you choose will depend upon the kind of fondue you are preparing. Cheese, meat, seafood, and vegetable fondues need more intense heat than do dessert fondues. For the latter, choose a candle warmer. The dessert fondue is usually prepared on the kitchen stove over very low heat and poured into the fondue pot. The only heat source needed is one sufficient to keep the dessert warm.

For all other fondues, you may choose your heat source from alcohol lamps, canned heat, or even electricity. Alcohol lamps are of two types. One has a wick which is raised and lowered by a screw. The other has cotton wool in the base of the lamp. The alcohol is poured over the cotton, ignited, and the degree of heat is controlled by a cover which opens and closes vents on the side of the lamp. When using an alcohol lamp, never fill it more than half full. One tablespoon of alcohol gives about twelve minutes cooking time. Denatured alcohol is the best kind to use in these lamps; it is less expensive, produces a more intense heat, and creates less odor.

Canned heat fits into special lamps which either come with fondue pots or can be purchased separately. The degree of heat is controlled by a vented cover similar to that on the alcohol lamp. In determining how much canned heat you will need, remember that a 2 5/8-ounce can burns for 50 to 60 minutes, while a 7-ounce can burns for four hours.

Electric fondue pots are now available. To use these, simply follow the manufacturers' directions.

When you are choosing your fondue equipment, look for sturdy pots with trays to catch spills and prevent burns. Generally, one pot will comfortably serve four people — more people than that, and you will have too much confusion.

In addition to pots and heat sources, you may want to invest in special forks and plates. Fondue forks are usually two or three-tined metal forks with wooden ends to prevent heat conduction. The best forks are color-keyed; each has a different color on the end so that your guests can easily tell which fork is theirs when the pot is filled with cooking food.

HORS D'OEUVRES

Planning and serving those little appetite teasers called hors d'oeuvres is one of the most pleasant areas of entertaining, for both the hostess and the guests. An imaginative hostess always welcomes the chance to create delectable little shapes and sizes of mouthwatering tidbits, and the guests will shower their hostess with praise as they savor delicious hot and cold finger food.

There are two very important things to remember when preparing hors d'oeuvres. First, remember that they are intended to excite, not satisfy the appetite. In most cases, hostesses serve them as a preview of good food to come. Naturally, you will want to plan on bite-sized goodies that are light on the palate and the stomach. Second, make sure that your hors d'oeuvres don't overlap your meal. In other words, be careful not to repeat food flavors. For example, you would not want to serve stuffed celery as an appetizer if you are intending to garnish your baked turkey with it. Neither would you want to serve tomato juice with the hors d'oeuvres if tomato soup is on your dinner menu.

You'll always be a popular hostess if you succeed in making hors d'oeuvres as appealing to the eye as they are to the taste. An artistic hostess doesn't just place the hors d'oeuvres on a serving tray — she designs them. Each selection is given her own personal touch. She may become totally absorbed in placing hot cheese canapes in a symmetrical design, or she may spend an hour arranging parsley around cucumber finger sandwiches on a silver tray. But all her efforts are worthwhile the moment she hears a chant of "oohs" and "ahs" from her arriving guests.

However, such a creative hostess always has two problems; she never has any goodies left over for the family and she is constantly pestered to prepare hors d'oeuvres for group gatherings.

BREWING COFFEE AND TEA

BREWING GOOD COFFEE

A cup of piping hot coffee welcomes most of us every morning to a new day. It magically opens our eyes and helps us out the door to a day filled with work and activities. It welcomes drop-in guests, especially if served with homemade pie or cake. It acts as a crutch to help us through late night work or unexpected "wee hour of the morning" events.

This very prevalent drink is a simple mixture of coffee and water, but this uncomplicated combination can be so unpredictable. All of us coffee drinkers have at one time or another been sickened by a harsh, bitter cup of coffee. We've frequently wondered why one pot turns out smooth and delicious, while another (usually the one we prepare for guests) turns out acrid and bitter. And we settle for the idea that turning out good coffee is simply a matter of chance.

Actually brewing good coffee doesn't have to be left to chance. There are a few simple procedures that will help eliminate error and insure that your coffee will be clear, full-bodied and aromatic. First, make sure that your cooking time is accurate. Fine grind, which is used in vacuum coffee makers, is usually ready in one to three minutes. Drip grind, used in drip and filter coffee makers, usually takes four to six minutes. Regular grind, for percolators, takes usually six to eight minutes.

Consider the strength of coffee you desire. Strength, of course, is determined by the proportion of coffee to water. Regular strength is most often two tablespoons of coffee to 3/4 cup of water per cup of coffee. Never perk coffee longer or pour it through the grounds again in order to make it stronger. These procedures serve only to make the coffee bitter.

BREWING GOOD TEA

When making tea, remember to start with fresh tea. Tea bags and loose tea are best kept fresh in a tightly covered container. (Tea should be used within six months.) Bring fresh cold water to a rolling boil. Measure one teaspoon of loose tea or one tea bag for each cup desired. Before placing tea in the pot, rinse the pot with boiling water to heat it and keep the tea warm. Porcelain and pottery teapots are preferable because they hold heat well. Put tea in the pot and immediately add boiling water. Steep the tea for about five minutes. Stir and serve at once. If you want weaker tea, dilute by adding hot water. However, never add fresh leaves to steeped tea in order to make it stronger or last longer; the brew will be extremely bitter.

Hot tea has been a popular drink in the Orient since 2737 B.C. However, iced tea is an American invention of the 20th Century. At the Worlds Fair in 1904 during the hot summertime, spectators refused to sample the hot tea of the Far East because the weather was too hot to enjoy it. But a brilliant Englishman decided to try pouring the tea over ice. Fair goers tried it and loved it. Since that day, iced tea has become a traditional beverage for the United States.

In brewing good iced tea, it is important to use twice as much tea as used when brewing hot tea. You must account for the melted ice. To make good iced tea, heat one quart of fresh, cold water till it boils rapidly. Add eight to twelve tea bags or three tablespoons of loose tea. Let the tea steep, uncovered, for five minutes. Remove tea bags or strain out loose tea. Add one quart of cold water. Serve over ice, preferably in tall glasses.

CARVING

Carving is an art that homemakers across America take pride in mastering. The instructions and illustrations that follow show the art of carving beef, ham, chicken and turkey. By following these instructions, you can be certain that the slices of meat you place on the table will be as attractive as they are delicious.

STANDING RIB ROAST

1. Place the roast on the platter with the largest end down to form a solid base. Insert the fork between the two top ribs. Starting across on the fat side, carve across the grain to the rib bone.

2. Use the tip of the knife to cut along the rib bone to loosen the slice. Be sure to keep close to the bone, to make the largest servings possible.

3. Slide the knife back under the slice, and steadying it with the fork, lift the slice to the side of the platter. If the platter is not large enough, place the slices on a heated platter close by.

WHOLE HAM

1. Place the ham on a platter with decorated side up and the shank to the carver's right. Remove several slices from the thinnest side to form a solid base on which to set the ham.

2. Turn the ham on its base. Starting at the shank end, cut a small wedge and remove; then carve perpendicular to the leg bone as shown.

3. Release slices by cutting under them and along the leg bone, starting at the shank end. For additional servings, turn ham over and make slices to the bone; release and serve.

CHICKEN AND TURKEY

1. To remove leg, hold the drumstick firmly with fingers, pulling gently away from the body. At the same time, cut skin between leg and body.

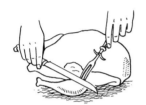

2. Press leg away from body with flat side of knife. Then cut through joint joining leg to backbone and skin on the back. If the "oyster", a choice oyster-shaped piece lying in the spoon-shaped section of the backbone, was not removed with the thigh, remove it at this point. Separate drumstick and thigh by cutting down through the joint.

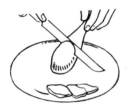

3. Slice drumstick meat. Hold the drumstick upright at a convenient angle to plate and cut down, turning drumstick to get uniform slices. Chicken drumsticks and thighs are usually served without slicing.

4. Slice thigh meat. Hold thigh tightly on plate with a fork. Cut slices of meat parallel to the bone.

5. Cut into white meat parallel to wing. Make a cut deep into the breast until the knife reaches the body frame, parallel to and as close to the wing as possible.

6. Slice white meat. Beginning at front, starting halfway up the breast, cut thin slices of white meat down to the cut made parallel to the wing. The slices will fall away from the bird as they are cut to this line. Continue carving for first servings. Additional meat may be carved as needed.

HERBS AND SPICES

Basil can be chopped and added to cold poultry salads. If your recipe calls for tomatoes or tomato sauce, add a touch of basil to bring out a rich flavor.

Bay leaf, the basis of many French seasonings, is nice added to soups, stews, marinades and stuffings.

Bouquet garni, a must in many Creole cuisine recipes, is a bundle of herbs, spices and bay leaf tied together and added to soups, stews or sauces.

Celery seed, from wild celery rather than our domestic celery, adds pleasant flavor to bouillon or stock.

Chervil is one of the traditional *fines herbes* used in French-derived cooking. (The others are tarragon, parsley and chive.) It is particularly good in omelets or soups.

Chives, available fresh, dried or frozen, can be substituted for raw onion in any poultry recipe.

Garlic, one of the oldest herbs in the world, must be carefully handled. When cooking, do not simmer until black or it will create an offensive odor. For best results, press or crush the garlic clove against the kitchen table; then cook. If your recipe calls for sliced garlic, substitute grated or pressed garlic. The flavor will improve noticeably.

Marjoram is an aromatic herb of the mint family. It is good in soups, sauces, stuffings and stews.

Mustard (dry) brings a sharp bite to sauces. Sprinkle just a touch over roast chicken for a delightful flavor treat.

Oregano is a staple herb in Italian, Spanish and Mexican cuisines. It is very good in dishes with a tomato foundation; it adds an excellent savory taste.

Paprika, a mild pepper, adds color to many dishes, and it is especially attractive with poultry. The very best paprika is imported from Hungary — there is a world of difference between it and the supermarket variety.

Rosemary, a tasty herb, is an important seasoning in stuffing for duck, partridge and capon.

Sage, the perennial favorite with all kinds of poultry, adds flavor to stuffings. It is particularly good with goose.

Tarragon, one of the *fines herbes*, has wonderful flavor and goes well with all poultry dishes except one; it is too pungent for poultry soups.

Thyme is used in combination with bay leaf in soups and stews.

Allspice, a pungent, aromatic spice, comes in whole or powdered form. It is excellent in marinades, particularly in game marinade, or curries.

Cinnamon, ground from the bark of the cinnamon tree, is important in preparing desserts as well as savory dishes.

Coriander adds an unusual flavor to soups, stews, chili dishes, curries and some desserts.

Cumin is a staple spice in Mexican cooking. To use, rub seeds together and let them fall into the dish just before serving. Cumin also comes in powdered form.

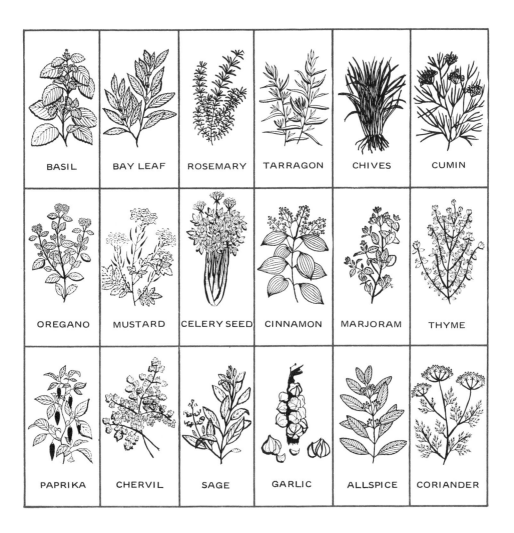

BASIL	BAY LEAF	ROSEMARY	TARRAGON	CHIVES	CUMIN
OREGANO	MUSTARD	CELERY SEED	CINNAMON	MARJORAM	THYME
PAPRIKA	CHERVIL	SAGE	GARLIC	ALLSPICE	CORIANDER

SELECTING MEATS

SELECTING MEATS FOR THE GRILL

Outdoor grilling usually brings to mind a lazy, sunny afternoon, billowing smoke, magnificent aromas of charcoal, onions and sauces, and lots of friendly conversation with friends and relatives. It is frequently an occasion which calls for the ultimate in meat, and whether you decide to grill poultry, lamb, pork or beef, you want the best available.

BEEF

Cattlemen have experimented, bred and cross-bred cattle for years in order to offer us the juiciest, most tender meat possible, and we Americans buy more beef than any other kind of meat. The average American consumes between 85 to 100 pounds of it a year. Statistics also prove that beef is our most popular meat for grilling. Maybe that's because most of us consider a thick, juicy charcoaled steak the ultimate in good eating.

For grilling, remember that the juice of the meat is very important because it helps keep the meat tender while cooking. Look for high quality rib, rolled or boneless roasts, high quality steaks or ground beef. These juicier cuts are the ones most suitable for grilling because they are well-marbled with fat which keeps them juicy and tender.

Use the following chart as a guide to help you select beef for grilling, or for any other occasion.

BEEF STEAKS

	Thickness	Grill Heat	Grilling Time In Minutes Per Side		
			Rare	Medium	Well-done
TENDER STEAKS (Sirloin, rib, rib eye, Porterhouse, T-bone, club)	1″	High	4-6	6-8	9-11
	1 1/2″	High	5-7	9-11	11-15
	2″	Medium	7-10	14-18	18-22
LESS TENDER STEAKS Chuck	1 1/2″	High	5-7	9-10	Chuck steak toughens if cooked well-done
	2″	High	8-10	14-17	
	3″	Medium	20-25	30-40	
Flank		High	4-7	Flank steak is always cooked only to the rare stage	
Round	1″	High	4-6	6-8	Round steak toughens if cooked well-done

 Flat Bone Sirloin Steak
 Rib Steak
 Delmonico (Rib Eye) Roast or Steak
 Porterhouse Steak
 T-Bone Steak
 Club Steak
 Flank Steak
 Round Steak

BEEF ROASTS

Type of Roast	Grill Heat	Roasting Time in Minutes Per Pound*		
		Rare	Medium	Well-done
Chuck or Round	Low to medium	(always well-done)		25-30
Rib eye	Low to medium	18-20	20-23	22-25
Rib, rolled	Low to medium	28-32	32-36	38-45
Rib, standing	Low to medium	22-24	27-30	32-35
Rolled Rump	Low to medium	(seldom rare)	22-25	25-30
Sirloin tip	Low to medium	20-25	23-27	28-32
Tenderloin, half	Medium to medium high	20-25	24-28	(seldom well-done)
Tenderloin, whole	Medium to medium high	12-15	15-18	(seldom well-done)

*If using a meat thermometer, rare = 140 degrees internal temperature
medium = 160 degrees internal temperature
well-done = 170 degrees internal temperature

  Heel of Round
 Inside Chuck Roll
Boneless Shoulder Pot roast or Steak
 Arm Pot roast or Steak
 Standing Rib Roast
 Rolled Rump
 Sirloin Tip

PORK

Pork is still another very popular meat featured in outdoor cookery. Some kinds of pork — sausage and ribs — require special cooking times. Follow recipe instructions when preparing these meats.

When planning to serve pork, allow one steak or chop per person, several sausages, and at least 3/4 pound of spareribs. If you're serving pork roast or ham, allow 1/3 to 1/2 pound boneless meat or 1/3 to 3/4 pound bone-in per serving.

Some pork cuts, such as canned hams, precooked shoulders and picnics, and precooked Canadian bacon, require only warming on a low to medium hot grill. Uncooked pork cuts need long, slow cooking and must always be well-done. If you are using a meat thermometer to check the internal temperature of rotisserie-roasted pork, be sure it registers 170 degrees. In cooking pork chops or steaks, cut into the meat to be certain that no trace of pink color remains.

Consult the chart that follows for approximate cooking times of various pork chops, steaks and roasts.

PORK		
	Cut	**Cooking Time**
	Canadian bacon	24-26 minutes per pound
Blade loin Roast	**Fresh pork** Loin Leg, bone-in Leg, boneless	35-40 minutes per pound 22-26 minutes per pound 24-28 minutes per pound
Sirloin Chop	**Chops and steaks** 1" thick 1 1/2" thick 2" thick	15-18 minutes per side 20-25 minutes per side 28-30 minutes per side
	Ham fully-cooked, whole fully-cooked, half fully-cooked, boneless smoked or fresh, whole smoked or fresh, half	15-18 minutes per pound 18-24 minutes per pound 15-18 minutes per pound 18-20 minutes per pound or to internal temperature of 170 degrees 22-25 minutes per pound or to internal temperature of 170 degrees
Center loin Roast	**Smoked pork butt or picnic**	30-40 minutes per pound
NOTE: All pork is cooked over low to medium grill heat.		

LAMB

Lamb has long been found on outdoor menus in the form of shish kabobs. But these skewered delights are just one way of preparing this delicate meat. There are lamb steaks, chops, and roasts that are delicious outdoor fare.

Allow 1/2 to 3/4 pound of bone-in or 1/4 to 1/3 pound boneless per serving. If you are featuring steaks or chops, allow 1 to 2 per person, depending on the size of the meat. Lamb is covered with a thin, clear, brittle membrane known as the fell. Beneath this paper-like covering is a layer of firm white fat. It is usually removed from chops but is left on roasts. Because the fell helps keep the juices in the meat, we suggest that you ask your butcher to leave it on chops you plan to broil on a grill. Tender cuts of lamb include the leg, loin, shoulder and rib roasts; steak; and loin, rib and shoulder chops. These cuts grill very well outdoors.

Less tender lamb cuts are from the breast and shank sections. With the exception of the rack of ribs, these are not recommended for outdoor cooking. But the rack of ribs is delicious when slowly rotisserie roasted. If you want to add a true Mediterranean touch to this delicacy, try basting it with a mixture of olive oil, lemon juice, and just a touch of marjoram. Consult the chart that follows for recommended cooking times for all cuts of lamb.

LAMB				
Cut	Grill Temperature	Cooking Time in Minutes Per Pound *		
		Rare	Medium	Well-done
Steaks and chops				
1″ thick	Medium	6-8 min. per side	10-15 min. per side	18-20 min. per side
2″ thick	Medium	15 min. per side	20 min. per side	22 min. per side
Roasts				
Leg, bone-in	Low to	19-16	18-20	25-30
Leg, boneless	medium	15-18	20-22	30-35
Rack of ribs		15-20	22-25	35-90
Shoulder, bone-in		14-18	20-22	25-30
Shoulder, boned		15-20	22-25	25-30

*If using a meat thermometer,   rare = 190 degrees internal temperature
medium = 150 degrees internal temperature
well-done = 175-180 degrees internal temperature

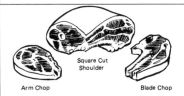

Arm Chop   Square Cut Shoulder   Blade Chop

American Leg

Boneless Sirloin Roast

Frenched Leg Roast

COOKING MEATS

It is easy to serve any cut of meat so that it is flavorful, tender and juicy — if that meat is cooked properly.

Broiling, roasting and panfrying are known as the dry-heat methods of cooking. They are used with tender cuts of meat — steak, chops, etc.

Braising and cooking in liquid are the moist-heat methods and are used with tougher cuts of meat. Moist heat creates steam which softens the tough connective tissues in this more sinewy meat.

BROILING

Tender, thick beef steaks, pork and lamb chops, sliced ham and bacon are delicious when broiled. For best results, steaks and chops should be 1 inch thick; ham slices, 1/2 inch thick. The broiler may be preheated if desired.

Steaks and chops 1 1/2 inches to 2 inches thick should be at least 3 inches from the heat. Those meats 1 inch thick or less should be placed about 2 inches from the heat.

When the top side is brown, season it as desired and turn. Ham and bacon do not need seasoning, but steaks and chops brown better if they are seasoned after they have been broiled. When the second side of the meat is done, season it, and place it on a heated platter. The heated platter helps retain the meat's heat; broiled meat cools very quickly and tastes best if it is served piping hot.

ROASTING

In roasting, the rule of slow heat applies — the oven should be set between 300 degrees F and 325 degrees F. Chunky, juicy, tender cuts of top quality beef, veal, pork, ham, lamb and mutton make the very finest roasts. A roast should weigh at least 3 to 4 pounds, but for best results, should be 5 pounds or more. If desired, the roast may be seasoned with salt and pepper. However, this seasoning will only penetrate 1/4 inch to 1/2 inch into the roast. Place the meat — fat side up — on a rack in an open shallow roasting pan.

Insert a meat thermometer so the bulb is in the center of the largest part of the meat. *A meat thermometer is the only foolproof way to tell if a roast is cooked to the desired temperature.* Do not take the roast out of the oven to read the meat thermometer; a household meat thermometer will indicate an accurate reading only when it is read inside a heated oven.

Do not add water, and do not cover. Do not sprinkle the meat with flour — it will brown naturally as it cooks. Do not open the oven door to baste; as the fat on a roast melts, it bastes itself. (This is why the meat is cooked fat side up.)

When the meat thermometer indicates the desired temperature, remove the roast from the oven. Allow the roast to set for 15 minutes after it is removed from the oven.

BRAISING

Meat to be braised may be dredged with flour, then slowly browned on both sides in a small amount of fat in a heavy cooking pan with a tight cover. Season with salt, pepper, herbs and spices. Vegetables may be added during the cooking process, and will take about 40 minutes to cook. Some of the less-tender cuts of meat may need some liquid added. Cover tightly and cook at a low temperature until tender. During cooking, the liquid should simmer, but not boil.

When done, remove the roast and vegetables, if any, to a heated platter and make gravy. The gravy is an essential part of any braised meat dish. It contains meat flavors and soluble food nutrients and should be used to accompany the meat.

COOKING IN LIQUID

Large Cuts: Meat may be browned if desired. Cover meat with stock or water. Season with salt, pepper, herbs and spices. Vegetables may be added if desired. Cover kettle and simmer until tender. If the meat is to be served cold, let it cool, and then chill in the stock in which it was cooked. If vegetables are to be cooked with the meat, as in "boiled" dinners, add them whole or in large pieces.

Stews: Cut the meat into uniform pieces, usually 1-inch to 2-inch cubes. Brown meat cubes on all sides if a brown stew is desired. Add just enough water, vegetable juices or soup stock to cover the meat. Season with salt, pepper, herbs and spices. Cover kettle tightly and simmer until meat is tender. Add vegetables to the meat about 40 minutes before the meat is done. When done, remove meat and vegetables to a pan, platter or casserole and keep hot. To thicken the stock, use a paste made of flour and a small amount of cold water or stock. Pour hot gravy over the meat and vegetables or serve separately in a sauce boat.

POULTRY ROASTING CHART

GAME BIRDS

GAME BIRD	READY-TO-COOK WEIGHT	OVEN TEMP.	ROASTING TIME	AMOUNT PER SERVING
Wild Duck	1-2 lbs.	350°	20-30 min.	1-1 1/2 lbs.
Wild Goose	2-4 lbs. 4-6 lbs.	325°	1-1 1/2 hrs. 1 1/2-2 1/2 hrs.	1-1 1/2 lbs.
Partridge	1/2-1 lb.	350°	30-45 min.	1/2-1 lb.
Pheasant	1-3 lbs.	400°	1-2 1/2 hrs.	1-1 1/2 lbs.
Quail	4-6 oz.	375°	15-20 min.	1/2-1 lb.
Squab	12-14 oz.	350°	30-50 min.	12-14 oz.

DOMESTIC BIRDS

DOMESTIC BIRDS	READY-TO-COOK WEIGHT	OVEN TEMP.	ROASTING TIME	
			UNSTUFFED	STUFFED
Chicken	1 1/2-2 lbs. 2-2 1/2 lbs. 2 1/2-3 lbs. 3-4 lbs.	375° 375° 375° 375°	3/4 hr. 1 hr. 1 1/4 hrs. 1 1/2 hrs.	1 hr. 1 1/4 hrs. 1 1/2 hrs. 2 hrs.
Capon	4-7 lbs.	375°	2 hrs.	3 hrs.
Turkey	6-8 lbs. 8-12 lbs. 12-16 lbs. 16-20 lbs. 20-24 lbs.	325° 325° 325° 325° 325°	3 1/2 hrs. 4 hrs. 4 1/2 hrs. 5 1/2 hrs. 6 1/2 hrs.	4 hrs. 4 1/2 hrs. 5 1/2 hrs. 6 1/2 hrs. 7 1/2 hrs.
Foil-Wrapped Turkey	8-10 lbs. 10-12 lbs. 14-16 lbs. 18-20 lbs. 22-24 lbs.	450° 450° 450° 450° 450°	2 1/4 hrs. 2 1/2 hrs. 3 hrs. 3 1/4 hrs. 3 1/2 hrs.	2 1/2 hrs. 3 hrs. 3 1/4 hrs. 3 1/2 hrs. 3 3/4 hrs.
Domestic Duck	3-5 lbs.	375° then 425°	1 1/2 hrs. 15 min.	2 hrs. 15 min.
Domestic Goos	4-6 lbs. 6-8 lbs. 8-10 lbs. 10-12 lbs. 12-14 lbs.	325° 325° 325° 325° 325°	2 3/4 hrs. 3 hrs. 3 1/2 hrs. 3 3/4 hrs. 4 1/4 hrs.	3 hrs. 3 1/2 hrs. 3 3/4 hrs. 4 1/4 hrs. 4 3/4 hrs.
Cornish Game Hen	1-1 1/2 lbs.	400°	1 1/2 hrs.	1 1/2 hrs.
Guinea Hen	1 1/2-2 lbs. 2-2 1/2 lbs.	375° 375°	3/4 hr. 1 hr.	1 hr. 1 1/2 hrs.

METHODS OF PREPARING POULTRY

Roasting takes place in an oven preheated to 325 degrees. Poultry to be roasted should be rubbed thoroughly with softened butter and placed on a rack in a shallow roasting pan. Turn the bird breast-side up for the last 15 minutes of cooking time for added color and crisper skin. Covering the roasting pan with a tent of foil will not only ensure good color and crispness, but will keep grease from spattering your oven surfaces. When the drumstick moves easily, the bird is cooked.

Broiling is a dry-heat cooking method. Preheat your broiler with the oven temperature set at 350 degrees. (Hotter than this and the poultry will singe.) Brush your broiler halves or quarters with melted butter — you may want to try seasoning the butter for added flavor. Place broiler pan as far away from the heat as possible and broil for 20 minutes on each side, brushing with melted butter frequently. After 40 minutes, prick the chicken with a skewer. If the juices run red, additional cooking time is needed.

Of all the cooking methods of poultry, none is more delicious than *frying*. Cover the cut-up pieces of your fryer with seasoned or plain flour. Meanwhile, heat 1/2 inch oil or shortening in a skillet. Beginning with the larger pieces, place chicken skin-side down in the pan of oil over moderate heat. Turn and brown other side. Reduce heat and cook for 15 to 25 minutes on each side.

Braising is much like frying, but the cooking is done in oil plus another liquid. To braise, season cut-up pieces of chicken and place them, skin-side down, in a skillet with 1/4 cup oil. Brown over high heat to seal in all the juices. Reduce heat and add 1/2 cup broth, consomme, vegetable juice or other liquid and cook covered, for 30 minutes or until tender.

Stewing is a good method to use with older poultry which may have somewhat tougher meat. Place chicken in a large kettle with water to cover. Add your favorite seasonings — celery, onion, peppercorns, salt and parsley are nice. Cover and simmer for one to three hours, or until the meat comes away from the bones easily. Cooking time will depend on the age and size of your bird.

SPECIAL METHODS FOR GAME

Both waterfowl — ducks and geese — and upland birds — grouse, pheasant, quail, pigeons, doves, woodcock, snipe and wild turkey — should be well larded before cooking. Larding is the process of adding fat to the poultry by placing strips of bacon over it or by inserting fat into the flesh with a larding needle. Roasting is the preferred cooking method for most game birds except quail. Quail is almost all white meat and can be cooked like domestic chicken. It may be sauteed, broiled, stewed or roasted.

COOKING AND SEASONING VEGETABLES

VEGETABLE	MINUTES COOKING TIME IN BOILING WATER	SUGGESTED SEASONINGS
ARTICHOKE	10-15	Dill, French dressing, lemon butter
ASPARAGUS spears tips, pieces	 10-20 5-15	Mustard seed, sesame seed, tarragon, lemon butter, nutmeg, dry mustard, caraway seed
BEANS (lima)	25-30	Savory, tarragon, thyme, marjoram, oregano, sage
BEANS (snap)	12-16	Basil, dill, marjoram, mint, mustard seed, oregano, savory, tarragon, thyme
BEETS young, whole older, whole sliced	 30-45 45-90 15-25	Allspice, bay leaves, caraway seed, cloves, dill, ginger, mustard seed, savory, thyme, orange, celery seed, nutmeg, vinegar
BROCCOLI	10-15	Seasoned butters, dill, lemon butter, caraway seed, mustard seed, tarragon
BRUSSELS SPROUTS	15-20	Basil, caraway seed, dill, mustard seed, sage, thyme, lemon butter
CABBAGE shredded wedges	 3-10 10-15	Caraway seed, celery seed, dill, mint, mustard seed, nutmeg, savory, tarragon, peppers
CARROTS young, whole older, whole sliced	 15-20 20-30 10-15	Allspice, bay leaves, caraway seed, dill, fennel, ginger, mace, marjoram, mint, nutmeg, thyme, cloves, curry powder, parsley flakes
CAULIFLOWER separated whole	 8-15 15-25	Caraway seed, celery salt, dill, mace, tarragon, seasoned butters, sesame seed, poppy seed
CELERY	15-18	Seasoned butters
CORN (on the cob)	5-15	Green pepper, paprika, garlic powder, onion salt
EGGPLANT	8-15	Marjoram, oregano, dill
GREENS	10-30	Meat drippings, peppers, onion
OKRA	10-15	Meat drippings
ONIONS	15-30	Caraway seed, mustard seed, nutmeg, oregano, sage, thyme
PARSNIPS whole quartered	 20-40 8-15	Parsley, onion, dill, lemon butter

VEGETABLE	MINUTES COOKING TIME IN BOILING WATER	SUGGESTED SEASONINGS
PEAS	12-16	Basil, dill, marjoram, mint, oregano, poppy seed, rosemary, sage, savory
POTATOES whole, medium quartered diced	25-40 20-25 10-15	Basil, bay leaves, caraway, celery seed, dill, chives, mustard seed, oregano, poppy seed, thyme
SPINACH	3-10	Basil, mace, marjoram, nutmeg, oregano, vinegar
SQUASH summer, sliced winter, cut-up	8-15 15-20	Allspice, basil, cinnamon, cloves, fennel, ginger, mustard seed, nutmeg, rosemary, garlic
SWEET POTATOES	30-55	Allspice, cardamom, cinnamon, cloves, nutmeg
TOMATOES (cut-up)	7-15	Basil, bay leaves, celery seed, oregano, sage, sesame seed, tarragon, thyme
TURNIPS and RUTABAGAS whole cut-up	20-30 10-20	Cloves, ginger, onion, caraway seed

The chart below details which vitamins and minerals are available in the most frequently served vegetables. Some vegetables contain traces of nutrients other than those listed, but vitamins A, B_1, B_2, and C as well as calcium and iron are the primary nutrients found in almost all vegetables. By serving your family a wide range of fresh, frozen, and canned vegetables in the course of a week's meals, you can ensure that they receive all the vitamins and minerals they need to maintain strong, healthy bodies.

VEGETABLE NUTRITIONAL CHART

VEGETABLE	SIZE SERVING Equivalent To 100 Grams	NUTRIENTS PER 100 GRAMS Vitamins	Minerals
Asparagus	6 spears	A, C	
Beans (lima)	2/3 cup	C, B_1	iron
Beans (snap)	¾ cup	A, C	iron
Beets	2 2¼-inch diam.	C	iron
Beet greens	¼ lb.	A*, C	iron*
Broccoli	¼ lb.	A*, C*, B_2	calcium, iron
Brussels sprouts	seven	C*	iron
Cabbage	¼ lb.	C*	
Carrots	2-4-inches long	A*	iron

VEGETABLE	SIZE SERVING Equivalent To 100 Grams	NUTRIENTS PER 100 GRAMS	
		Vitamins	Minerals
Cauliflower	1/3 small head	C*	
Celery	6 stalks	C	
Chard	¼ lb.	A*, C	iron
Collard greens	¼ lb.	A*, C*, B_1, B_2	calcium*, iron
Corn	1 ear	C, B_1	
Cucumbers	14 slices	C	
Dandelion greens	¼ lb.	A*, C, B_1	calcium, iron*
Eggplant	1 4-inch slice		
Endive	¼ lb.	A*, C	iron
Kale	¼ lb.	A*, C*, B_2	calcium*, iron
Lettuce (iceberg)	1/3 head	A, C	
Lettuce (leaf)	10 lg. leaves	A, C	iron
Mustard greens	¼ lb.	A*, C*, B_2	calcium*, iron
Okra	5-10 pods	A, C*	calcium
Onions	2 medium	C	
Parsley	1 bunch	A*, C*	calcium, iron*
Parsnips	1 small	C	
Peas (green)	¾ cup	A, C*, B_1	
Peppers	1 large	A, C*	
Potatoes	1 small	C	
Pumpkin	½ cup	A*, C	
Radishes	10 small	C	iron
Rutabagas	¾ cup	C	
Spinach	¼ lb.	A*, C*, B_2	
Squash (summer)	¾ cup	C	
Squash (winter)	½ cup	A*, C	
Sweet potatoes	2/3 medium	A*, C	
Tomatoes	1 small	A, C	
Turnips	¾ cup	C	
Turnip greens	¼ lb.	A*, C*, B_2*	calcium*, iron
Watercress	1 bunch	A*, C*	calcium, iron

* Indicates excellent source of vitamin or mineral.

COOKING TECHNIQUES

Bake — To cook by dry heat in an oven or under hot coals.

Baste — To moisten, especially meats with melted butter, pan drippings or liquid during cooking.

Beat — To mix by vigorous stirring or whipping.

Blanch — To immerse, usually vegetables or fruit, briefly into boiling water so as to inactivate enzymes, loosen skins, or soak away excess salt.

Blend — To combine a number of ingredients so as to produce a mixture of uniform consistency.

Boil — To heat liquid until it bubbles; the boiling point for water is usually about 212 degrees.

Braise — To cook, especially meats, covered in a small amount of liquid or in steam.

Brew — To prepare a beverage by allowing boiling water to extract flavor and/or color from certain substances.

Broil — To cook by direct exposure to intense heat such as a flame or an electric heating unit.

Chill — To cool in the refrigerator or in cracked ice.

Cream — To blend butter, usually softened, with a granulated or crushed ingredient until the mixture is soft and creamy.

Curdle — To congeal milk with rennet or heat until solid lumps or curds are formed.

Cut in — To disperse solid shortening into dry ingredients with a knife or pastry blender. The texture of the mixture should resemble coarse cracker meal.

Deep-fry — To cook in a deep pan or skillet containing hot cooking oil. Deep-fried foods are generally completely immersed in hot oil.

Dice — To cut into small cubes about a quarter inch in size.

Dissolve — To create a solution by thoroughly mixing a solid or granular substance with a liquid.

Dredge — To sprinkle with flour, bread crumbs, and so on to form a coating.

Ferment — To change the chemical composition of certain foods through the action of microorganisms. For example, yeast acts on malt to produce beer.

Fillet — To remove the bones of meat and fish.

Fold in — To blend a delicate, frothy mixture into a heavier one, preferably with a rubber spatula so that none of the lightness or volume is lost. The motion used is one of turning under and bringing up.

Fry — To cook in a pan or skillet containing hot cooking oil. The fat should not totally cover the food.

Glaze — To cover or coat with sauce, syrup, egg white or a jellied substance. After applying, it hardens and becomes firm adding color and flavor.

Grate — To rub food against a rough perforated utensil reducing the food to slivers, chunks, curls and so on.

Grill — To broil usually on an open grating over heat.

Grind — To cut, crush, or force through a chopper so as to produce small bits.

Jell — To become semisolid either through chilling or the addition of gelatin or pectin.

Julienne — To cut vegetables and fruit especially into long thin strips.

Knead — To press, fold, and stretch dough until it is smooth and uniform.

Lard — To insert strips of fat or bacon into or on lean meat so as to keep it moist and juicy during cooking. Larding is an internal basting technique.

Leaven — To cause batters and doughs to rise usually by means of a chemical leavening agent. This process may occur before or during baking.

Marinate — To soak usually in a highly seasoned oil-acid solution so as to flavor and/or tenderize food.

Melt — To liquify solid foods by the action of heat.

Mince — To cut or chop into very small pieces.

Mix — To combine ingredients so as to distribute them uniformly.

Mold — To shape into a particular form. Gelatin and rice are two foods which can be molded easily.

Panbroil — To cook in a skillet or pan using no fat other than what is needed to prevent sticking.

Panfry — To cook in a skillet or pan containing only a small amount of fat.

Parboil — To partially cook in boiling water. Most parboiled foods require additional cooking.

Parch — To dry or roast slightly through exposure to intense heat.

Pit — To remove the hard inedible seed from peaches, plums, and so on.

Plank — To broil and serve on a board or wooden platter.

Plump — To soak fruits, usually dried, in liquid until they appear puffy and swollen.

Poach — To cook in a small amount of gently simmering liquid.

Preserve — To prevent food spoilage by pickling, slating, dehydrating, smoking, boiling in syrup, and so on. Preserved foods have excellent keeping qualities.

Puree — To reduce the pulp of cooked fruit and vegetables to a smooth and thick liquid by straining or blending.

Render — To extract animal fat.

Roast — To cook by dry heat either in an oven or over hot coals; or to dry or parch by intense heat.

Saute — To fry quickly in shallow fat or oil.

Scald — To heat a liquid almost to the boiling point; or to soak, usually vegetables or fruit, in boiling water until the skins are loosened.

Scallop — To bake with a sauce in a casserole. The food may either be mixed or layered with the sauce.

Score — To cut diagonally across in parallel lines, especially to cut meat.

Scramble — To cook and stir simultaneously.

Sieve — To pass dry and liquid ingredients through a closely meshed metal utensil so as to separate liquid from solid and fine from coarse.

Skewer — To thread usually meat and vegetables onto a sharpened rod (as a shish kabob); or to fasten closed the opening of stuffed fowl with small pins.

Skim — To ladle or spoon off excess fat or skum from the surface of a liquid.

COOKING AIDS

Substitute 1 teaspoon dried herbs for 1 tablespoon fresh herbs.

Try 1 cup minus 2 tablespoons all-purpose flour as a substitute for 1 cup cake flour.

Add 1/4 teaspoon baking soda and 1/2 cup buttermilk to equal 1 teaspoon baking powder. The buttermilk will replace 1/2 cup of the liquid indicated in the recipe.

Use 3 tablespoons dry cocoa plus 1 tablespoon butter or margarine instead of 1 square (1 ounce) unsweetened chocolate.

Make custard with 1 whole egg rather than 2 egg yolks.

Mix 1/2 cup evaporated milk with 1/2 cup water (or 1 cup reconstituted non-fat dry milk with 1 tablespoon butter) to replace 1 cup whole milk.

Make 1 cup of sour milk by letting stand for 5 minutes 1 tablespoon lemon juice or vinegar plus sweet milk to make 1 cup.

Substitute 1 package (2 teaspoons) active dry yeast for 1 cake compressed yeast.

Add 1 tablespoon instant minced onion, rehydrated, to replace 1 small fresh onion.

Substitute 1 tablespoon prepared mustard for 1 teaspoon dry mustard.

Use 1/8 teaspoon garlic powder instead of 1 small pressed clove of garlic.

Substitute 2 tablespoons of flour for 1 tablespoon of cornstarch to use as a thickening agent.

Mix 1/2 cup tomato sauce with 1/2 cup of water to make 1 cup tomato juice. Make catsup or chili with 1 cup tomato sauce, 1/2 cup sugar and 2 tablespoons vinegar.

ABBREVIATIONS USED IN THIS BOOK

Cup . . . . c.
Teaspoon . . . . tsp.
Tablespoon . . . . tbsp.
Pound .lb.
Ounce . . . . oz.
Gallon . . . . gal.
Minutes . . . . min.

Large . . . . .lg.
Small . . . . sm.
Package . . . . pkg.
Pint . . . . pt.
Quart . . . . qt.
Square . . . . sq.
Slice .sl.

EQUIVALENTS

3 tsp. = 1 tbsp.
2 tbsp. = 1/8 c.
4 tbsp. = 1/4 c.
8 tbsp. = 1/2 c.
16 tbsp. = 1 c.
5 tbsp. + 1 tsp. = 1/3 c.
12 tbsp. = 3/4 c.
4 oz. = 1/2 c.
8 oz. = 1 c.
1 oz. = 2 tbsp. fat or liquid
2 c. fat = 1 lb.

2 c. = 1 pt.
2 c. sugar = 1 lb.
5/8 c. = 1/2 c. + 2 tbsp.
7/8 c. = 3/4 c. + 2 tbsp.
1 lb. butter = 2 c. or 4 sticks
2 pt. = 1 qt.
1 qt. = 4 c.
A few grains = less than 1/8 tsp.
Pinch = as much as can be taken between tip of finger and thumb
Dash = less than 1/8 tsp.

OVEN TEMPERATURE

Temperature (°F)	Term
250-300	Slow
325	Moderately slow
350	Moderate
375-400	Moderately hot
425-450	Hot
475-500	Extremely hot

OUR MEN IN THE KITCHEN

APPETIZERS

Appetizers are those delicious hot and cold finger foods that none of us can seem to get enough of. They are savory foods that are intended to excite our appetites, and no matter how many we eat, they never seem to satisfy us. That's because they aren't supposed to — that's why we call them "appetizers" — they only whet our appetites.

Appetizers can include fruit juices, mixed drinks and snacks of all kinds. It would be impossible to even attempt to make a list of all the possibilities. But we give you quite a broad selection in our following recipes.

Some people always seem to have the knack of throwing together a little of this and a little of that, and coming up with a prized delicacy everytime. If you're interested in acquiring that "knack", you have only to thumb through the following pages for some great ideas.

BUTTER SAUCE FOR SNAILS

1/4 c. butter or margarine
1 3/4 tsp. minced parsley
1 tsp. minced shallots
1 tsp. garlic powder
1/2 tsp. salt
Snails in shells

Combine all ingredients except snails in small pan; cook over low heat until butter melts. Pour over snails, using all sauce. Broil until bubbly. Serve at once.

Lt. Cmdr. J. Michael Lents
Key West Navy Base, Key West, Florida

BLENDED CHEESE BALL

1   3-oz. package cream cheese
1 jar Old English cheese
1 sm. package Roquefort cheese
1/2 lb. mellow Cheddar cheese, grated
1 clove of garlic, minced
1 tbsp. Worcestershire sauce
Chili powder to taste

Have cream cheese, Old English and Roquefort cheeses at room temperature; combine with Cheddar cheese. Blend thoroughly with garlic and Worcestershire sauce until smooth. Shape into ball; roll in chili powder. Chill until ready to serve.

Maj. Mark Dierlam
Andersen AFB, Agana, Guam

WALNUT-CHILI-CHEESE BALL

1 lb. grated Cheddar cheese
1 1/2 c. walnuts, finely chopped
2   3-oz. packages cream cheese
1/4 tsp. garlic powder
1 tbsp. Worcestershire sauce
2 tbsp. onion flakes
1 tbsp. chili powder

Combine cheese and 1 cup walnuts; blend thoroughly. Add cream cheese, garlic powder, Worcestershire sauce and onion flakes; mix well. Shape mixture into ball 5 inches in diameter. Roll ball in chili powder and remaining walnuts. Chill until firm. Serve with assorted crackers. May be frozen, well wrapped, for future use.

Maj. Ben E. Killebrew
Fort Monmouth, New Jersey

PARTY CHEESE BALL

1/4 lb. blue cheese
1/4 lb. Old English cheese
1   8-oz. package cream cheese
2 tbsp. chopped parsley
1 sm. onion, chopped
1 tbsp. Worcestershire sauce
1/2 c. chopped pecans

Soften cheeses, then mash together until well blended. Add remaining ingredients except pecans and mix well. Shape into a ball. Roll ball into chopped pecans. Chill and serve with desired crackers.

Maj. Paul J. Rice
Judge Advocate General's Sch.
Charlottesville, Virginia

CHEESE BREAD

1 lg. onion, chopped
1 c. grated Parmesan cheese
1 c. mayonnaise
1 tsp. garlic salt
1 loaf cocktail rye bread, sliced thin

Mix onion, cheese, mayonnaise and garlic salt; spread on slices of bread. Place slices on baking sheet; Broil 4 to 5 inches from source of heat until lightly browned. French bread may be substituted for rye bread.

Capt. Ronald R. Ravescroft
Wasserkuppe, Germany

CHEESE OLIVES

4 oz. Cheddar cheese, grated
1/2 c. flour, sifted
1/4 tsp. salt
1/8 tsp. dry mustard
3 tsp. melted butter
1 tbsp. milk
Dash of hot sauce
Pitted green olives

Combine cheese, flour, salt and mustard; blend well. Stir in butter, milk and hot sauce to form dough. Coat olives with dough. Bake at 400 degrees for 15 minutes or until lightly browned. Ripe olives may be used, if desired. Yield: 25 balls.

Lt. Walt Cunningham
USN Dental, Taipei, Taiwan

CHEESE MARBLES

2 c. grated Cheddar cheese
1/2 c. butter
1 c. flour
1/4 tsp. salt
2 tsp. dry mustard

Blend cheese and butter until smooth and creamy. Sift flour, salt and mustard together. Add dry ingredients to cheese mixture; gradually mix thoroughly. Form into marble-sized balls. Place on greased cookie sheet. Bake 15 minutes in 350-degree oven. Stuffed olives may be coated with thin layer of dough and bake as above. Yield: 30-40 balls.

Lt. Col. Albert E. Manning
Defense Indus. Supply Center
Philadelphia, Pennsylvania

CHILI CON QUESO DIP

4 strips bacon
2 med. onions, chopped
1/2 green pepper, chopped
2 cloves of garlic, chopped
1 lg. fresh tomato, chopped
2 or 3 hot cherry peppers, chopped
1 1/4 lb. Velveeta cheese, cubed
Salt to taste

Fry bacon strips until crisp; remove bacon and drain on paper towel. Pour off all but 2 tablespoons bacon fat. Add onions, green pepper, garlic, tomatoes and hot peppers to bacon fat and cook until mushy, stirring frequently. Add cheese and salt. Cook over low heat until cheese is melted. Crumble the bacon into the cheese mixture. Keep warm while serving.

Maj. Paul J. Rice
Judge Advocate General's Sch.
Charlottesville, Virginia

EASY CHILI CON QUESO DIP

3 lg. onions
3 cloves of garlic
3 sm. cans green chili peppers, drained
3 No. 2 cans tomatoes
2 lb. Velveeta cheese, cubed
Salt to taste

Chop onions, garlic and peppers. Drain tomatoes; add to onion mixture. Simmer in saucepan for 1 hour. Add cheese; stir until cheese melts.

Add salt. May be processed in blender for greater smoothness. Serve with corn chips, if desired. Yield: 2 quarts.

Maj. Conrad E. Schray
Hq 570th USA AB, Handorf, West Germany

FRESH AVOCADO DIP

2 ripe avocados
1 tbsp. minced onion
1/4 tsp. chili powder
1/4 tsp. salt
Dash of pepper
1/8 tsp. garlic powder
1/3 c. mayonnaise
6 slices crisp bacon, crumbled
2 or 3 drops of lemon juice

Mash avocados. Add remaining ingredients and mix well. Chill.

Lt. Jr. Grade William E. Tanner
NAS, Agana, Guam

PEPPERED CHEESE-VEGETABLE DIP

1 1/2 c. sour cream
1 c. shredded sharp Cheddar cheese
1/4 c. finely chopped onion
3 tbsp. minced green pepper
1/4 tsp. salt
1/8 tsp. hot sauce
1 tbsp. milk

Combine all ingredients in mixing bowl and mix well. Add 1 tablespoon more milk to make of dipping consistency if necessary. Cover and refrigerate for at least 3 hours. Serve as dip for assorted fresh vegetables.

Capt. Carl L. Durst
AFIT, Columbia, Missouri

ROKA BLUE VEGETABLE DIP

1 jar roka blue cheese spread
1 8-oz. package cream cheese
Grated or dehydrated onion to taste
Milk

Let cheeses come to room temperature; mix in onion. Stir in enough milk to blend well and to make a creamy consistency. Serve with cauliflower pieces, carrot sticks and celery sticks.

Cmdr. Eugene M. Riddick
US Naval Station, San Francisco, California

TOMATO DIP

1 lg. package cream cheese
1   14-oz. bottle catsup
1 sm. onion, finely chopped
Dash of hot sauce

Soften cream cheese in a bowl; mash until smooth. Blend in catsup gradually. Add onion and hot sauce. Refrigerate for 24 hours for flavors to blend. Serve with potato chips or corn chips.

Col. Charles R. Burton
Langley AFB, Virginia

GERMAN BEER-CHEESE

1 lb. sharp Cheddar cheese
2 8-oz. packages cream cheese, softened
Few drops of hot sauce
1/2 to 3/4 c. beer, at room temperature
2 tsp. Worcestershire sauce
2 cloves of garlic, minced
Salt and pepper to taste

Grate Cheddar cheese and bring to room temperature. Combine with cream cheese. Add remaining ingredients; beat until mixed. Chill. May be placed in plastic tubs and frozen. Bring to room temperature. Sprinkle with paprika, chopped parsley or ground nuts before serving; serve with hearty crackers and party rye bread.

Maj. Charles G. Simpson
Vandenberg AFB, California

BEEF JERKY

1 flank steak
Soy sauce
Garlic powder to taste
Hickory salt to taste
Lemon pepper to taste

Cut steak with grain into thin strips; marinate in soy sauce. Spread steak on wire rack; sprinkle with garlic powder, hickory salt and lemon pepper. Dry in 150-degree oven for 15 hours or overnight; serve with beer, if desired.

Lt. Col. Jimmy L. Wood, USAF
NATO, Keflavik, Iceland

STEAK HORS D'OEUVRES

3/4 c. soy sauce
2 tbsp. sugar

2 tbsp. oil
2 tbsp. cornstarch
Flank steak

Combine soy sauce, sugar and oil. Dissolve cornstarch in small amount of water; add to marinade. Cut flank steak on the diagonal in 1-inch squares; marinate for 2 hours or overnight. Have guests spear steak on bamboo sticks; cook on habachi.

Cmdr. Dick Anderson
Dam Neck Naval Base, Virginia Beach, Virginia

HAM BALLS

1 lb. ground ham
1 lb. ground pork
1 lb. ground beef
1 c. saltine crumbs
2 eggs, slightly beaten
1 c. milk
2 c. (packed) brown sugar
1/2 c. vinegar
1/2 c. water
2 tsp. dry mustard

Combine meats, crumbs, eggs and milk; shape into bite-sized balls. Combine remaining ingredients in saucepan; bring to a boil. Place meatballs in baking dish; pour sauce over balls. Bake, covered, at 325 degrees for 45 minutes. Uncover. Bake for 15 minutes longer. Baste occasionally.

Lt. Col. John C. Allison
Blytheville AFB, Arkansas

VIRGINIA HAM APPETIZERS

1 c. ground Virginia ham
1 c. chutney
1/3 c. (about) thick cream
Toast rounds
Parmesan cheese

Mix ham and chutney together, then add enough cream to moisten to spreading consistency. Spread thickly on toast rounds. Sprinkle with cheese. Bake in 375-degree oven 5 minutes. Yield: 18 appetizers.

Lt. Col. F. Lee Early, Jr.
Ft. Campbell, Kentucky

THE DUTCHMAN

1 lb. braunschweiger
1 med. onion, minced

3 tbsp. hot mustard
Chopped parsley
Beer

Combine all ingredients, adding just enough beer to handle easily. Shape into large ball. Chill until firm; roll in parsley. Serve with assorted crackers. May be frozen.

Lt. Col. T. L. Richards
MAAG, Oslo, Norway

GLAZED CHICKEN LIVER PATE

1 env. unflavored gelatin
1 lb. chicken livers
1 chicken bouillon cube
2 tbsp. onion flakes
1/2 tsp. salt
1/4 c. buttermilk
1 tbsp. prepared mustard
1/4 tsp. pepper
1/4 tsp. thyme
1/4 tsp. nutmeg
2 tbsp. parsley flakes
2 tsp. sugar

Soften gelatin in 1/4 cup water in blender container. Place chicken livers in saucepan with 3/4 cup water, bouillon cube, onion flakes and salt; cover. Simmer for 5 to 6 minutes or until livers are tender. Pour chicken liver mixture and remaining ingredients into blender container; blend until livers are finely chopped. Pour into 7 1/2 x 3 1/2 x 2 1/4-inch loaf pan; chill until firm. Unmold onto platter.

Tangy Glaze

1 env. unflavored gelatin
1 c. buttermilk
2 tsp. prepared mustard
1/4 tsp. onion salt

Soften gelatin in 1/4 cup water in small saucepan. Place over low heat, stirring constantly, for 2 to 3 minutes or until gelatin dissolves. Remove from heat; stir in buttermilk, mustard and onion salt. Chill until slightly thickened. Coat top and sides of loaf with glaze, removing excess from platter; chill until firm. Repeat glaze coating several times, chilling after each coating. Soften glaze to spreading consistency by placing over bowl of warm water and stirring vigorously, if necessary. Garnish top with pimento flowers, scallion stems and green pepper leaves.

HOT PICKLED MUSHROOMS

2/3 c. tarragon vinegar
1/2 c. salad oil
1 med. clove of garlic, crushed
1 tbsp. sugar
2 tbsp. water
1 1/2 tsp. salt
Dash of freshly ground pepper
Dash of hot sauce
1 med. onion
2 6-oz. cans broiled mushroom crowns,
    drained

Combine first 8 ingredients for marinade. Slice onion; separate into rings. Add onions and mushrooms to marinade. Cover; refrigerate for 8 hours or overnight, stirring occasionally. Drain; serve as appetizers. Yield: 12 servings.

Mrs. David B. Bates, 1st VP, OWC
Minot AFB, North Dakota

MAGIC MUSHROOMS

1/2 c. butter
1 sm. onion, minced
12 to 24 lg. fresh mushrooms
1/4 tsp. dried basil
1/4 tsp. crushed oregano
1/2 tsp. garlic salt
1/4 tsp. celery salt
1 or 2 dashes of hot sauce
1 or 2 dashes of Worcestershire sauce
2 to 3 tbsp. lemon juice
1/2 tsp. salt
1/4 c. cooking sherry

Melt butter in large skillet. Add onion; saute until soft. Add mushrooms; coat well with butter. Add basil, oregano, garlic salt, celery salt, hot sauce, Worcestershire sauce, lemon juice, salt and sherry. Mix well; cover. Simmer until mushrooms are cooked; serve with toothpicks.

Mrs. Stuart B. McCurdy, W and M Chm., OWC
MacDill AFB, Tampa, Florida

STUFFED MUSHROOM CAPS

3 doz. fresh mushroom caps
1/8 lb. butter
Salt to taste
Onion salt to taste
Pepper to taste
1/2 lb. mild sausage
1/4 tsp. oregano
1 egg, slightly beaten
1/4 c. corn flake crumbs
Parmesan cheese to taste

Remove stems from mushroom caps. Melt butter in skillet; saute mushrooms, stem side up, for 10 minutes. Sprinkle with salt, onion salt and pepper. Combine sausage, oregano, egg and corn flake crumbs in saucepan. Fry until brown and crumbly. Drain off grease. Add cheese. Stuff mushroom cavities with sausage dressing; place on baking sheet. Broil for 5 minutes; serve immediately. Yield: 6 servings.

Mrs. Noel Widdifield, OWC
Beale AFB, California

MINI PIZZAS

1 can 8-count refrigerator biscuits
1 can tomato paste
1 sm. onion, chopped
1/2 lb. ground beef
Garlic salt to taste
1 tsp. Worcestershire sauce
1/2 sm. can tomato sauce

Separate each biscuit into 2 thin layers; place on cookie sheet. Spread tomato paste over each biscuit half. Combine remaining ingredients in skillet; cook over medium heat, stirring frequently until browned. Spread ground beef mixture over tomato paste. Bake at 375 degrees for 10 minutes. Yield: 16 pizzas.

Capt. Henry J. Zabinski
Sembach AFB, Germany

TINY PIZZAS

1 lb. bulk pork sausage
2 tsp. catsup
2 tsp. Worcestershire sauce
1 lb. Velveeta cheese
1 1/2 loaves party rye bread
Oregano

Brown sausage; pour off excess fat. Add catsup and Worcestershire sauce. Cut the Velveeta cheese in small chunks and add to the sausage mixture. Cook, stirring, until melted. Place bread on cookie sheet. Place 1 teaspoon sausage mixture on each slice; sprinkle with small amount of oregano. Freeze until firm; store in plastic bags until needed. Place frozen pizza on a baking sheet. Bake at 400 degrees for 7 minutes. May add mushrooms to pizzas before baking, if desired.

Lt. Col. Oliver J. Bussen
Defense Depot, Ogden, Utah

AVOCADO HALF SHELLS WITH CAVIAR

3 fully ripe California avocados
Lemon juice
6 tbsp. black caviar

Cut avocados lengthwise, twisting gently to separate halves. Insert sharp knife directly into seeds; twist gently to lift out. Brush cut surfaces with lemon juice; spoon caviar into cavities. Arrange caviar halves on crushed ice; garnish with chopped egg and onion or sour cream. May ripen avocados at home in paper bag or cool, dark place. May use red caviar, chopped smoked oysters, devilled ham, sardines and mustard sauce, marinated small canned shrimp with chives, anchovy paste and sour cream, a well-seasoned pate or crumbled crisp bacon with sauteed mushrooms instead of black caviar. Yield: 6 servings.

Photograph for this recipe on page 116.

CRISPY WON TON

3/4 c. ground pork
6 fresh shrimp, chopped fine
3 water chestnuts, chopped fine
1 egg, slightly beaten
2 tbsp. chopped onion
1 tsp. cornstarch
1/2 tsp. sugar
1/4 tsp. salt
1/2 tsp. shoyu
1/2 lb. won ton pi, cut into quarters
Peanut oil

Combine all ingredients except pi and oil; cook in skillet, stirring constantly, until pork is partially done. Line a colander with paper toweling, then place pork mixture in toweling. Chill. Place 1/2 teaspoon pork mixture in center of each pi and fold into a triangle. Fold tip of triangle over straight edge, extending about 1/2 inch. Dampen 2 remaining tips; bring to center, folding about 1 inch over on each side. Dampen

tips; pinch together. Place on waxed paper until ready to fry. Heat oil in deep fat fryer to 400 degrees. Place won ton in oil; fry until light brown. Do not overcook.

Maj. Frank Takeshi Sanpei
Wright-Patterson AFB, Dayton, Ohio

PICKLED SHRIMP

2 lb. cleaned cooked shrimp
1 c. sliced onions
5 bay leaves
1 1/2 c. vegetable oil
3/4 c. white vinegar
3 tbsp. capers and juice
2 1/2 tsp. celery seed
1 1/2 tsp. salt
Hot sauce

Place alternate layers of shrimp, onions and bay leaves in a large dish. Combine oil, vinegar, capers, celery and salt and several drops of hot sauce; mix well. Pour over shrimp mixture; chill for at least 2 hours. Good for a cocktail buffet. Yield: 15 servings.

Lt. Col. Carl H. Irwin, Jr.
Oakland Army Base, Oakland, California

SEVICHE

1 lb. uncooked white fish fillets
1 med. onion
3 crisp lettuce leaves
1 c. white wine
1/2 c. lemon juice
1/2 c. vinegar
1/2 tsp. salt
1/4 tsp. pepper
1/4 tsp. marjoram (opt.)
1/4 tsp. basil (opt.)

Cut fish fillets into cubes or strips; place in glass bowl. Slice onion thinly, separate into rings. Shred lettuce finely. Combine onion and lettuce with fish. Combine lemon juice, vinegar, salt, pepper, marjoram, and basil with 1/2 cup water in small bowl; blend well. Pour marinade over fish mixture; chill for at least 4 hours, stirring occasionally. Serve with assorted crackers. Yield: 10 servings.

Col. John B. Watkins, Jr.
White Sands Missile Range, New Mexico

MEATS

On those occasions when you want to serve the very best and show your friends how highly you think of them, turn your culinary talents toward roasting a tempting standing rib roast of beef. Your friends will talk about that party for months, and you can be guaranteed that the compliments will last longer than that!

Or, explore the epicurian world of seldom served lamb, veal or specialty cuts. Because lamb and mutton are so pleasing to the eye, as well as the palate, they are ideal to serve at parties and on occasions when you want your menu very special. In addition to their visual attractiveness, these meats are delicious to the taste.

If your family and friends are like most Americans, the sight and taste, not to mention the sound of the sizzling of T-bone steaks, will be greeted with enthusiastic raves. We Americans prefer our meats without heavy sauces and gravies, and many of the following recipes will show the creative cook how to combine the right spices and herbs to bring out the flavors of grilled, roasted or fried meats.

BEST BEEF BRISKET

1 3 to 4-lb. beef brisket
2 tbsp. lard or drippings
2 tsp. salt
1/2 tsp. mustard seed
1 bay leaf
4 peppercorns
1 clove of garlic, sliced
8 to 10 whole white onions
1/3 c. flour
2 tbsp. prepared horseradish
Paprika (opt.)

Brown brisket on all sides in lard; pour off drippings. Add salt, mustard seed, bay leaf, peppercorns, garlic and 1 1/2 cups water; cover. Simmer for 2 hours. Turn brisket; add onions. Cover; simmer for 1 hour longer or until brisket is done. Remove brisket to serving board or platter; let stand for about 15 minutes for easier carving. Remove onions; keep warm. Discard bay leaf. Measure cooking liquid; add enough water, if necessary, to make 2 1/2 cups liquid. Blend flour with 1/2 cup water. Stir into cooking liquid; cook, stirring constantly, until thickened. Stir in horseradish. Sprinkle brisket and onions with paprika; serve with horseradish gravy. Yield: 10-12 servings.

FREDDIE'S MARINADE FOR SHISH KABOBS

1 3 to 4-lb. boneless chuck roast
1 clove of garlic, pressed
1 c. oil
1/2 c. vinegar
1 tsp. salt
1/4 tsp. pepper
2 tsp. dry mustard
2 tsp. Worcestershire sauce
Dash of cayenne pepper
Dash of hot sauce
Onion wedges
Green pepper cubes
Cherry tomatoes
Whole mushrooms
Pineapple chunks

Cut the roast into 1-inch cubes. Mix garlic, oil, vinegar, salt, pepper, mustard, Worcestershire sauce, cayenne pepper and hot sauce in a bowl. Add roast cubes and marinate for 6 to 8 hours.

Place roast cubes, onion wedges, green pepper, tomatoes, mushrooms and pineapple chunks alternately on skewers; place over low coals on grill. Cook for 15 minutes, turning frequently and brushing with remaining marinade. Serve with cooked rice. Yield: 6 servings.

Capt. Bruce Fredrick
Vint Hill Farms Sta., Virginia

SMOKED BRISKET

1 beef brisket
Salt and pepper to taste

Soak a large supply of hickory chips well in advance. Start charcoal fire in grill with cover in only one end of the grill. Trim excess fat from brisket, leaving a 1/4-inch layer of fat for moisture. Season with salt and pepper. When coals are ready, open vents only beneath the coals and over the beef to make a draft of smoke over beef. Place brisket at far end of grill away from fire for indirect cooking. Cook for 6 to 7 hours, maintaining a low heat, adding more charcoal and wet chips as needed. Slice and serve with sandwich rolls and favorite spread or sauce. May be frozen for later use.

Maj. Billy G. Edenfield
Robins AFB, Georgia

SMOKED BEEF BRISKET

1 6-lb. boneless beef brisket
Garlic salt to taste
Onion salt to taste
Celery salt to taste
1 sm. bottle liquid smoke
Barbecue sauce

Place brisket in shallow baking pan. Sprinkle with seasonings; add liquid smoke. Cover with foil; marinate overnight. Bake, covered, at 250 degrees for 6 hours. Remove roast to platter; cool. Slice roast; return to roasting pan with favorite barbecue sauce. Heat through. Yield: 8-10 servings.

Maj. Manley W. Crider, Jr.
Maxwell AFB, Alabama

BARBECUED BRISKET

1/2 c. vegetable oil
1/4 c. soy sauce
1/4 c. vinegar

1/8 c. smoke sauce
Pepper to taste
Garlic salt to taste
Celery salt to taste
1 8-lb. beef brisket

Mix all ingredients together except beef in pint jar and shake well. Marinate beef in sauce for 8 hours, turning occasionally. Bake at 200 degrees for 8 hours. Slice thin and serve on bun and with favorite barbecue sauce. For each pound of beef, marinate and roast for 1 hour. Yield: 16 servings.

Lt. Col. Donald S. Johnson
Kincheloe AFB, Michigan

BEEF CUBES IN SOUR CREAM

2 lb. beef chuck
Flour
2 med. onions, thinly sliced
1/2 c. sour cream
2 tbsp. grated sharp Cheddar cheese
1 tsp. salt
Freshly ground pepper to taste

Cut beef into 1-inch cubes; roll in flour. Brown on all sides in small amount of fat in large skillet. Combine onions, sour cream, cheese, salt and pepper with 1/2 cup water; pour over beef. Simmer, covered, for 1 hour and 45 minutes or until beef is tender. Yield: 6 servings.

Vice Adm. Arthur Robert Gralla
Washington, D. C.

CAMPER'S STEW

1 lb. lean ground beef
3 c. water
2 env. vegetable soup mix
2 cans potatoes, drained
1 sm. can onions, drained
1 can whole kernel corn
1 1-lb. can tomatoes

Brown ground beef in large, heavy kettle. Add water and stir in soup mix. Bring to a boil, stirring constantly. Add potatoes, onions, corn and tomatoes; heat thoroughly. Yield: 6-8 servings.

Lt. Cmdr. Walter L. Czerwonka
Roosevelt Roads Naval Sta., Ceiba, Puerto Rico

CABBAGE ROLLS

1 med. head cabbage
1 lb. hamburger
1 lb. bulk sausage
3 c. rice
2 eggs
1/2 tsp. salt
1/2 tsp. pepper
8 slices bacon, cut in 1-in. lengths
2 med. tomatoes, cut into quarters
1 can whole tomatoes
1 can tomato sauce
1 tsp. parsley flakes
2 tbsp. vinegar
1 tbsp. oil

Remove core from cabbage and cook in boiling water till leaves are soft. Mix hamburger, sausage, rice, eggs, salt and pepper; shape into balls. Remove outside leaves of cabbage. Place a meatball in each cabbage leaf; roll up. Shred remaining cabbage; place about 2 inches deep in large kettle. Place bacon and tomato quarters on shredded cabbage. Place cabbage rolls on bacon mixture; add canned tomatoes, tomato sauce, parsley flakes, vinegar and oil. Simmer for 2 hours or until hamburger mixture is done.

CWO Frank Kellueskie
Ft. Devens, Massachusetts

ZIPPY CREAMED BEEF

1 lb. lean ground beef
Salt and pepper to taste
Monosodium glutamate
4 tbsp. flour
2 c. milk
1/4 tsp. cayenne pepper
8 dashes of hot sauce
2 beef bouillon cubes
1 tbsp. butter

Brown ground beef in skillet over low heat, stirring with wooden spoon to separate; pour off excess grease. Add salt, pepper and monosodium glutamate. Sprinkle flour over ground beef; cook, stirring constantly, until flour is browned. Add milk gradually, stirring constantly until mixture is smooth and thickened; stir in cayenne pepper, hot sauce and bouillon cubes. Simmer, stirring constantly, until cubes are dissolved. Add butter, stirring until melted. Simmer for 10 minutes longer; add milk if desired. Serve over toast. Yield: 4 servings.

J. Robert Lucas
Heidelberg, Germany

CREAMED BEEF FOR MORNING AFTER

1 lb. ground beef
1/4 c. sweet dry vermouth
1/2 c. chopped onions
1/2 c. sliced mushrooms
1/2 garlic clove, crushed
1/4 c. flour
2 c. milk
1/2 c. sour cream
2 oz. cream cheese
1 tsp. salt
1 tsp. pepper
1 tsp. paprika
1/2 tsp. hot sauce

Cook ground beef in vermouth over medium heat in a large skillet until brown. Add onions, mushrooms and garlic; simmer for 5 minutes. Push to one side of skillet, then add flour to the pan juices and stir until blended. Add 1 cup milk and stir all ingredients together. Stir in sour cream, cream cheese and remaining milk. Add salt, pepper, paprika and hot sauce; simmer over low heat for 10 minutes. Serve over toast or biscuits. Yield: 8 servings.

Capt. William C. Godfrey
Panzer Kaserne, Boeblingen, Germany

SWEET AND SOUR MEATBALLS

8 lb. lean ground beef
3 onions, chopped
Salt and pepper to taste
3/4 bottle A-1 sauce
3/4 bottle steak sauce
1/2 bottle Worcestershire sauce
Hot sauce
Hot mustard
2 boxes brown sugar
1 pt. vinegar
1 lg. can pineapple juice

Combine ground beef, onions, salt and pepper, A-1 sauce, steak sauce, Worcestershire sauce, 20 to 25 drops of hot sauce and 6 tablespoons hot mustard; blend well. Form into bite-sized balls. Brown in large skillet, stirring to brown on all sides; drain well. Combine brown sugar, vinegar, 1 jar hot mustard, pineapple juice and dash of hot sauce in large saucepan. Simmer for several minutes. Add meatballs to sauce; heat through. Serve in chafing dish.

Lt. Col. T. L. Richards
MAAG, Oslo, Norway

FLORIDA GRAPEFRUIT BASKETS

3 Florida grapefruit

Cut grapefruit in half. Insert 2 wooden picks 1/2 inch apart on each side of grapefruit. Cut through the peel 1/4 inch below the top of the half to make handle; do not cut between the picks. Cut around each section of fruit loosening from membrane. Cut around entire edge of grapefruit. Remove picks. Lift handles and tie together. Attach flower to handle.

Photograph for this recipe on page 129.

ROAST TURKEY
WITH ORANGE-RICE STUFFING

1   12 to 14-lb. turkey
Salt and pepper to taste
Orange-Rice Stuffing

Wash turkey in cold running water. Pat inside dry with paper toweling, leaving outside moist. Sprinkle turkey cavities with salt and pepper. Stuff turkey with Orange Rice Stuffing. Fasten neck skin to body with skewer. Push legs under band of skin at tail or tie to tail. Place turkey, breast side up, on rack in shallow open roasting pan. Cover with a loose covering or tent of aluminum foil, if desired. Bake in a preheated 325-degree oven for 4 hours and 30 minutes to 5 hours or until tender.

Orange-Rice Stuffing

1 c. butter or margarine
1 c. chopped onion
4 c. water
2 c. Florida orange juice
3 tbsp. grated orange rind
4 c. chopped celery
2 tbsp. salt
1 tsp. poultry seasoning
5 1/3 c. packaged precooked rice
1/2 c. chopped parsley

Melt butter in a large saucepan; add onion and cook until tender but not brown. Add water, orange juice, orange rind, celery, salt and poultry seasoning. Bring to a boil; stir in rice. Cover; remove from heat and let stand for 5 minutes. Add parsley and fluff with fork. Any leftover stuffing may be wrapped in foil and placed in oven last 30 minutes of baking time.

Photograph for this recipe on page 129.

BAKED TANGERINES
WITH ORANGE-CRANBERRY RELISH

6 Florida tangerines or Temple oranges
2 tbsp. sugar
2 tbsp. butter or margarine
2/3 c. Florida orange juice
Orange-Cranberry Relish

Make 8 vertical cuts in the tangerine skin from the blossom end to about 1 inch from the bottom. Pull peel down and turn pointed ends in. Remove white membrane. Loosen sections at the center and pull apart slightly. Fill each center with 1 teaspoon sugar and dot with 1 teaspoon butter. Pour orange juice over tangerines. Bake in preheated 325-degree oven for 30 minutes. Garnish center with a small amount of Orange-Cranberry Relish. Serve with turkey.

Orange-Cranberry Relish

2 Florida oranges, quartered and seeded
4 c. fresh cranberries
2 c. sugar

Force orange quarters with peel and cranberries through food chopper. Add sugar and mix well. Chill in refrigerator for several hours before serving. This relish will keep well in refrigerator for several weeks.

Photograph for this recipe opage 129.

ORANGE CREPES
WITH ORANGE SAUCE

3 eggs
2 egg yolks
1/2 c. milk
1/2 c. Florida orange juice
2 tbsp. salad oil
1 c. all-purpose flour
3/4 tsp. salt
1 tbsp. sugar
1 tsp. grated orange rind

Beat eggs and egg yolks together. Add remaining ingredients and beat until smooth. Let stand at room temperature for at least 1 hour. Brush hot 7 or 8-inch skillet lightly with additional salad oil. Add 2 tablespoons batter to skillet; turn and tip skillet so mixture covers bottom evenly. Batter will set immediately into thin lacey pancake. Loosen with spatula and flip over in about 15 to 20 seconds or when browned. Brown other side and turn crepe out onto foil or waxed paper. Repeat with remaining batter.

Orange Sauce

1/2 c. soft butter
1/2 c. confectioners' sugar
1 tbsp. grated orange rind
3 tbsp. orange liqueur
1/3 c. Florida orange juice
1 c. Florida orange sections

Cream butter with confectioners' sugar and orange rind. Blend in orange liqueur gradually. Spread about 1/2 teaspoon mixture over side of crepe that was browned second. Roll up crepes. Place remaining mixture with orange juice in large skillet or chafing dish; heat until bubbly. Add rolled crepes and heat, spooning sauce over tops. Add orange sections; heat for just 2 to 3 minutes longer. Yield: 6 servings.

Photograph for this recipe on page 129.

LAMB CHOP AND TOMATO BROIL
WITH HORSERADISH SAUCE

6 1-in. thick loin lamb chops
3 med. tomatoes, halved
1/4 c. butter, melted
1/2 tsp. salt
1/8 tsp. pepper
12 sm. boiled potatoes
Chopped parsley
3 tbsp. drained horseradish
1 c. sour cream

Place lamb chops and tomato halves on rack in shallow pan. Broil 4 to 6 inches from source of heat for 8 to 12 minutes or to desired degree of doneness, turning once. Combine butter, salt and pepper; brush chops and tomatoes frequently with butter mixture. Peel potatoes; brown lightly in additional butter in skillet. Arrange chops, tomatoes and potatoes on heated platter; sprinkle tomatoes with parsley. Blend horseradish with sour cream. Season to taste with additional salt. Serve sauce with lamb chop dish. Yield: 6 servings.

Photograph for this recipe on page 130.

SWEDISH MEATBALLS

1 lb. ground chuck
1/4 c. fine dry bread crumbs
1 tbsp. instant minced onion
1 tsp. salt
Dash of pepper
1/2 tsp. allspice
1 2/3 c. evaporated milk
3 tbsp. butter
2 tbsp. flour
1 beef bouillon cube
1 c. boiling water
1 tbsp. Worcestershire sauce

Mix ground chuck, crumbs, onion, salt, pepper, allspice and 2/3 cup evaporated milk; shape into meatballs, using 1 teaspoon for each. Melt butter in large, heavy skillet over medium heat. Add meatballs; fry, turning meatballs frequently, until brown on all sides. Remove skillet from heat. Sprinkle flour evenly over meatballs, stirring to blend well. Dissolve bouillon cube in boiling water; add to skillet. Stir in remaining evaporated milk and Worcestershire sauce until smooth. Place skillet over low heat; cook, stirring frequently, until gravy is thickened. Serve over hot, cooked noodles. Yield: 6 servings.

COWBOY HAMBURGERS

Butter
6 hamburger buns
Mustard
Catsup
6 hamburger patties
Sliced onion rings
Sliced dill pickles

Spread butter lightly over both sides of hamburger buns. Spread mustard on one side and catsup on the other side. Place uncooked hamburger patty on one side of bun; add onion ring and dill pickles. Cover with remaining bun half. Wrap in foil. Bake at 400 degrees for 40 minutes. Cool slightly before eating. Yield: 6 servings.

Lt. Cmdr. Robert L. Boyd
Naval Air Facility, El Centro, California

OLD-FASHIONED MEAT LOAF

3/4 lb. ground beef
1/4 lb. ground pork
4 slices dry bread, cut in cubes
1 egg
1 1/2 tsp. salt
Dash of pepper
1 med. onion, chopped
1/2 c. chopped celery
Catsup

Preheat oven to 325 degrees. Mix all ingredients well, adding enough catsup to hold ingredients together. Shape into loaf; place in heavy pan or casserole. Pour catsup over top of meat loaf; add small amount of water to pan to prevent sticking. Bake for 3 hours and 30 minutes, covering pan when meat loaf is brown. Reduce oven temperature to 200 degrees and keep hot until served. Yield: 4 servings.

Cmdr. Ronald D. Baker
Naval Grad. Dental Sch., Bethesda, Maryland

POOR MAN'S STROGANOFF

1 med. onion, chopped
1 tbsp. vegetable oil
1 lb. hamburger
1 can cream of mushroom soup
1/2 c. red wine
1/2 tsp. dillseed
Salt and pepper to taste
1/4 c. canned sliced mushrooms (opt.)

Saute onion in oil until tender. Add hamburger and cook until brown. Add soup, wine, dillseed, salt, pepper and mushrooms; heat until bubbly. May add more dillseed, if desired. Serve over mashed potatoes.

Lt. Michael T. Hanst
Harold E. Holt Naval Base Exmouth, Western Australia

JERRY'S ENCHILADAS

1 lb. hamburger
1 med. onion, finely chopped
1/2 tsp. garlic salt
Salt and pepper to taste
1 sm. can tomato sauce
1/2 tsp. oregano
3/4 pkg. chili mix
1 pkg. extra thin corn tortillas
1 1/2 c. grated Cheddar cheese

Fry hamburger in skillet till brown; pour off grease. Add onion, garlic salt, salt, pepper, tomato sauce, oregano and enough water to fill skillet 3/4 full. Simmer for about 30 minutes. Add chili mix and stir well. Cover skillet and cook for 10 minutes longer. Dip the tortillas in skillet liquid till saturated; place, flat side down, in an oblong 2-quart baking dish. Place hamburger mixture, then cheese on 1 end of each tortilla; roll. Place close together in the baking dish; pour remaining hamburger mixture over top. Bake at 300 degrees for 1 hour or until cheese melts. Chopped onion may be placed on cheese before rolling enchiladas, if desired. Yield: 3-4 servings.

Lt. Jerry A. Weber
NAS, Kingsville, Texas

CHILI-TORTILLA CASSEROLE

2 lb. ground beef
1 lg. onion, chopped
2 cans tomato sauce
1 tbsp. Worcestershire sauce
Salt and pepper to taste
1/2 tsp. minced garlic
3 tbsp. chili powder
1/2 lb. broken spaghetti
1 can pinto beans
1 lb. Cheddar cheese, grated
1 can chopped ripe olives, drained
8 to 10 corn tortillas

Combine ground beef and onion in large skillet; cook, stirring frequently, until beef is browned. Stir in tomato sauce, Worcestershire sauce, salt, pepper, garlic and chili powder; heat through. Add spaghetti and water to cover; simmer until spaghetti is tender. Remove from heat; stir in pinto beans. Combine cheese and olives in small bowl. Layer, in 9 x 13-inch baking dish, half the beef mixture, half the cheese mixture, tortillas, remaining beef mixture and remaining cheese

mixture. Bake at 325 degrees for 30 minutes. Yield: 6-8 servings.

Cmdr. Dick Anderson
Dam Neck Naval Base, Virginia

PATIO DELIGHT

1 lb. hamburger
1 Bermuda onion, sliced
1 lg. baking potato, sliced
1 lg. tomato, sliced
1 lg. carrot, sliced lengthwise
Salt and pepper to taste
Worcestershire sauce to taste

Shape hamburger into 6 patties; top with onion, potato, tomato and carrot slices. Place the stacks in 6 individual 12-inch squares of aluminum foil; season with salt, pepper and Worcestershire sauce. Wrap in the foil, allowing a tiny air hole in the top. Light charcoal in outdoor grill; let burn until coals are hot. Cook directly on hot coals for 20 minutes. May be baked in preheated 450-degree oven for 30 minutes.

Maj. Frank M. Stewart
Ft. Lee, Virginia

KIDNEY AND EGG STEW

1 beef kidney
6 c. boiling water
1 sm. onion, minced
1/2 c. flour
2 tsp. salt
1/4 tsp. pepper
1/4 tsp. paprika
3 tbsp. butter
2 hard-cooked eggs, minced
1/2 c. white wine

Cut kidney into 1/4-inch slices; remove fat and gristle. Soak in cold water for 30 minutes; drain. Add boiling water, then add onion. Simmer, uncovered, for 1 hour; cool. Mix flour with 1/2 cup cooled liquid to make a paste. Heat kidney mixture. Add flour paste gradually and cook, stirring constantly, until thickened. Add salt, pepper, paprika, butter, eggs and wine; heat through. Serve over noodles, toast points or hash brown potatoes. Yield: 4 servings.

Capt. Walter T. Michnal
Kincheloe AFB, Michigan

EASY BEER ROAST

1 3-lb. eye of round roast
2 tbsp. soy sauce
1 can beer
2 tbsp. freshly ground pepper

Place roast in baking pan; pour soy sauce over roast. Pour beer over roast; sprinkle pepper on top. Let stand for 3 to 4 hours or longer, basting or turning every 30 minutes. Bake at 325 degrees for 55 to 60 minutes. Remove from oven and let stand for 10 minutes. Slice very thin. Excellent for a cocktail buffet. Yield: 8-12 servings.

Lt. Col. Carl H. Irwin, Jr.
Oakland Army Base, Oakland, California

PETE'S OVEN POT ROAST

1 can cream of mushroom soup
1 pkg. onion soup mix
1 3 to 4-lb. chuck roast

Line shallow roasting pan with heavy-duty foil, leaving enough to fold over roast. Spread 3/4 can mushroom soup on foil; sprinkle with 1/2 package soup mix. Place roast on top of soup mix; spread remaining soup and soup mix over top of roast. Fold foil over top and ends of roast, sealing well. Bake at 325 degrees for 3 hours. Yield: 6 servings.

Col. Charles E. Weddle
Wiley Barracks, Neu Ulm, Germany

SAUERBRATEN

1 6-lb. beef rump roast
5 c. vinegar
3 onions, sliced
1 lemon, sliced
12 whole cloves
6 bay leaves
6 peppercorns
3 tbsp. salt

Place roast in large bowl. Combine vinegar, onions, lemon, cloves, bay leaves, peppercorns and salt with 5 cups water; mix well. Pour vinegar mixture over roast. Marinate, turning occasionally, for 48 hours. Remove roast from marinade; reserve marinade. Brown roast on all sides in Dutch oven in small amount of fat over medium heat; pour 1 cup marinade over roast. Reduce heat. Simmer, covered, for 2 hours or until roast is tender; add reserved marinade or water, if necessary. Marinate roast for just 24 hours if milder flavor is desired. Yield: 8-10 servings.

Vice Adm. Arthur Robert Gralla
Washington, D. C.

POT ROAST IN BEER

1 3 1/2 to 4-lb. lean pot roast
1 can of beer
1 sm. bottle chili sauce

Trim all fat from roast; brown in small amount of fat in Dutch oven. Combine beer and chili sauce; pour over roast. Simmer, covered, for 2 hours or until roast is tender. Skim excess fat from liquid. Serve with rice, if desired. Yield: 4 servings.

Vice Adm. John Victor Smith
Washington, D. C.

OVEN-BARBECUED SHORT RIBS

2 1/2 lb. beef short ribs
Salt and pepper
Onion slices
Green pepper rings
1 8-oz. can tomato sauce
1 1/2 c. water
2 tsp. (or more) chili powder
2 tbsp. Worcestershire sauce
3 or 4 drops of hot sauce

Place short ribs in roasting pan and season lightly with salt and pepper. Place desired amount of onion slices and green pepper rings on ribs. Mix 1 teaspoon salt, 1 teaspoon pepper and remaining ingredients in saucepan; bring to a boil. Pour over ribs; cover. Bake at 350 degrees for 1 hour and 30 minutes to 2 hours.

Lt. Thomas C. Gannon
Naval Aerospace Recovery Facility
El Centro, California

STANDING RIB ROAST

1 5 to 6-lb. standing rib roast

Preheat oven to 375 degrees. Place roast in shallow baking pan. Bake for 1 hour. Turn off heat; do not open oven door. Reheat oven at 375 degrees. Bake for 30 minutes longer or to desired degree of doneness.

Lt. James R. Clarke
Ft. Sheridan, Illinois

BEEF WELLINGTON

1 5 to 6-lb. fillet of beef
Salt and pepper
1 clove of garlic, halved
4 pieces of suet
1/4 c. chopped onion
1/2 c. chopped filberts
1 1/4 c. butter or margarine
1/4 lb. mushrooms, chopped
1/4 c. cognac
1/2 lb. ground veal
1/2 lb. ground pork
1 egg, slightly beaten
1/4 c. heavy cream
1/4 c. chopped parsley
1/4 tsp. basil
1/4 tsp. thyme
1/4 tsp. rosemary leaves
1/8 tsp. ground allspice
4 c. sifted all-purpose flour
2/3 c. all-vegetable shortening, chilled
1 egg white, slightly beaten

Trim all fat from beef. Place beef on rack in shallow roasting pan; sprinkle with salt and pepper. Rub with garlic; cover with suet. Roast in 425-degree oven for 1 hour or until meat thermometer registers 140 degrees for rare. Cool slightly; remove suet. Wrap beef; refrigerate for 24 hours. Saute onion and filberts in 1/4 cup butter until onion is tender and filberts are toasted. Stir in mushrooms and cognac; cook over medium heat for 5 to 10 minutes. Combine mushroom mixture with veal, pork, egg, cream, parsley, 1 teaspoon salt, basil, thyme, rosemary leaves, allspice and 1/8 teaspoon pep-

per in large bowl. Cover; refrigerate for 24 hours. Cut remaining butter into 1/2-inch pieces. Mix flour and 1 teaspoon salt in large mixing bowl. Cut butter pieces and shortening into flour mixture until mixture resembles large bread crumbs. Sprinkle 10 tablespoons cold water over mixture; work quickly until mixture forms ball. Sprinkle with small amount of additional flour; wrap in waxed paper. Refrigerate for 24 hours. Roll out 3/4 of the pastry on floured board to 18 x 18-inch square or large enough to enclose beef. Place beef along 1 edge of pastry; cover with veal forcemeat. Lift pastry up over beef, overlapping under beef and sealing edges; brush pastry with egg white. Roll out remaining pastry; cut into shapes, using small cookie cutters. Arrange on top of pastry; brush with egg white. Place beef on ungreased cookie sheet carefully. Bake in 425-degree oven for 40 minutes or until pastry is golden brown. Remove carefully with 2 broad spatulas to large serving platter. Yield: 12 servings.

Brussels Sprouts

1/2 c. butter or margarine
3 10-oz. packages frozen California
   Brussels sprouts
1 c. chicken broth
1 tsp. salt
1/2 tsp. marjoram leaves
1/4 tsp. coarsely ground pepper
2 slices lemon peel
1 1/2 c. sliced cooked chestnuts (opt.)

Melt butter in large saucepan. Saute Brussels sprouts in butter for 5 to 10 minutes, separating with fork. Stir in broth, seasonings and lemon peel; cover. Simmer for 10 minutes or until crisp-tender, stirring in chestnuts during last 5 minutes. Place on platter with Beef Wellington.

ALPINE GOULASH

2 1/2 lb. boneless round steak
2 tbsp. shortening
3 c. coarsely chopped onions
1 clove of garlic, minced
2 8-oz. cans tomato sauce
2 tbsp. brown sugar
2 tbsp. paprika
1 1/2 tsp. salt
1 tsp. caraway seed
1 tsp. dillseed

1/4 tsp. pepper
1 c. sour cream

Cut steak into small cubes. Brown steak in shortening, then add remaining ingredients except sour cream. Cover and simmer for 2 hours and 30 minutes or until steak is tender, stirring occasionally. Stir in sour cream just before serving. Serve over hot noodles. Yield: 4-5 servings.

Maj. John F. Snyder
Pentagon, Washington, D. C.

CUBE STEAK

3 tbsp. oil
6 slices cube steak
1/2 c. chopped green peppers
1/4 c. chopped onion
1 can whole tomatoes
1 can tomato sauce

Heat oil in skillet. Add cube steaks and 3/4 cup water; boil till all the water has evaporated, then brown steaks. Add green peppers, onion, tomatoes and tomato sauce; simmer for 1 hour, turning steaks occasionally.

CWO Frank Kellueskie
Ft. Devens, Massachusetts

EASY TERIYAKI STEAK

4 ribe eye steaks, cut 1 in. thick
1   10-oz. bottle teriyaki sauce

Marinate steaks in teriyaki sauce for 24 hours, turning occasionally. Grill over charcoal fire for 6 minutes on each side or to desired doneness. Serve on hot steak plates.

Lt. Col. Donald S. Johnson
Kincheloe AFB, Michigan

BOURBON FLANK STEAK TERIYAKI

8 tbsp. soy sauce
4 tbsp. bourbon
1/2 c. hot water
1 clove of garlic, finely minced (opt.)
1/4 tbsp. ginger
1/4 tsp. freshly ground pepper
4 lb. flank steak

Blend marinade ingredients together; pour over steak. Let stand for at least 2 hours to mari-

nate, turning the steak several times. Broil to desired doneness. Slice steak thin on an angle across the grain to serve. Store remaining marinade in a closed container in refrigerator for future use. Yield: 6 servings.

Cmdr. Don F. Hummel
USS Niagara Falls, FPO, San Francisco
Lt. Col. William J. Vaughn
Davis Monthan AFB, Arizona

BURGUNDY-MARINATED FLANK STEAK

1 c. Burgundy
1/2 c. olive oil
1 tsp. salt
1/2 tsp. pepper
1 clove of garlic, minced
1 bay leaf
1 onion, finely minced
1 tsp. chopped fresh rosemary
1   2 1/2-lb. flank steak

Simmer marinade ingredients in saucepan for 10 minutes. Score flank steak on one side; place in shallow pan. Pour hot marinade over steak; refrigerate, covered, for 2 to 3 days, turning daily. Broil as close as possible to hot coals for 4 minutes on each side. Cut steak thinly across the grain. Good served with hashed brown potatoes and broiled tomatoes. Marinade will keep for 2 to 3 weeks; may use in stew, if desired. Yield: 3-4 servings.

Capt. Herbert F. Butler, Jr.
Naval Supply Ctr., Pearl Harbor, Hawaii

DELICIOUS MARINATED FLANK STEAK

3 tbsp. minced scallion
2 tbsp. soy sauce
1/2 tsp. thyme
2 tbsp. olive oil
Juice of 1/2 lemon
Pinch of pepper or several drops of
    hot sauce
1   2-lb. flank steak

Mix marinade ingredients together in bowl. Place steak in broiler pan; spread marinade on both sides of steak. Let marinate for 24 hours or longer. Broil for 5 to 7 minutes on each side.

Col. E. S. Stenberg, Jr.
Fort Myer, Virginia

DO-AHEAD FLANK STEAK

3/4 sm. bottle soy sauce
3 tbsp. oil
1 c. vinegar
2 tbsp. sugar
Salt and pepper to taste
Worcestershire sauce to taste
Garlic salt to taste
1 flank steak

Combine soy sauce, oil, vinegar, sugar and seasonings. Place steak in shallow dish; pour marinade over steak. Let marinate for 10 hours.
Score steak. Broil for 20 minutes or to desired
degree of doneness. Yield: 4 servings.

CWO Donald Wayne Bullen
Selfridge Air National Guard, Michigan

FLANK STEAK SUPREME

1/3 c. soy sauce
1/3 c. bourbon
1/3 c. salad oil
1 tsp. basil
Garlic powder to taste
1 tbsp. chopped onion
Salt and pepper to taste
1   2-lb. flank steak

Combine first 7 ingredients in bowl. Place
steak in glass dish. Pour marinade over steak;
place in refrigerator for 6 hours or overnight,
turning occasionally so that all parts are marinated. Drain steak. Broil for 3 to 4 minutes on
each side or to desired degree of doneness. Slice
thinly on diagonal to serve.

Lt. Col. Wendell E. Johnson
Fort Myer, Virginia

PARTY FLANK STEAK

1/2 c. soy sauce
2 tbsp. water
2 tbsp. salad oil
1 tsp. ground ginger
2 to 3 tbsp. sugar
1 clove of garlic, crushed
Pinch of monosodium glutamate

Salt and pepper to taste
2 flank steaks

Combine soy sauce, water, salad oil, ginger,
sugar, garlic and seasonings in jar. Cover; shake
well. Pour over flank steak; marinate for at least
3 to 4 hours. Broil steak for 5 minutes on each
side or to desired degree of doneness. Yield: 4-6
servings.

Maj. Manley W. Crider, Jr.
Maxwell AFB, Alabama

HONEY-MARINATED FLANK STEAK

1/4 c. soy sauce
3 tbsp. honey
2 tbsp. vinegar
1 1/2 tsp. garlic powder
1 1/2 tsp. ground ginger
1/3 to 1/2 c. salad oil
1 green onion, finely chopped
1   1 1/2-lb. flank steak

Mix soy sauce, honey and vinegar together;
blend in garlic powder and ground ginger. Add
oil and chopped green onion. Place steak in
shallow pan; pour marinade over steak. Let
stand for a minimum of 4 hours. Broil or barbecue for about 5 minutes per side for medium
rare, basting occasionally with the marinade.
Slice on the diagonal to serve. Yield: 4 servings.

Capt. Duarte Alvaro Lopes
Wright-Patterson AFB, Ohio

98

SUPER-GOOD FLANK STEAK

1 flank steak
Meat tenderizer
1 c. red wine
2 or 3 cloves of garlic, halved
1 tbsp. wine vinegar
1 tbsp. olive oil or salad oil

Rub flank steak with meat tenderizer; place in
glass dish with wine, garlic, vinegar and oil. Let
stand for several hours, turning occasionally.
Broil for approximately 5 minutes on each side.
Slice diagonally 1/2 inch thick to serve. Yield:
4 servings.

Col. Charles E. Weddle
Wiley Barracks, Neu Ulm, Germany

ROAST PORK
WITH SAUERKRAUT AND APPLE

1 3 1/2-lb. pork loin roast
Onion salt to taste
Marjoram to taste
Pepper to taste
1 qt. drained sauerkraut
2 red apples, thinly sliced
1/2 c. apple brandy
1 tbsp. light brown sugar
2 tbsp. butter

Sprinkle pork with onion salt, marjoram and
pepper; score fatty side. Secure on spit. Insert
meat thermometer. Adjust spit about 8 inches
from prepared coals, placing foil pan under
pork to catch drippings. Roast for 15 to 20
minutes per pound or until meat thermometer
registers 185 degrees. Place on heated serving
platter; keep warm. Combine sauerkraut, apple
slices, brandy, brown sugar and butter in skillet.
Simmer, covered, for 5 minutes or until apples
are tender. Spoon into serving dish. Garnish
with additional apple slices and parsley. Serve
with pork.

Photograph for this recipe on page 139.

FILBERT TORTE
WITH STRAWBERRY WHIPPED CREAM

Graham cracker crumbs
2 c. sugar
1/2 tsp. ground allspice
1 lb. filberts, ground
1 tsp. grated lemon peel
6 eggs, separated
1/4 tsp. salt
1 tbsp. light corn syrup
1 tsp. water
1 egg white, slightly beaten

Grease 9-inch 6 1/2-cup ring pan; sprinkle with
graham cracker crumbs. Set aside. Mix sugar
and allspice together; mix in filberts and lemon
peel with tossing motion. Beat egg yolks until
thick and lemon colored; blend into filbert mixture, working in well with hands. Beat egg
whites until frothy; add salt. Beat until stiff but
not dry; fold into filbert mixture. Turn into
prepared ring pan. Bake at 350 degrees for 35
to 40 minutes or until cake tests done. Cool for
5 minutes. Loosen cake with spatula; turn out
onto ungreased baking sheet. Blend corn syrup
and water; brush over top of torte. Brush entire
torte with egg white. Bake for 5 minutes longer.
Cool; place torte on serving plate.

Strawberry Whipped Cream

2 pt. fresh strawberries
1 1/2 c. heavy cream
3 tbsp. kirsch

Slice strawberries, reserving 1 cup for garnish.
Whip cream until stiff, adding kirsch gradually.
Fold in sliced strawberries. Mound in center of
torte; garnish with reserved strawberries.

Photograph for this recipe on page 139.

HOT POTATO SALAD WITH BACON

4 lb. pared potatoes, sliced
1/2 c. chopped onion
2/3 c. bacon drippings
1/2 c. vinegar
2 tbsp. chopped parsley
2 tsp. sugar
1 tsp. paprika
1/2 tsp. salt
1/4 tsp. pepper
12 slices fried bacon, crumbled

Cook potatoes in saucepan in 2 inches salted
water until tender; drain. Saute onion in bacon
drippings until tender; stir in vinegar, parsley,
sugar, paprika, salt and pepper. Combine potatoes, bacon and onion mixture. Toss gently.
Serve warm with pork roast and sauerkraut.

Photograph for this recipe on page 139.

GRILLED CHICKEN
WITH KRAUT RELISH

6 c. sauerkraut
1   4-oz. jar pimento
2 med. green peppers, chopped
2 med. onions, chopped
1/4 tsp. paprika
Freshly ground pepper to taste
1 clove of garlic, minced
1/2 c. melted butter
1/4 c. wine vinegar
1/2 c. (firmly packed) dark brown sugar
2 tbsp. Worcestershire sauce
2 tbsp. cornstarch
1/4 c. water
12 chicken legs with thighs

Drain the sauerkraut and reserve liquid. Drain the pimento and chop. Toss sauerkraut with green peppers, pimento, half the onions, paprika and pepper in a bowl and chill. Saute remaining onion and the garlic in butter in a saucepan until golden. Add the vinegar, sugar, Worcestershire sauce, pepper and reserved sauerkraut liquid and stir until sugar is melted. Bring to a boil over medium heat. Blend the cornstarch with water and stir into onion mixture. Boil for 30 seconds, stirring constantly, then remove from heat. Place chicken on grill 7 to 8 inches from source of heat; cook for 10 minutes. Brush with sauce and continue grilling for 10 minutes. Turn chicken and grill an additional 10 minutes or until done, brushing frequently with sauce to glaze. Serve kraut relish with grilled chicken.

Photograph for this recipe on page 140.

OLD-FASHIONED
STRAWBERRY SHORTCAKE

2 c. sifted all-purpose flour
4 tsp. baking powder
1/2 tsp. salt
1/2 tsp. cream of tartar
1/4 c. sugar
1/2 c. vegetable shortening
1/3 c. milk
1 egg
Butter
3 pt. fresh California strawberries,
*   sliced and sweetened*
Whipped cream

Sift flour, baking powder, salt, cream of tartar and sugar together. Cut in shortening until mixture resembles coarse meal. Combine milk with egg; stir into flour mixture with a fork until soft dough is formed. Turn out onto lightly floured board and pat or roll into 8-inch circle, 1/2 inch thick. Place on ungreased baking sheet. Bake in preheated 425-degree oven for 10 to 12 minutes or until golden brown. Split and spread butter on both halves. Pile strawberries and whipped cream between layers and on top. Yield: 8 servings.

Photograph for this recipe on page 140.

ORIENTAL PEPPER STEAK

2 lb. sirloin steak, cubed
2 tbsp. cooking oil
2 tsp. beef bouillon
2 c. water
1 tsp. garlic powder
2 tsp. Worcestershire sauce
1 tsp. A-1 steak sauce
2 onions, sliced
1 c. fresh or canned mushrooms
1 1/2 c. sliced green peppers
3 tomatoes, cut in wedges
1/3 c. slivered almonds
2 tsp. cornstarch
2 tsp. soy sauce

Saute steak cubes in oil. Add bouillon, water, garlic powder, Worcestershire sauce and steak sauce. Simmer, covered, for 10 minutes. Add onions, mushrooms, green peppers and tomatoes; cook for 10 minutes longer. Sprinkle almonds over vegetable mixture. Combine cornstarch and soy sauce; stir into mixture. Cook until thickened. Serve over rice or noodles. Yield: 4-6 servings.

Maj. Conrad E. Schray
Handorf, West Germany

STEAKS A LA JACK

1 T-bone or rib steak per person
Tenderizer
Garlic powder to taste
Seasoning salt to taste
Onion powder to taste
1/4 c. Worcestershire sauce
1/2 c. melted butter or margarine

Trim excess fat from steak. Sprinkle on both sides with tenderizer, garlic powder, seasoning salt and onion powder; let stand for 30 minutes. Place steaks on rack over white-hot coals. Baste with mixture of Worcestershire sauce and butter. Dampen coals with water if coals flame up. Cook to desired degree of doneness.

CWO Hubert W. Moore
Ft. Gulick, Canal Zone

TERIYAKI STEAK SPECIAL

2 cloves of garlic, split
1/2 c. soy sauce
1/4 c. (packed) brown sugar
2 tbsp. olive oil
1/4 tsp. freshly ground pepper
1/2 tsp. ground ginger
2 or 3 steaks

Combine all ingredients for marinade. Pour over steaks. Marinate for 1 hour to 1 hour and 30 minutes, turning occasionally. Cook over hot coals on charcoal brazier. Baste with marinade and cook to desired degree of doneness.

Col. William A. Meikle
Hickam AFB, Hawaii

T-BONE SPECIAL

2 T-bone steaks
Salt and freshly ground pepper to taste
Garlic salt to taste
Oregano to taste

Prepare barbecue grill with briquettes or charcoal; ignite. Let coals burn to medium heat. Season steaks with salt, pepper, garlic salt and oregano. Place over hot coals on barbecue grill; cook to desired degree of doneness.

Col. Worth M. Speed
Richards-Gebaur AFB, Missouri

SWEET AND SOUR BEEF STEW

2 tbsp. salad oil
2 lb. boneless lean beef chuck, cut into
    1-in. cubes
1 c. catsup
1/2 c. (firmly packed) brown sugar
1/2 c. red wine vinegar
1 tbsp. Worcestershire sauce
2 c. water
1 lg. onion, chopped
4 lg. carrots, cut into 3/4-in. chunks
4 lg. potatoes, cubed
4 sm. whole onions, peeled

Heat oil over medium heat in a large heavy frypan or Dutch oven. Add beef and brown on all sides. Drain off excess oil. Combine catsup, brown sugar, wine vinegar, Worcestershire, water and chopped onion; pour over beef. Cover and simmer for 30 minutes. Add carrots and cook for 1 hour, stirring occasionally. Add potatoes and whole onions and cook until all ingredients are tender. Remove cover and cook until sauce is of desired thickness. Serve with chunks of Italian bread and butter. Yield: 4-6 servings.

Maj. George A. Moore
Fort Buchanan, Puerto Rico

GLAZED CORNED BEEF

1 5-lb. brisket of corned beef
Whole cloves
4 tsp. powdered mustard
1/4 c. dark corn syrup
2 tsp. cider vinegar
1/4 tsp. ground allspice

Place corned beef in 4-quart saucepan; add enough water to cover. Cover; bring to boiling point. Reduce heat; cook for 4 hours or until corned beef is tender. Remove from water; drain. Place on rack in shallow baking pan, fat side up. Score fat; stud each square with 1 whole clove. Set aside. Mix mustard with 2 teaspoons water; let stand for 10 minutes for flavor to develop. Add remaining ingredients; mix well. Spoon half the glaze over corned beef. Bake in preheated 325-degree oven for 20 minutes. Remove from oven; spoon remaining glaze over top. Bake for 20 minutes longer or until corned beef is glazed and browned. Yield: 8 servings.

SHISH KABOB FOR A KING

1 1/2 c. salad oil
3/4 c. soy sauce
1/4 c. Worcestershire sauce
1 1/2 tsp. salt
1 tbsp. pepper
1/2 c. wine vinegar
1 1/2 tsp. parsley flakes
2 cloves of garlic, crushed
1/3 c. lemon juice
2 lb. beef tenderloin, cut into 2-in. cubes

Sm. onions to taste
Green peppers, cut in squares
Mushrooms to taste
Quartered tomatoes to taste

Combine oil, soy sauce, Worcestershire sauce, salt, pepper, vinegar, parsley, garlic and lemon juice; mix well. Marinate beef in sauce for 4 hours; drain. Soak onions in 2 cups water for 30 minutes. Alternate beef, green peppers, onions, mushrooms and tomatoes on skewers. Cook over hot coals to desired degree of doneness, turning frequently. Marinade may be refrigerated for future use. Yield: 4 servings.

Maj. F. Cregg Crosby
Andersen AFB, Guam

TENDERLOIN HAWAIIAN

1 c. soy sauce
2 tbsp. dry mustard
1 1/2 tsp. salt
1 tbsp. fresh pepper
1/2 c. wine vinegar
1 1/2 tsp. chopped parsley
2 cloves of garlic, minced
1/3 c. lemon juice
1 1/2 c. olive oil or salad oil
1 beef tenderloin

Combine soy sauce, mustard, salt, pepper, vinegar, parsley, garlic, lemon juice and olive oil; blend thoroughly. Pour sauce over tenderloin in shallow bowl. Marinate for 24 hours, turning once. Cook tenderloin on grill over medium coals to desired degree of doneness, turning occasionally. Baste with remaining marinade, if desired. May be broiled in oven. Yield: 8 servings.

Col. David W. Meyer
Defense Electronic Supply Ctr., Dayton, Ohio

TERIYAKI DIVINE

3/4 c. shoyu sauce
1/2 c. sugar
1/4 c. saki or mirin
1 sm. piece of gingerroot, crushed
1 sm. clove of garlic, minced
1/2 tsp. monosodium glutamate
3 to 4 lb. thinly sliced sirloin tip

Combine shoyu sauce, sugar, saki, gingerroot, garlic and monosodium glutamate; mix well. Marinate beef in sauce for at least 3 hours.

Cook over hibachi; do not overcook. Yield: 6-7 servings.

Maj. Frank Takeshi Sanpei
Wright-Patterson AFB, Ohio

SAUSAGES AND DIXIE CORN PUDDING

3 pkg. frozen cut corn in butter sauce
2 tbsp. flour
1/2 c. light cream, scalded
2 eggs, separated
1/2 tsp. salt
1/4 tsp. pepper
1/4 c. frozen chopped onions
1/4 c. frozen chopped green peppers
1/4 c. diced pimento
12 pork sausages, grilled

Heat pouches of corn in boiling water according to package directions. Separate butter sauce from corn by emptying pouches into strainer or colander over saucepan. Blend flour into butter sauce; add cream, stirring to blend. Beat egg yolks with salt and pepper; stir into sauce. Mix corn with onions, green peppers and pimento. Whip egg whites until stiff peaks form; fold into sauce mixture. Stir in vegetables gently; pour into buttered baking dish. Bake at 350 degrees for 30 minutes; place pork sausages on top. Yield: 6-8 servings.

LAMB ON A SPIT

1/2 c. catsup
2 tbsp. olive oil
2 tbsp. red wine vinegar
2 tbsp. Worcestershire sauce
1/4 c. fresh lemon juice
1 tsp. hot sauce
1 onion, grated
1 clove of garlic, pressed
1 tsp. dry mustard
1 tsp. paprika
1 tsp. salt
1 tsp. rosemary
1 8-lb. leg of lamb, boned and rolled

Combine all ingredients except lamb with 1 cup water in saucepan; bring to a boil. Boil for 5 minutes, stirring frequently. Place lamb in large bowl; pour sauce over lamb. Cover; let stand in refrigerator for 3 days, turning occasionally. Remove lamb from sauce, reserving sauce; place on spit of rotisserie. Balance evenly; place meat thermometer in thickest part, making sure thermometer does not touch the spit. Cook until thermometer registers desired degree of doneness, basting frequently with reserved sauce. Yield: 14 servings.

Lt. Col. Charles A. Bell
Maxwell AFB, Alabama

DILLED LAMB

1   3 to 4-lb. lamb shoulder
1 med. onion, quartered
1/2 tsp. dillseed
Salt and pepper to taste
2 to 3 tsp. butter
2 to 3 tsp. flour
Dillweed to taste

Skin or trim off excess fat from lamb shoulder. Place in large pot; add enough water to fill pot 1/2 full. Add onion, dillseed, salt and pepper; bring to a boil. Reduce heat and cover. Simmer for 2 hours and 30 minutes to 3 hours, adding water, if needed, to measure 1 cup after lamb is done. Remove lamb and place on platter. Pour liquid from pot and reserve. Melt butter in pot; stir in flour. Stir in reserved liquid and cook until thickened. Stir in dillweed; serve with lamb.

Lt. Michael T. Hanst
Harold E. Holt Naval Base
Exmouth, Western Australia

LAMB AND BEEF SHISH KABOBS

3 lamb steaks, cut 1 in. thick
3 beef steaks, cut 1 in. thick
3 cloves of garlic, minced
1/3 c. salad oil
3 tbsp. soy sauce
3 tbsp. vinegar
1 1/2 tsp. sugar
1/4 tsp. pepper
2 lg. onions, minced
6 sm. onions
12 sm. potatoes
1 green pepper, cut in 1 1/2 x 1-in.
   pieces
20 to 24 lg. whole mushrooms

Cut lamb and beef into 1-inch cubes; place in shallow pan. Combine garlic, oil, soy sauce, vinegar, sugar, pepper and minced onion; blend well. Marinate lamb and beef cubes in sauce for several hours or overnight. Cook onions and potatoes in water in saucepan for 10 minutes; drain well. Arrange lamb and beef cubes, green pepper, onions, potatoes and mushrooms alternately on skewers. Broil over hot coals for 20 minutes, turning frequently. Baste with remaining marinade. Yield: 4 servings.

Lt. Cmdr. Larry C. Selgelid
US Naval Supply Ctr., Newport, Rhode Island

FRUITED LAMB RACK

1   3-lb. rack of lamb
1 tsp. salt
1/2 tsp. pepper
1   8-oz. jar maraschino cherries
1   1-lb. 14-oz. can sliced peaches
3/4 tsp. cloves
1/2 tsp. ginger
1 tbsp. lemon juice
1 bunch seedless green grapes
1 egg white, beaten
Sugar

Sprinkle lamb with salt and pepper; place on rack in shallow roasting pan. Roast in 325-degree oven for 1 hour. Drain cherry and peach syrups into saucepan; heat. Stir in cloves, ginger and lemon juice. Roast lamb for 30 minutes longer or until meat thermometer registers 175 degrees, basting frequently with syrup mixture. Dip small clusters of grapes in egg white, then in sugar; allow to dry on rack. Garnish roast with frosted grapes, cherries and peaches. Yield: 4-6 servings.

Photograph for this recipe on page 124.

MONGOLIAN BARBECUE

3 lg. green peppers
1 med. cabbage
1 doz. scallions
6 lg. carrots
1 stalk celery
1 lb. flank steak
1 lb. pork steak
1/4 c. vegetable oil
1 tsp. hot sauce
1 c. soy sauce
1   8 1/2-oz. can sliced bamboo shoots
1   16-oz. can bean sprouts
1   5-oz. can water chestnuts
1/2 tsp. sesame oil
2 tsp. garlic salt
1 tbsp. salt
4 c. cooked rice

Slice green peppers into thin strips; shred cabbage. Slice scallions lengthwise thru bulb and tops; chop into 2-inch pieces. Sliver carrots with vegetable peeler. Slice celery into thin strips lengthwise; chop into 2-inch pieces. Slice flank steak and pork steak into thin 2 to 3-inch strips. Saute steak strips in hot oil in large Dutch oven, stirring constantly, over medium heat until just lightly browned. Stir in green peppers, cabbage, scallions, carrots and celery; mix well. Reduce heat; add hot sauce and soy sauce. Simmer for 5 minutes. Drain bamboo shoots and bean sprouts; drain and sliver water chestnuts. Add sesame oil, bamboo shoots, bean sprouts, water chestnuts, garlic salt and salt; mix well. Simmer for 5 minutes longer; stir in rice. Simmer for 5 minutes longer. Rice may be served as side dish, if preferred. Yield: 8 servings.

Lt. Col. Clyde Markley, Jr.
Duluth AFB, Minnesota

PORK SHISH KABOBS

3 lb. pork tenderloin
3/4 tsp. salt
Pepper to taste
1 tbsp. ground coriander
1 tbsp. cumin seeds
1/2 c. salad oil
1 c. onion slices
1 tbsp. (packed) brown sugar
1/4 c. soy sauce
1 tbsp. monosodium glutamate
Dash of ground ginger

Cut pork into 1-inch cubes. Combine salt, pepper, coriander, cumin seeds, oil, onion slices, brown sugar, soy sauce, monosodium glutamate and ginger; mix well. Place pork in shallow dish; pour sauce over meat. Marinate for several hours. Arrange pork on skewers. Cook over hot coals far enough from source of heat to cook slowly. Baste with remaining marinade. Serve with lime wedges. Yield: 6-8 servings.

Capt. William E. Cummins, USN
Pearl Harbor, Hawaii

BRAISED GINGER PORK

2 lb. lean pork, cubed
Flour
3 tbsp. oil
2/3 c. chicken broth
1/3 c. soy sauce
4 tbsp. dry sherry
1/2 c. chopped onion
1 sm. clove of garlic, minced
2 tbsp. sugar
3/4 tsp. ginger
Dash of pepper

Dredge pork cubes in flour; brown in oil in large skillet over medium heat. Drain off excess fat. Combine broth, soy sauce and sherry with pork; stir in onion, garlic, sugar, ginger and pepper. Simmer, covered, for 30 minutes or until meat is tender. Serve over rice. Yield: 4 servings.

Lt. Col. John C. Allison
Blytheville AFB, Arkansas

CAPTAIN'S PIZZA

1 pkg. yeast
5 1/4 c. flour
1 1/2 tbsp. olive oil
1 1/2 tsp. salt
2 8-oz. cans tomato sauce
1 tsp. ground oregano
1 tsp. aniseed
1 tsp. Italian seasoning
4 cloves of garlic, minced
Pepper to taste
Sausage
6 oz. provolone
6 oz. Romano
8 oz. mozzarella
Chopped green onions
Mushrooms to taste
Ripe olives to taste

Dissolve yeast in 1 1/2 cup warm water in large bowl; beat in 2 cups flour. Stir in olive oil and salt; add remaining flour. Knead on lightly floured surface for 15 minutes or until dough is smooth and elastic. Place dough in greased bowl, turning to grease top. Let rise, covered, in warm place until doubled in bulk. Punch down; let rise one or two times more. Divide dough in half; roll out 1 piece on lightly floured surface 3/16 inch thick and fit into 16-inch greased pan. Roll out remaining dough 3/16 inch thick and fit into 12-inch greased pan. Combine tomato sauce, oregano, aniseed, Italian seasoning, garlic and pepper; mix well. Spread sauce over dough. Brown sausage; drain. Grate provolone, Romano and mozzarella; mix well. Spread 1/3 of cheese mixture over sauce. Spread green onions, mushrooms, ripe olives and sausage over cheese; top with remaining cheese. Bake at 500 degrees for 15 minutes or until crust is browned and cheese melted. Yield: 2 pizzas.

Capt. Loyal Gordon Bassett
Robins AFB, Georgia

SWEET AND SOUR PORK

Corn oil
1 lg. green pepper, cut in chunks
1 lg. onion, quartered
1 sm. can pineapple chunks
Sm. sweet pickles, sliced
Maraschino cherries, cut in half
1   16-oz. can sweet and sour sauce
Soy sauce
Cornstarch
1 1/2 to 2 lb. cooked pork roast,
     cut into 1-in. cubes

Pour small amount of corn oil into a large iron skillet and heat. Add green pepper and onion and saute for several minutes. Drain the pineapple, pickles and cherries; reserve liquids. Add pineapple chunks and desired amount of pickles and maraschino cherries to skillet. Pour in the sweet and sour sauce and enough reserved liquid from pineapple, pickles and cherries to taste. Sauce may be thin but will thicken from cornstarch-coated fork. Make a paste with soy sauce and cornstarch; coat pork cubes in paste. Heat oil in deep fat fryer to 400 degrees; fry small amounts of coated pork in oil for 2 to 3 minutes or until golden brown, watching closely. Combine pork and sauce; simmer for 5 to 10 minutes. Serve over a bed of fried Chinese noodles or rice. Yield: 6 servings.

Lt. Cmdr. James R. Finn
Naval Construction Bn. Ctr.
Port Hueneme, California

NICK'S BREAKFAST

4 thin slices ham
2 tbsp. butter
1 tbsp. flour
6 tbsp. heavy cream
5 mushrooms, thinly sliced
4 eggs
2 English muffins, split
Gouda or Edam cheese, grated

Place ham in broiler pan. Broil until brown. Melt butter in small saucepan; stir in flour until smooth. Add cream and mushrooms; cook, stirring, until thick and creamy. Set aside. Fry eggs over easy, one at a time, in small amount of fat. Place English muffin halves in broiler pan; spoon 1 tablespoon sauce on each muffin half. Cover with ham slice, then egg. Spoon remaining sauce over eggs; sprinkle generously with cheese. Broil until cheese melts. Yield: 4 servings.

Capt. Paul A. Nicholson
Merrell Barracks, Nurnberg, Germany

PIG IN THE CORN

1 lb. lean bulk sausage
1 1/2 c. yellow cornmeal
1/2 c. all-purpose flour
1 tsp. salt
2 tsp. sugar
3 tsp. baking powder
3 eggs, well beaten
1 1/4 c. half and half
1/4 c. melted butter

Crumble sausage; fry until well done. Drain off fat; cool slightly. Sift dry ingredients together into a bowl. Add eggs, half and half and butter; mix well. Pour layer of cornmeal mixture into greased muffin tins; add layer of sausage. Fill muffin tins 2/3 full with remaining cornmeal mixture. Bake at 400 degrees for 15 minutes or until brown.

Lt. Col. F. Lee Early, Jr.
Ft. Campbell, Kentucky

GENUINE GEORGIA PORK BARBECUE

3/4 c. catsup
1 tbsp. wine vinegar
1 tsp. ground oregano
4 to 6 cloves of garlic, sliced thin
1 tbsp. salt
1 tsp. paprika
1 tsp. pepper
1 tsp. chili powder
1 tbsp. sugar
4 lb. country-style pork spareribs

Combine catsup, vinegar, oregano, garlic, salt, paprika, pepper, chili powder and sugar in saucepan; mix well. Simmer, stirring occasionally, for 20 minutes. Arrange spareribs in shallow baking dish; pour sauce over spareribs. Bake, covered, at 350 degrees for 2 hours; remove cover. Bake for 20 minutes longer. Half teaspoon cayenne pepper may be substituted for pepper, if desired. Yield: 6 servings.

Lt. Col. William G. Richardson
Davis-Monthan AFB, Arizona

STRAWBERRY MOCHA
CREAM TARTLETS

4 c. sifted all-purpose flour
2 tsp. salt
1 1/2 c. vegetable shortening
2 pt. fresh strawberries
Light corn syrup
1/2 c. strong coffee
1/2 c. sugar
6 egg yolks
1 tbsp. instant coffee powder
2 tbsp. cocoa
1 c. softened sweet butter

Combine the flour and salt in bowl. Cut in the shortening until uniform but coarse. Sprinkle with 1/2 cup water; toss with fork, then press into ball. Roll out 1/2 of the dough at a time on a lightly floured surface to a 1/8-inch thickness. Cut into 3-inch circles, then fit inside 2 1/4-inch tart pans. Prick with fork. Place on a baking sheet. Bake in a 425-degree oven for 10 minutes or until lightly browned. Cool; remove from tart pans. Brush the strawberries with corn syrup and let dry on racks. Combine the coffee and sugar; boil to the thread stage or until candy thermometer registers 234 degrees. Beat the egg yolks with the instant coffee powder and cocoa until fluffy and thick. Add the hot syrup gradually to yolks, pouring in a thin steady stream and beating constantly. Continue beating until light in color and cold, then beat in butter. Chill slightly, if necessary. Pipe a ring of the butter mixture around the inside edge of each cooled tartlet shell. Place a strawberry in each shell and chill until served. Yield: 50 servings.

Photograph for this recipe on page 149.

BLACK BEANS AND RICE

1 6-oz. package herb rice
1/4 c. chopped onion
1 c. cooked black beans or kidney beans
1 tomato, cut in wedges
Finely chopped parsley

Cook rice according to package directions, adding onion at beginning of cooking. Stir in part of the beans. Turn out onto a large square of heavy-duty aluminum foil. Top with tomato; add remaining beans. Fold foil over top, sealing to make a tight package. Place on grill for 10 to 15 minutes or until heated through. Sprinkle with parsley when ready to serve. Rice mixture may be cooked the day before and chilled, if desired. Yield: 6 servings.

Photograph for this recipe on page 150.

SEAFOOD CREAM
WITH AVOCADO HALVES

1 lb. fresh mushrooms, sliced
1 c. sliced onion
1 c. butter or margarine
2/3 c. flour
2 1/2 tsp. salt
1 tsp. monosodium glutamate
1/2 tsp. dry mustard
1/2 tsp. pepper
1/4 tsp. thyme leaves
5 c. milk
2 c. light cream
2 eggs, slightly beaten
2 c. grated Swiss cheese
8 7-oz. cans solid white tuna
1 c. sauterne
2 tsp. grated lemon peel
Lemon juice
6 5-oz. cans lobster, drained
2/3 c. chopped toasted blanched almonds
12 ripe avocados
Watercress

Saute the mushrooms and onion in butter until lightly browned; remove with slotted spoon. Quickly stir in the flour and seasonings. Stir in the milk and cream gradually. Cook and stir until the sauce boils for 1 minute. Stir a small amount of hot sauce into eggs, then return to the saucepan. Stir the cheese into hot sauce over low heat until melted. Drain the tuna; separate into large pieces. Add sauterne, lemon peel, 2 tablespoons lemon juice, tuna, lobster, almonds, sauteed mushrooms and onion to the sauce. Heat to serving temperature. Cut the avocados in half lengthwise, twisting gently to separate halves. Whack a sharp knife directly into seeds and twist to lift out. Peel avocado halves and brush with lemon juice. Arrange on a serving platter with watercress. Garnish with lime slices. Serve hot seafood mixture over avocado halves. Garnish with buttered, toasted fine bread crumbs and sliced truffles. Yield: 24 servings.

Photograph for this recipe on page 149.

BAHAMIAN-BARBECUED CHICKEN

1/4 c. lime juice
1/4 c. honey
1/4 c. light rum
4 1/2 tsp. monosodium glutamate
1/4 c. salad oil
2 tbsp. soy sauce
1/2 tsp. dried leaf tarragon
4 broiler-fryer chickens, halved
4 tsp. salt
1 tsp. pepper
Lime slices (opt.)

Line bottom of grill with heavy-duty aluminum foil and prepare fire. Blend the lime juice and honey in a bowl. Warm the rum slightly, then ignite. Add to honey mixture when flame has burned out. Add 1/2 teaspoon monosodium glutamate, oil, soy sauce and tarragon and beat until blended. Sprinkle both sides of chickens with the salt, pepper and remaining monosodium glutamate. Place chickens, skin side up, on grate 6 inches from heat and cook, turning occasionally, for 45 minutes to 1 hour and 15 minutes depending on weight of chicken. Brush with barbecue sauce during last 30 minutes of cooking time. Chicken leg should twist easily out of thigh joint and pieces should feel tender when probed with a fork when done. Garnish chicken with lime slices.

Photograph for this recipe on page 150.

TROPICAL FRUIT BAKE

1/2 c. (packed) brown sugar
1/4 c. butter, melted
1 tsp. grated lemon rind
2 tbsp. lemon juice
1/8 tsp. nutmeg
3 bananas
1 papaya
1 c. honeydew melon balls
1 c. cantaloupe balls
Flaked coconut

Combine brown sugar, butter, lemon rind and juice and nutmeg. Peel bananas; cut in half crosswise and lengthwise. Peel papaya; discard seeds and cube fruit. Combine all fruits; divide among 6 squares of heavy-duty aluminum foil. Sprinkle brown sugar mixture over each and sprinkle with coconut. Seal foil to make tight packages. Place on grill for 10 to 15 minutes or until heated through. Yield: 6 servings.

Photograph for this recipe on page 150.

HERBED PINWHEELS

1 c. butter, softened
1/4 c. chopped parsley
1/2 tsp. oregano leaves
1/4 tsp. tarragon leaves
1/4 tsp. ground thyme
1/8 tsp. pepper
4 c. sifted all-purpose flour
2 tbsp. baking powder
2 tsp. salt
2/3 c. vegetable shortening
1 1/2 c. milk
1 egg

Whip the butter with parsley, oregano, tarragon, thyme and pepper; let stand for 1 hour to blend flavors. Mix the flour, baking powder and salt in a bowl; cut in shortening until mixture looks like coarse meal. Stir in the milk. Knead about 10 times on a floured board and divide the dough in half. Roll out each half into a 12 x 10-inch rectangle. Spread half the herb mixture on each rectangle; roll up each rectangle from 12-inch side and seal edge. Cut each roll into 24 1/2-inch pinwheels and place pinwheels in ungreased muffin pans. Beat the egg with 2 tablespoons water and brush over pinwheels. Bake in a 425-degree oven for 10 to 15 minutes or until golden brown.

Photograph for this recipe on page 149.

BARBECUED SPARERIBS

2 tbsp. Worcestershire sauce
1 tbsp. wine vinegar
1 tbsp. thick meat sauce
1 tbsp. sugar
1/4 c. catsup
Dash of hot sauce
2 to 3 lb. spareribs

Combine Worcestershire sauce, vinegar, meat sauce, sugar, catsup and hot sauce; blend thoroughly. Cook spareribs over hot charcoal for 45 minutes or until tender; turn frequently. Cook, turning and basting frequently with sauce for 15 minutes longer. Sauce may be used with chicken or pork chops baked in oven. Yield: 3 servings.

Col. William A. Meikle
Hickam AFB, Hawaii

VEAL SCALLOPINI

1 1/2 lb. veal steak, cut 1/2 in. thick
1 tsp. salt
1 tsp. paprika
1/2 c. salad oil
1/4 c. lemon juice
1 clove of garlic
1 tsp. prepared mustard
1/4 tsp. nutmeg
1/2 tsp. sugar
1/4 c. flour
1/4 c. shortening
1 med. onion, sliced
1 green pepper, cut in strips
2 chicken bouillon cubes
1 4-oz. can sliced mushrooms
1 tbsp. butter
6 pimento-stuffed olives, sliced

Cut veal into serving pieces. Combine salt, paprika, salad oil, lemon juice, garlic, mustard, nutmeg and sugar in small bowl; beat well. Arrange veal in shallow baking pan; pour sauce over veal, turning pieces to coat well. Marinate for 15 minutes. Remove garlic; discard. Remove veal from marinade; coat with flour. Brown veal in hot shortening in skillet; add onion and green pepper. Combine bouillon cubes with 1 cup boiling water, stirring until dissolved; add to remaining sauce. Pour sauce mixture over veal. Simmer, covered, for 40 minutes or until veal is tender. Saute mushrooms lightly in butter in small skillet; add to veal mixture. Stir in olives. Simmer, covered, for 5 minutes longer. Yield: 4-6 servings.

Capt. Owen Connell
Wasserkuppe AFS, Fulda, Germany

TEXAS BARBECUE

8 lb. cooked boned fresh ham
3 lb. cooked chuck roast
6 tbsp. butter or margarine
1/2 c. minced onion
1 clove of garlic, minced
2 c. catsup
1/2 c. Worcestershire sauce
1/4 c. hot sauce
1/4 c. liquid smoke
1 tsp. dry mustard
1 tsp. sugar
1 tbsp. lemon juice
Peppercorns to taste

Remove fat from fresh ham and chuck roast; shred or slice thinly. Melt butter in large saucepan; saute onion and garlic in butter until tender. Stir in catsup, Worcestershire sauce, hot sauce, liquid smoke, dry mustard, sugar, lemon juice, peppercorns and 2 cups water. Blend well. Simmer, stirring occasionally, for 25 minutes. Pour sauce over meats in large saucepan; marinate overnight. Heat through before serving. Serve on sesame seed buns, if desired. Yield: 16 servings.

Col. Thomas E. Wesson
Fort Hood, Texas

TERIYAKI SAUCE FOR STEAK

1/2 c. soy sauce
1/4 c. (firmly packed) dark brown sugar
2 tbsp. oil
1/2 tsp. monosodium glutamate
1 tsp. ginger
1/2 tsp. cracked pepper
2 cloves of garlic, sliced

Combine all ingredients; stir until the sugar is dissolved. May be kept in refrigerator for several weeks.

Mrs. Jean K. Pfister, W and M Chm., Tacom OWC
Utica, Michigan

POULTRY AND SEAFOOD

Poultry and seafood are two of the most versatile and economical dishes we will present in this Party Book. It would be an understatement to say that either one of these dishes could be made a hundred ways. They have been, and yet new recipes are being created every day.

There are few dishes more appealing than these two foods. Both lend themselves admirably to large gatherings and are easy to prepare. Both are well suited to sauces and seasoning, grilling, broiling or roasting. Both have mild flavors which are extremely compatible with many highly or unusually seasoned foods. In fact, the variety of foods with which poultry and seafood can be combined is genuinely impressive.

In the following section, you will find a diverse collection of appetite-arousing recipes for delectable entrees, dishes featuring marinades, sauces and stuffings. For truly enjoyable eating, be sure and turn to this unique chapter each time you plan to serve poultry or seafood.

CRANBERRY-GLAZED
CORNISH GAME HENS

6 Cornish game hens
Salt and pepper to taste
1   1-lb. can whole berry cranberry
    sauce
1/4 c. melted butter or margarine
1/4 c. concentrated frozen orange juice
2 tsp. grated orange rind
Pinch of poultry seasoning

Truss hens; sprinkle inside and out with salt and pepper. Place on rack in roasting pan. Roast according to package directions for Cornish hens. Heat cranberry sauce with remaining ingredients; brush on hens liberally every 5 minutes during last 30 minutes of roasting. Garnish with parsley. Yield: 6 servings.

Photograph for this recipe on page 156.

BRONZED BIRDS

6   1-lb. Cornish hens
1 clove of garlic
1 tsp. salt
1/2 tsp. pepper
1/4 c. clover honey
1/4 c. whiskey
1/2 c. melted butter

Wash and dry Cornish hens. Grease shallow baking pan; arrange hens in pan. Crush garlic with salt, then combine with pepper, honey, whiskey and butter. Brush hens with butter mixture. Bake at 350 degrees for 35 to 40 minutes, basting frequently with remaining butter mixture. Yield: 6 servings.

Lt. Col. Miles E. Burgenheim
Edwards AFB, California

BRAISED BREAST OF PHEASANT

1/2 c. shortening
2 pheasant or chicken breasts, halved
Salt and pepper to taste
1 1/2 c. cold water
1 sm. carrot, sliced
1 sm. onion, sliced
1 stalk celery, sliced
2 sprigs of parsley
1/2 bay leaf
4 tbsp. flour
3/4 c. canned tomatoes

1 tsp. lemon juice
1 tsp. minced parsley
1/2 c. sauteed mushrooms

Melt 1/4 cup shortening in skillet. Add pheasant; saute until brown. Season with salt and pepper; add water. Add carrot, onion, celery, parsley sprigs and bay leaf; simmer until pheasant is tender. Remove pheasant; strain stock. Melt remaining shortening. Add flour; blend. Add stock and tomatoes gradually, stirring constantly. Add lemon juice, minced parsley, mushrooms, salt and pepper; bring to a boil. Add pheasant; heat through. Yield: 4 servings.

Col. John A. Herberg
Homestead AFB, Florida

ZAGREB-STYLE CREAMED CHICKEN

4 tbsp. butter or margarine
4 sprigs of parsley, chopped
1/4 lb. large mushrooms, sliced
6 eggs, slightly beaten
3/4 c. sour cream
3/4 c. grated Parmesan cheese
1/2 tsp. hot sauce
1 tsp. salt
1/2 tsp. paprika
1 c. diced chicken
6 baked puff pastry shells, heated

Melt butter in large skillet. Saute parsley and mushrooms in butter lightly, turning gently; remove from heat. Combine eggs, sour cream, cheese, hot sauce, salt and paprika. Add chicken to mushrooms; reheat over low heat. Add egg mixture; increase heat to high. Lift and turn mixture with spatula until slightly thickened. Turn into pastry shells. Yield: 6 servings.

CASHEW CHICKEN

3 chicken breasts, split
1/2 lb. fresh or frozen Chinese pea pods
1/2 lb. mushrooms
4 green onions
1   15-oz. can bamboo shoots
1 can water chestnuts
1 tbsp. chicken base
1 c. water
1/2 c. soy sauce
2 tbsp. cornstarch
1/2 tsp. sugar
1/2 tsp. salt
4 tbsp. salad or peanut oil
1   4-oz. package cashew nuts

Bone chicken breasts; remove skin. Slice horizontally in 1/8-inch thick slices, then cut in 1-inch squares. Arrange on tray. Remove ends and strings from Chinese pea pods. Wash and slice mushrooms. Cut green part of the onions into 1-inch lengths; slash both ends several times, making small fans. Slice white part 1/4 inch thick. Drain bamboo shoots and slice; drain water chestnuts. Arrange all vegetables on tray in individual piles. Mix chicken base and water; pour into small pitcher. Mix soy sauce with cornstarch, sugar and salt; pour into small pitcher. Heat 1 tablespoon oil over moderate heat to 350 degrees. Add nuts; cook for 1 minute or until lightly toasted, shaking pan constantly. Remove from pan; set aside. Add remaining oil to pan. Add chicken; cook quickly, turning until chicken turns opaque. Add mushrooms; pour in stock. Cover; simmer for 2 minutes. Uncover and add bamboo shoots and water chestnuts. Stir in cornstarch mixture; cook until sauce is thickened, stirring constantly. Simmer for 1 minute. Mix in green onions and peas; heat through. Sprinkle with nuts; serve with rice. Yield: 4 servings.

Maj. John A. Knutzen
USMA, West Point, New York

CHICKEN BREASTS PIQUANT

3 chicken breasts, split
1/4 c. soy sauce
3/4 c. rose wine
1/4 c. salad oil
2 tbsp. water
1 tsp. ginger
1/4 tsp. oregano
1 tbsp. brown sugar
1 clove of garlic, sliced

Arrange chicken breasts in baking dish. Combine remaining ingredients; pour over chicken breasts. Marinate for at least 2 hours or overnight. Cover. Bake in 375-degree oven for 2 hours or until tender; may be served on rice.

1st Lt. Robert G. Taylor, Jr.
Los Angeles AFS, Los Angeles, California

PECHO DE POLLO

3 c. sour cream
3 tbsp. lemon juice
3 cloves of garlic, crushed
3/4 tsp. salt
1/4 tsp. pepper
1 tsp. celery seed
3/4 tsp. paprika
1 1/2 tsp. Worcestershire sauce
12 chicken breast halves, boned
6 whole green chilies, seeded and
   halved
Butter
Corn flake crumbs

Mix sour cream, lemon juice, garlic, salt, pepper, celery seed, paprika and Worcestershire sauce in large bowl. Add chicken and marinate overnight in refrigerator. Drain chicken; reserve marinade. Roll each chicken breast half with a green chili half; place in baking dish, skin side out. Pour reserved marinade over chicken. Place 1 pat butter on each breast; sprinkle with corn flake crumbs. Bake, covered, at 350 degrees for 45 minutes. Yield: 6 servings.

Lt. Ernest V. Bruchez, Jr.
US Naval Ammunition Depot, Hawthorne, Nevada

PIZZA-STYLE CHICKEN BREASTS

1 chicken breast per person
1 c. tomato juice
Oregano to taste
Sliced Swiss or Monterey Jack cheese

Remove skins from chicken breasts; place in broiler pan. Broil chicken breasts, basting with tomato juice every 10 minutes, for about 40 minutes. Sprinkle oregano on each breast; place cheese on top of breasts. Broil for about 5 minutes longer or until cheese is golden brown. Oregano may be mixed with tomato juice, if desired; grated Parmesan cheese may be substituted for sliced cheese.

Capt. David E. Lowe
Beale AFB, Marysville, California

POLLO DA GAETA

4 chicken breasts
Flour
Salt and pepper to taste
Butter
Sliced tomatoes
Mushrooms
Oregano to taste
Fresh chopped parsley to taste
1 c. white wine
Muenster cheese slices

Bone chicken breasts; pound very thin. Mix flour, salt and pepper; dredge chicken with seasoned flour. Saute in generous amount of butter for about 3 minutes on each side; set aside until 15 minutes before serving. Place tomatoes on chicken; add generous amount of mushrooms. Sprinkle with oregano and parsley; pour wine over chicken. Cover with cheese slices. Bake at 325 degrees until cheese melts and chicken is thoroughly heated.

Cmdr. Donald Wayne Kellerman
NAS, Patuxent River, Maryland

COUNTRY CAPTAIN

1 broiler-fryer chicken
1 tsp. salt
1/4 tsp. pepper
1/4 c. butter
1 med. onion, chopped
1 sm. green pepper, chopped
1 clove of garlic, crushed
2 tsp. curry powder
1/2 tsp. leaf thyme
1   1-lb. can stewed tomatoes
Hot cooked rice
Toasted blanched almonds

Cut chicken into serving pieces and sprinkle with salt and pepper. Melt butter in a large skillet; add chicken and brown on all sides. Remove chicken from skillet. Add onion, green pepper, garlic, curry powder and thyme to skillet; cook until onion is tender but not brown. Add tomatoes and chicken; cover. Cook for 20 to 30 minutes or until chicken is tender. Serve over rice; sprinkle with almonds. Yield: 4 servings.

Capt. Stevan R. De Soer
Ft. Sheridan, Chicago, Illinois

POULET BLANC

4 chicken breasts
Salt and pepper to taste
6 tbsp. butter
1/4 c. white wine
1/3 c. chopped onion
1 c. sour cream
1/4 c. pitted sliced olives
Cooked rice
1/4 c. chopped chives

Remove skin from chicken breasts; season with salt and pepper. Melt 4 tablespoons butter in electric frying pan or skillet; saute chicken in butter for about 20 minutes or until golden brown. Pour wine over chicken slowly; cover. Steam for 20 to 25 minutes. Remove chicken; place in warming pan. Add remaining butter and onion to frying pan; saute until onion is brown. Add sour cream and olives; heat through, stirring slowly. Place chicken on rice. Sprinkle chives into sauce; pour over chicken.

Capt. Richard D. Forman
Offutt AFB, Omaha, Nebraska

DEEP-FRIED CHICKEN

3 fryers
2 tbsp. salt
1 med. onion, chopped
5 c. water
1/4 c. milk
1 egg
1/2 tsp. baking powder
1 1/2 c. flour
Fine cracker meal

Split chickens into halves; place in pot, cut side down, with 1 tablespoon salt, onion and 4 cups water. Cover; steam until tender. Drain chicken; cool. Place remaining water, milk, egg, baking powder, remaining salt and flour in mixing bowl; beat until smooth and consistency of pancake batter. Add flour if too thin; add water if too thick. Heat fat in deep fryer to 350 degrees. Coat chicken with batter, holding up to drain off excess; coat with cracker meal. Cook in deep fat until golden brown; serve piping hot. Uncooked shellfish or fish may be substituted for chicken.

Capt. James S. Martin
Keesler AFB, Biloxi, Mississippi

PATE MAISON

1/2 env. unflavored gelatin
1/2 c. bouillon or consomme
Pimento
Capers
Truffles and ripe olives
1 lb. chicken livers
1/2 tsp. monosodium glutamate
2 tbsp. minced onion
6 tbsp. butter or margarine
1/2 tsp. salt
1 tsp. dry mustard
1/4 tsp. cloves
1/8 tsp. nutmeg
2 tbsp. brandy

Sprinkle gelatin over bouillon in saucepan. Place over low heat, stirring constantly, until gelatin is dissolved. Pour thin layer of bouillon mixture in bottom of 8 x 4 x 2 1/2-inch pan. Chill until thickened. Press a design of pimento, capers, truffles and ripe olives into thickened bouillon. Pour remaining bouillon mixture over design and chill while preparing pate. Sprinkle chicken livers with monosodium glutamate. Saute with onion in 2 tablespoons butter for 6 to 7 minutes. Remove from heat. Turn into blender. Sprinkle with salt, dry mustard, cloves and nutmeg. Blend until smooth. Add remaining butter and brandy. Blend until smooth. Turn into prepared pan. Chill. Dip quickly into pan of hot water up to top to unmold. Loosen with sharp knife. Turn onto platter. Yield: 24 servings.

Photograph for this recipe on page 160.

RIPE OLIVE RIGOLETTOS

2 c. canned pitted ripe olives
2 8-oz. packages cream cheese
1 tsp. salt
6 drops of hot sauce
2 tbsp. lemon juice
2 tbsp. tomato paste
1/2 c. mashed avocado
8 candied cherries, chopped
1 tbsp. chopped sugared ginger
1/4 c. chopped nuts
1 bunch hearts of celery
1 cucumber
1 green pepper
1 tomato
1 red onion
1 pkg. Cheddar cheese

Chop 1 1/2 cups ripe olives very fine. Cut remaining olives into halves, quarters and rings for garnish. Soften the cream cheese in a bowl. Add the chopped olives, salt, hot sauce and lemon juice and mix well. Spoon equal amounts into 3 bowls. Add tomato paste to 1 bowl, mashed avocado to 1 bowl and cherries, ginger and nuts to remaining bowl. Stuff celery with cherry mixture and press together to form bunch. Roll in waxed paper and chill. Cut the cucumber into slices. Cut green pepper and tomato into wedges, scooping out seeds and membrane. Cut the onion into wedges and separate. Cut cheese into triangles. Pipe cream cheese mixtures onto canape bases with a pastry tube and garnish with reserved ripe olives. Cut celery into slices. Chill all canapes well before serving.

Photograph for this recipe on page 159.

LOBSTER BARQUETTES

1 10-oz. package pie crust mix
1 tbsp. butter
1 5-oz. can lobster, finely chopped
1 tbsp. chopped onion
1 tbsp. chopped parsley
2 tbsp. brandy
1/2 tsp. monosodium glutamate
2 tsp. lemon juice
1/3 c. warm light cream
1 egg yolk
Grated Parmesan cheese
Buttered bread crumbs

Prepare pie crust mix according to package directions. Roll dough on lightly floured board to 1/8-inch thickness. Invert 3-inch barquette molds on dough. Cut 1/3 inch around each mold with knife. Fit piece of pastry into each mold; press to bottom and sides. Trim excess around rim of mold. Prick bottom with a fork. Fill pastry shells with rice to prevent pastry from bubbling. Bake at 375 degrees for 10 to 12 minutes or until shells are golden brown. Remove rice. Cool. Melt butter in a skillet. Add lobster, onion and parsley. Cook until onion is tender but not brown. Stir in brandy. Sprinkle with monosodium glutamate and lemon juice. Combine cream and egg yolk; stir into skillet. Spoon mixture into baked barquettes. Sprinkle with Parmesan cheese and bread crumbs. Brown under broiler to serve immediately. Refrigerate until ready to serve if prepared in advance. Reheat in a 350-degree oven for 15 minutes. Brown lightly under broiler.

Photograph for this recipe on page 160.

CRAB MEAT QUICHE

1 8-in. unbaked pie shell
2 eggs
1 c. light cream
1 tsp. monosodium glutamate
3/4 tsp. salt
Dash of cayenne pepper
3 oz. Swiss cheese, grated
3 oz. Gruyere cheese, grated
1 tbsp. flour
1 6 1/2-oz. can crab meat, flaked

Prick bottom and sides of pie shell with fork. Bake in a 450-degree oven for about 10 minutes or until delicate brown. Combine eggs, cream, monosodium glutamate, salt and cayenne pepper; beat well. Combine cheeses, flour and crab meat; sprinkle evenly in pie shell. Pour in cream mixture. Bake at 325 degrees for 45 minutes to 1 hour or until tip of knife inserted in center comes out clean. Cut into small wedges.

Photograph for this recipe on page 160.

ALMOND MUSHROOMS

18 lg. mushrooms
Monosodium glutamate
1/3 c. fine dry bread crumbs
2 tsp. lemon juice
1/8 tsp. rosemary
1 tsp. marjoram
1/4 tsp. salt
1/4 c. finely chopped almonds
1 tbsp. capers
3 tbsp. butter
3 tbsp. chopped parsley

Wash mushrooms and remove stems. Sprinkle inside of mushroom caps with monosodium glutamate. Chop stems finely; combine with bread crumbs, lemon juice, herbs, salt, almonds and capers. Spoon mixture into caps. Place in greased shallow baking pan. Dot each mushroom with butter. Bake at 350 degrees for 20 to 25 minutes. Sprinkle with parsley.

Photograph for this recipe on page 160.

RIPE OLIVE QUICHE

1 10-oz. package frozen patty shells
1 8-oz. package cream cheese
2 eggs
2 c. canned pitted ripe olives, drained
1 2-oz. can rolled anchovies with capers

1/2 c. grated Fontina or imported
  Swiss cheese
1/2 c. grated Parmesan cheese

Thaw patty shells in refrigerator. Knead patty shells together and roll out. Press into 10-inch fluted tart pan. Mix cream cheese with eggs; pour into pastry. Cut olives into halves and chunks. Sprinkle evenly over cheese filling. Arrange anchovies on top; sprinkle with cheeses. Bake in 400-degree oven for 40 minutes or until brown. Serve warm or cold.

Photograph for this recipe on page 159.

VEGETABLES VINAIGRETTE

White Beans

3 c. cooked white beans
1/2 tsp. monosodium glutamate
1 onion, chopped
2 tbsp. chopped parsley
1/2 c. French dressing
1 clove of garlic, slashed

Place beans in a large bowl; add remaining ingredients. Mix well. Chill for several hours. Remove garlic before serving.

Cucumbers

3 cucumbers
1/2 tsp. monosodium glutamate
1/2 c. vinegar
2 tbsp. sugar
1 clove of garlic, slashed
Chopped dill

Peel cucumbers and slice thinly. Sprinkle with monosodium glutamate. Combine vinegar, sugar and 2 tablespoons water; pour over cucumbers. Add garlic. Sprinkle with dill. Chill. Remove garlic before serving.

Artichoke Hearts

2 1-lb. cans artichoke hearts
1 tsp. monosodium glutamate
1/2 c. French dressing
2 tbsp. lemon juice

Drain artichoke hearts and place in bowl. Sprinkle with monosodium glutamate. Add dressing and lemon juice. Marinate for several hours. Garnish with diced pimento and capers.

Photograph for this recipe on page 160.

CHICKEN SOPA

1 canned whole chicken
1 4-oz. can green chilies
1 onion, chopped
2 cans cream of chicken soup
Salt and pepper to taste
18 corn tortillas, torn into pieces
1 c. grated cheese
1 c. chicken broth

Bone chicken; cut into small pieces. Drain green chilies; chop. Cook onion in small amount of fat until soft; add green chilies. Add chicken, soup, salt and pepper; mix well. Place 1/3 of the tortillas in 9 x 13-inch baking pan; add 1/3 of the chicken mixture. Repeat layers twice; top with cheese. Pour broth over cheese; cover. Bake at 350 degrees for 30 minutes. Uncover; bake for 15 minutes longer. Yield: 6 servings.

Col. Richard E. Chandler
George AFB, Victorville, California

CHICKEN CASSEROLES

Toast slices, crusts removed
Cooked chicken slices
Whole mushrooms, sauteed
Rich cream sauce
Grated cheese
Bread crumbs
Sherry

Place slices of toast in bottoms of individual casseroles. Place slices of chicken over toast, then place mushrooms on chicken. Pour cream sauce over all. Sprinkle with cheese and bread crumbs. Add 1 teaspoon of sherry. Bake at 350 degrees until cheese is melted.

Col. Clayton C. Fenton, Jr., USMC
Defense Elec. Supply Ctr., Dayton, Ohio

SPAGHETTI WITH CHICKEN CREOLE

3 lb. broiler-fryer chicken pieces
Salt
3 slices bacon, diced
2 tbsp. salad oil
2 c. chopped onion
1 clove of garlic, minced
1 1/2 c. chopped celery
1 med. green pepper, diced
2 tbsp. flour
1 28-oz. can tomatoes
1 8-oz. can tomato sauce
1/2 tsp. crushed thyme leaves
1 tbsp. chili powder
2 bay leaves
1/2 tsp. hot sauce
2 tbsp. Worcestershire sauce
1 tbsp. dark brown sugar
1 10-oz. package frozen cut okra, thawed
12 oz. spaghetti

Sprinkle chicken lightly with salt. Cook bacon in Dutch oven or large skillet until crisp; drain on paper towel. Add oil to drippings; brown chicken in hot oil mixture. Remove chicken; set aside. Add onion and garlic to oil; saute until onion is soft. Stir in celery and green pepper; saute for 3 minutes. Stir in flour, then tomatoes, tomato sauce, 2 1/2 teaspoons salt, seasonings and sugar. Add chicken and okra; bring to a boil. Cover; simmer for 25 to 30 minutes or until chicken is tender. Remove bay leaves. Add 1 1/2 tablespoons salt to 4 to 5 quarts rapidly boiling water; add spaghetti gradually so that water continues to boil. Cook, uncovered, stirring occasionally, until tender; drain in colander. Place spaghetti in deep serving platter; spoon sauce and chicken on top. Sprinkle with bacon. Yield: 6 servings.

GRILLED CHICKEN

1 c. water
1 c. vinegar
1/2 c. cooking oil
1 tsp. salt
12 pieces of chicken

Mix water, vinegar, oil and salt in bowl. Place chicken on grill over coals; baste with vinegar mixture. Cook for about 1 hour, turning chicken several times and basting with remaining vinegar mixture. Yield: 6 servings.

Capt. Richard H. Frantz
Seymour Johnson AFB, North Carolina

TWIRLY BIRDS

1 stick margarine
4 tsp. cinnamon
1 tsp. curry powder
1/4 tsp. garlic powder
2   2-lb. fryers
1 lg. onion, sliced
1/4 c. honey

Melt margarine. Stir in 3 teaspoons cinnamon, curry powder and garlic powder; heat until bubbly. Sprinkle 1/2 teaspoon cinnamon in cavity of each chicken; place 1/2 of the onion slices in each cavity. Skewer neck skin to body; tie legs tightly to tail. Place chickens on barbecue spit; brush with part of the margarine mixture. Start rotisserie. Roast chickens, basting, for about 1 hour and 15 minutes. Stir honey into remaining margarine mixture. Roast chickens for 15 minutes longer, basting with honey mixture.

Maj. Edward Furchak
Offutt AFB, Omaha, Nebraska

DILLY CHICKEN

1 med. onion, chopped
1/4 c. butter
2 c. uncooked diced chicken
1 c. sauterne
Dash of garlic salt
1/4 tsp. dillweed
1/8 tsp. poultry seasoning
2 dashes of paprika
1/4 tsp. sugar
Salt and pepper to taste
1 c. sour cream

Cook onion in butter until soft. Add chicken; cook until brown. Add remaining ingredients except sour cream; cover. Cook over low heat for 30 minutes. Add sour cream; mix well. Cover; keep warm until sauce is homogenized. Serve over noodles or rice. Yield: 3-4 servings.

1st Lt. Robert G. Taylor, Jr.
Los Angeles AFS, Los Angeles, California

HOT SHOT CHICKEN

Chicken thighs, drumsticks and breasts
Monosodium glutamate
Seasoned pepper and salt
Heavy cream

Arrange chicken in 1 layer, closely packed, in shallow baking pan; season generously with monosodium glutamate, pepper and salt. Bake at 300 degrees for about 1 hour or until skin is dry. Pour enough cream over chicken to partially cover. Bake, basting frequently, for 1 hour and 30 minutes longer, adding cream, if needed.

Robert F. Froehlke
Sec. of the Army
Washington, D. C.

LEMON CHICKEN

1 clove of garlic, mashed
1/2 tsp. salt
1/2 tsp. pepper
1/2 tsp. thyme
1/4 c. salad oil
1/2 c. lemon juice
2 tbsp. grated onion
2 broilers, halved

Mix all ingredients except broilers: add broilers. Marinate for several hours or overnight. Prepare barbecue grill, having coals white hot. Drain broilers; place on grill. Cook until done, brushing several times with remaining marinade.

Capt. Keith Bennett
Pearl Harbor Naval Shipyard, Honolulu, Hawaii

MALLARD WITH RICE DRESSING

2 mallards
1 box long grain and wild rice
2 tsp. salt

2 tbsp. minced onion
2 tbsp. minced green pepper
2 tbsp. minced celery
1   4-oz. can chopped mushrooms, drained
1/4 tsp. pepper
1/2 c. melted butter
2 c. orange juice

Soak mallards in salt water for 2 to 3 hours, then wrap in a wet towel. Refrigerate overnight. Stir long grain and wild rice into 2 1/2 cups boiling water; add salt, onion, green pepper, celery, mushrooms and pepper. Cover and simmer for about 25 minutes or until all water is absorbed. Add butter. Stuff mallards with rice mixture; place in baking pan. Mix orange juice with 2 cups water. Bake mallards in 350-degree oven for 2 hours, basting frequently with orange juice mixture. Yield: 4 servings.

Cmdr. R. A. Esposito
NAS, Fallon, Nevada

DUCKS FOR DUCK HATERS

2 ducks, cut in half
Salt and pepper to taste
1 onion, finely chopped
Butter
1 peeled apple, grated
1 tsp. grated orange peel
4 tbsp. currant jelly
5 tbsp. sherry or port

Season ducks with salt and pepper. Cook onion in small amount of butter until limp. Add apple and orange peel; cook for several minutes. Add jelly and sherry; cook until reduced to consistency of molasses. Remove from heat. Place ducks, cavity side down, about 3 inches over medium charcoal fire for about 5 minutes or until well browned. Turn ducks; pierce each half 15 or 20 times with ice pick. Spoon 1 tablespoon onion mixture into cavity of each half; cook for 5 to 10 minutes or until done. Do not overcook. Place on platter, meaty side up; keep warm. Serve with remaining sauce.

Maj. Lucius F. Hallett, III
Elmendorf AFB, Anchorage, Alaska

FILLET OF SOLE
WITH LOBSTER SAUCE

1 lb. fillet of sole
2 tbsp. butter

2 1/2 tbsp. flour
1/2 c. milk
1/2 c. cream
1 tsp. chopped chives
1 tsp. chopped parsley
2 tsp. minced carrot
2 tsp. minced green pepper
1 tsp. grated lemon rind
1/2 tsp. salt
1/8 tsp. pepper
Dash of nutmeg
1/2 c. white dry wine
1/2 lb. fresh cooked lobster, chopped
1 egg yolk, slightly beaten

Preheat oven to 350 degrees. Place fish on well-buttered heatproof serving platter. Bake for 15 minutes. Remove all liquid on platter with spoon or towel. Melt butter in saucepan, then add flour and stir until well blended. Add milk and cream. Stir and cook until thickened. Add vegetables, lemon rind and seasonings. Cook over low heat for 3 to 4 minutes. Add wine and lobster; cook until heated through. Add small amount of sauce to egg yolk, then stir egg mixture back into sauce. Cook for 1 minute. Pour sauce over fish. Return to oven for 5 minutes. Place under broiler to brown. Garnish with parsley and lemon wedges. Serve immediately. Yield: 4 servings.

Col. Clayton C. Fenton, Jr.
Def. Elec. Supply Ctr., Dayton, Ohio

BROILED FISH FILLETS

6 fish fillets
Salt and pepper to taste
2 tbsp. grated onion
2 tomatoes, diced
2 tbsp. melted butter
1/8 tsp. garlic powder
1 c. grated Cheddar cheese

Place fillets on foil in broiler pan; season with salt and pepper. Top with onion and tomatoes. Pour butter over tomatoes; sprinkle with garlic powder. Broil for 8 to 12 minutes or until done. Sprinkle with cheese; broil until cheese bubbles.

Capt. Bob Buster, Jr.
Ft. Benjamen Harrison, Indianapolis, Indiana

BAKED STRIPED BASS

1/4 c. butter
1/2 lb. sliced bacon
1 c. rice
1 tbsp. basil
1 tbsp. parsley
5 lb. cleaned whole bass
Carrots
Potatoes
Celery
Green pepper
Onions
Salt and pepper to taste

Place large sheet of foil in 8 x 16-inch baking pan, having enough foil to cover all ingredients in pan. Cut butter into small pieces; place on foil. Separate bacon slices and line foil; add rice, basil and parsley. Place bass over rice; add enough vegetables for desired amount of servings. Add about 2 1/2 cups water, salt and pepper. Bring foil around all ingredients; seal. Bake at 350 degrees for 3 hours.

Cmdr. Roger P. Hartgen
Tracen, Petaluma, California

BAKED STUFFED FISH

1 1/2 lb. fillets of haddock or flounder
1 can frozen shrimp soup, thawed
1/4 c. melted butter
30 round buttery crackers, crushed
1 tbsp. minced onion
1/2 tsp. Worcestershire sauce
1/4 tsp. garlic salt

Place fillets in baking pan; pour soup over fillets. Bake at 350 degrees for 20 minutes. Combine remaining ingredients; spread over fillets. Return to oven; bake for 10 minutes longer. Yield: 6 servings.

Maj. James W. Davis
Seymour Johnson AFB, Goldsboro, North Carolina

BAKED FISH

5 to 10 flounder, halibut or codfish
    fillets
1 onion, diced
Butter
1 can cream of mushroom or celery soup
1 med. can stewed tomatoes
2 c. cooked sliced carrots

1/2 tsp. curry powder
1/2 tsp. nutmeg
1/2 tsp. dry mustard
Salt to taste
1/2 c. semisweet wine

Arrange fillets in shallow baking pan lined with aluminum foil. Bake at 400 degrees for 15 minutes. Cook onion in small amount butter until soft. Add soup, tomatoes, carrots, curry, nutmeg, mustard and salt; simmer while fillets are baking. Add wine; pour over fillets. Bake for 15 minutes longer.

Cmdr. Robert Russell
Coast Guard Air Station, Bell Chasse, Louisiana

BAKED FLOUNDER IN WHITE WINE

2 lb. flounder fillets
3 c. thinly sliced cooked potatoes
1 4-oz. can sliced mushrooms, drained
1 tsp. paprika
1/2 tsp. salt
1/4 tsp. pepper
1 c. sour cream
1/2 c. dry white wine
2 tbsp. flour
1 tbsp. grated onion
Chopped parsley to taste (opt.)

Thaw fillets, if frozen. Skin fillets; cut into serving portions. Arrange potatoes in well-greased 12 x 8 x 2-inch baking dish; top with mushrooms. Combine paprika, salt and pepper; sprinkle half the seasonings over mushrooms. Combine sour cream, wine, flour and onion; spread

half the sour cream mixture over mushrooms. Top with fillets. Sprinkle fillets with remaining seasonings; spread with remaining sour cream mixture. Bake in 350-degree oven for 35 to 45 minutes or until fish flakes easily when tested with fork. Remove from oven; let stand for 10 minutes for easier serving. Sprinkle with parsley. Yield: 6 servings.

FISH ROLL-UPS WITH BLUE CHEESE STUFFING

1/2 c. butter
1/4 c. minced parsley
1 med. tomato, coarsely chopped
1/2 c. minced celery
1/4 c. (firmly packed) blue cheese
3 c. soft bread crumbs
1 egg, well beaten
1/2 tsp. salt
6 flounder fillets
Juice of 1 lemon

Melt 1/4 cup butter in 10-inch skillet over low heat. Add parsley, tomato and celery and cook, stirring frequently, for 10 minutes. Remove from heat. Crumble in cheese. Add bread crumbs, egg and salt and mix well. Spread over fish fillets. Roll each fillet up and fasten with toothpick. Place fish roll-ups in greased 1 1/2-quart baking dish. Melt remaining butter; mix in lemon juice. Pour over fish. Bake at 350 degrees for 30 minutes. Yield: 6 servings.

Maj. James W. Davis
Seymour Johnson AFB, Goldsboro, North Carolina

HALIBUT IN BEER BATTER

2 lb. halibut
1 can warm stale beer
3 eggs
1 tsp. salt
1/4 tsp. pepper
3 tsp. baking powder
1 c. flour
1/4 c. grated Parmesan cheese
1/4 tsp. garlic powder

Cut halibut into 1-inch cubes; set aside. Combine remaining ingredients for batter. This should be consistency of thin pancake batter. Dip fish cubes in batter, then fry in hot, 350 to 375-degree, fat for about 5 minutes or until done. This batter is very good for onion rings and green peppers. One envelope cheese sauce mix may be used for the Parmesan cheese. Yield: 6 servings.

Lt. David I. Scott
USCG Air Sta., Annette, Alaska

ONION FILLET

2 tbsp. butter
1 can French-fried onion rings
4 to 6 walleye pike or bass fillets
Salt and pepper to taste
1 pt. sour cream
1 pkg. dried onion soup mix
Grated Cheddar or Parmesan cheese
    to taste
Paprika

Grease 8 x 8-inch baking dish with butter. Place onion rings over bottom of dish; place pike fillets on onion rings. Season with salt and pepper. Mix sour cream and onion soup mix; spread evenly over fillets. Bake at 325 degrees for 30 minutes. Sprinkle cheese and dash of paprika over top; bake until cheese melts.

Lt. Col. Phil Serrin
Pentagon, Washington, D. C.

POACHED FISH WITH WINE SAUCE

1 1/2 lb. fish fillets
1/2 c. butter
Juice of 1/2 lemon
1/2 c. sherry
Salt and pepper to taste
2 tbsp. flour
1 c. milk
1/4 lb. cooked sm. shrimp

Slice fillets into 1/4-inch thick slices 1/2 inch wide and 4 to 5 inches long; roll and fasten with toothpick. Melt 1/4 cup butter in saucepan; add lemon juice and 1/4 cup sherry. Place fish in shallow baking pan; season with salt and pepper, then brush with lemon juice mixture. Bake in preheated 350-degree oven for 15 minutes. Melt remaining butter in saucepan. Sprinkle flour over butter; stir in thoroughly. Stir in milk and remaining sherry. Cook over medium heat, stirring constantly, until moderately thick. Add shrimp; pour over fish. Bake for 30 minutes longer; serve with rice. Yield: 6 servings.

Maj. Richard S. Ribinski
Wurtsmith AFB, Oscoda, Michigan

BAKED SALMON DELUXE

1 whole fresh salmon, cleaned
Salt to taste
1/4 lb. margarine, thinly sliced
1 or 2 lemons, thinly sliced
White wine or lemon-lime carbonated
*   beverage*

Spray broiler pan with cookwear coating; place salmon in broiler pan. Sprinkle salt on inside of salmon, then place slices of margarine and lemon inside salmon. Bake at 550 degrees for 10 to 15 minutes. Reduce temperature to 425 degrees; bake salmon 10 minutes per pound for first 4 pounds and 5 minutes for each additional pound, basting frequently.

Col. Marion G. Smith
Ft. McPherson, Georgia

OUTDOOR-BROILED SALMON

Brown sugar
Lemon juice
Worcestershire sauce
Butter
Wine (opt.)
1 fresh salmon fillet

Mix desired amounts of brown sugar, lemon juice, Worcestershire sauce, butter and wine into paste; rub paste into salmon fillet. Cook salmon on a grill over hot coals until brown on both sides.

Col. Charles R. Burton
Langley AFB, Virginia

SPAGHETTI WITH
CLAM AND ANCHOVY SAUCE

2 doz. cherrystone clams
4 or 5 tbsp. olive oil
3 tbsp. butter
2 shallots, finely chopped
3 (or more) cloves of garlic, chopped
6 anchovy fillets
1/4 c. chopped parsley
1/2 tsp. rosemary
1/2 c. dry white wine
Freshly ground pepper to taste
1/2 lb. spaghetti

Open clams; drain and reserve juice. Chop clams fine. Heat oil and butter. Add shallots; cook until golden brown. Add garlic and anchovies; cook, stirring, until anchovies make a paste. Add parsley, rosemary, 1 cup reserved clam juice, wine and pepper; simmer for 10 minutes. Add clams; simmer for 1 minute longer. Remove from heat. Cook spaghetti in large amount of boiling, salted water until of desired doneness. Drain; serve with clam sauce. Yield: 4 servings.

Cmdr. Richard L. Ferrarini
Whiting Field, Milton, Florida

QUICK CLAM FRITTERS

2 eggs, slightly beaten
2 c. minced clams
1/2 c. cracker meal
1/4 tsp. salt

Combine all ingredients; shape into patties. Fry in well-greased electric skillet at 380 degrees until golden brown on both sides.

Capt. S. R. De Soer
Ft. Sheridan, Chicago, Illinois

SPAGHETTI AND WHITE CLAM SAUCE

4 tbsp. oil
4 tbsp. butter
2 cloves of garlic, minced
1 lg. onion, chopped
1 can minced clams
Salt and pepper to taste
1/2 c. white wine
Dried or fresh parsley to taste
1 pkg. spaghetti, cooked and buttered
Grated Parmesan cheese
Dash of crushed red pepper (opt.)

Heat oil. Add butter; heat until melted. Add garlic; saute for 2 minutes. Add onion; saute until translucent. Drain clams; reserve juice. Add reserved clam juice to garlic mixture; bring to a rapid boil. Add salt and pepper; stir in clams. Add wine slowly to keep boiling; cook to desired consistency. Add parsley. Fold into hot spaghetti; serve with Parmesan cheese and red pepper. One-fourth cup vermouth may be substituted for wine. Yield: 4 servings.

Maj. Robert L. Graetzel
Woodbridge RAF, Suffolk, England

CRAB AU GRATIN

2 tbsp. butter
2 tbsp. flour
1 c. milk
3/4 c. grated sharp and mild cheese
Salt and pepper to taste
Dried chives to taste
Chopped parsley to taste
2 or 3 dashes of Worcestershire sauce
1/2 sm. can pimento, diced
1/2 sm. can mushrooms
1/3 tsp. hot mustard
1   6 1/2-oz. can crab meat
1/4 c. dry sherry

Melt butter; stir in flour. Add milk slowly; cook, stirring constantly, until thickened. Add cheese; stir until melted. Add salt, pepper, chives, parsley, Worcestershire sauce, pimento, mushrooms and mustard; mix well. Drain crab meat; reserve 1/2 of the liquid. Add crab meat and reserved liquid to cheese mixture; heat through, stirring frequently. Stir in sherry; place in casserole. Bake at 350 degrees for 10 to 15 minutes or until hot. Serve on toasted bread. Yield: 6 servings.

Maj. Gen. George G. Loving, Jr.
Maxwell AFB, Alabama

CRAB CAKES

3 eggs
1 med. onion, chopped
1/2 green pepper, chopped
2 tbsp. prepared mustard
1/4 tsp. salt
Dash of pepper
1/2 c. melted butter or margarine
6 slices bread, crusts removed
1 lb. crab meat
Cooking oil

Place eggs, onion, green pepper, mustard, salt, pepper and melted butter in large mixing bowl; mix thoroughly. Crumble bread. Add to egg mixture; mix until bread absorbs most of the liquid. Add more butter if too dry; add more bread if too moist. Remove all bits of shell from crab meat. Fold crab meat into bread mixture, being careful not to break up lumps of crab meat. Form into patties about 3 inches in diameter and 1 to 1 1/2 inches thick. Place in refrigerator for at least 1 hour. Heat oil in deep fryer to 350 degrees. Cook patties in oil for 4 to 8 minutes or until golden brown; serve piping hot.

Capt. James S. Martin
Keesler AFB, Mississippi

HANGTOWN FRY

6 eggs
8 Eastern oysters
Flour
1/2 c. dry bread crumbs
1/4 c. butter
4 slices bacon, halved and cooked
Salt and pepper to taste
Dash of hot sauce

Beat 1 egg in small bowl. Dip oysters in flour, then in beaten egg, then in bread crumbs. Melt butter in skillet; saute oysters for 1 minute on each side. Arrange bacon slices in skillet between oysters. Beat remaining eggs; add salt, pepper and hot sauce. Pour egg mixture in skillet and cook slowly until eggs are set, lifting sides gently to let eggs run underneath. Slide under broiler flame to brown top lightly. Serve with Bloody Marys or Screwdrivers to begin, then garlic toast, strong black coffee and fruit and cheese platter as a follow-up. Yield: 4 servings.

Lt. Cmdr. John S. Ahl
NROTC, Stanford U, Stanford, California

SHRIMP SCAMPI

2 lb. fresh jumbo shrimp
4 cloves of garlic
1 tbsp. salt
1 c. olive oil
1/4 c. minced fresh parsley
1 tbsp. lemon juice

Split shrimp shells up back; devein. Crush garlic in salt. Add remaining ingredients; blend well. Add shrimp; marinate for 4 hours. Drain shrimp. Grill over medium charcoal fire for 3 minutes on each side. Yield: 4 servings.

Cmdr. Joseph H. Burke
NAS, Barbers Point, Oahu, Hawaii

CAJUN SHRIMP

1   10-oz. package shrimp
1 to 1 1/2 sm. onions, chopped
1/3 bell pepper, chopped
Butter
Pinch of thyme
Hot sauce to taste
1 can stewed tomatoes
Dash of garlic powder
Salt and pepper to taste
Parsley flakes to taste
Several dashes of lemon juice
Sliced okra to taste (opt.)

Peel and devein shrimp. Saute onions and bell pepper in butter until onions are light brown. Add shrimp; cook until shrimp turn pink. Add remaining ingredients, breaking up tomatoes and keeping shrimp whole; cover. Cook until okra is done, stirring frequently. Serve on rice. Yield: 4 servings.

Capt. John H. Elledge, Jr.
Joint Refugee Operations Ctr., Berlin, Germany

SHRIMP A LA JACQUES

5 egg yolks
1 recipe hollandaise sauce
White wine to taste
Jumbo shrimp
Garlic butter
Grated Gouda cheese to taste

Add egg yolks to hollandaise sauce; stir quickly until blended. Add wine. Arrange desired number of shrimp on heatproof shells; cover with sauce. Top with pat of garlic butter and Gouda cheese. Broil for 2 minutes or until browned.

Col. Sidney L. Davis
MacDill AFB, Tampa, Florida

SHRIMP FLAMBE

1 lb. shrimp
4 tbsp. butter
1/2 tbsp. Worcestershire sauce
4 dashes of hot sauce
1 clove of garlic, minced
Juice of 1 sm. lemon
1/2 c. dry vermouth
1/4 c. chopped parsley

Salt and pepper to taste
1/4 c. cognac or brandy

Wash and dry shrimp. Heat butter in 10 to 12-inch frying pan over high heat until brown. Add Worcestershire sauce, hot sauce and garlic. Add shrimp; cook for 1 minute. Add lemon juice; cook for 1 minute. Add vermouth, parsley, salt and pepper; cook over high heat for 3 minutes. Add cognac; ignite. Remove shrimp with slotted spoon to hot serving plate. Cook liquid until medium sauce is formed; spoon over shrimp. One teaspoon garlic salt may be substituted for minced garlic. Two tablespoons bottled lemon juice may be used in place of fresh lemon juice; 1 tablespoon dried parsley may be substituted for fresh parsley.

Col. Robert G. Taylor
USAF Acad., Colorado

BROILED SHRIMP

2 lb. jumbo shrimp
1 clove of garlic, pressed
1 c. olive oil
1/2 c. sauterne
Juice of 1/2 lemon
1 1/2 tbsp. chopped parsley
1 1/2 tbsp. chopped basil
1 tsp. salt
1/4 tsp. pepper
1 recipe lemon-butter sauce

Shell, clean and devein shrimp, leaving tails on. Mix 1 clove of garlic and remaining ingredients except lemon-butter sauce. Add shrimp; marinate in refrigerator for several hours. Drain shrimp; grill or broil for about 10 minutes, watching carefully so as not to burn. Serve at once with lemon-butter sauce mixed with remaining garlic. Yield: 3-4 servings.

Lt. Jr. Grade David H. Graves
NAS, Kingsville, Texas

SPAGHETTI SAUCE WITH LOBSTER

2 cans anchovies with capers
1/2 c. chopped parsley
1 clove of garlic, chopped
4 No. 303 cans Italian-style tomatoes
2 tbsp. sugar
1 tsp. salt
2 tbsp. oregano

1 tbsp. basil
6 med. lobster-tails
3 cans tomato paste

Drain anchovies; reserve oil. Cook anchovies, parsley and garlic in reserved oil for about 10 minutes. Add tomatoes, sugar, salt, oregano and basil; simmer for 2 hours, stirring occasionally and breaking up tomatoes. Add lobster-tails; cook for 10 minutes longer. Add tomato paste; heat through. Yield: 6 servings.

Col. John E. Wolter
Castle AFB, Atwater, California

HERBED SHRIMP DIABLE

2 lb. fresh shrimp
1/2 c. butter
1/2 lb. fresh mushrooms, sliced
12 cherry tomatoes, stems removed

1 c. sliced celery
1 tsp. parsley flakes
2 tsp. freeze-dried chives
1/2 tsp. tarragon leaves
1/2 tsp. ginger
1 tsp. dry mustard
2 tsp. season-all
1/8 tsp. garlic powder
1/4 tsp. monosodium glutamate
1/4 tsp. coarsely ground pepper
3 tbsp. lemon juice
1/4 c. brandy, heated

Shell and devein shrimp. Melt butter in large skillet. Add mushrooms, tomatoes and celery; saute for 2 to 3 minutes. Push to one side of skillet. Add the shrimp. Mix seasonings; sprinkle over shrimp mixture. Cook, stirring, for 2 minutes. Add lemon juice; stir well. Cover; simmer for 5 minutes. Transfer to chafing dish. Flame with heated brandy just before serving. Serve over rice. Yield: 4-6 servings.

EGGS AND SOUPS

Versatility is the most outstanding and the most wonderful
characteristic of both eggs and soups. We can make them
as simple or as lavish as we want — and either way they have
classic appeal.

Soups or eggs may serve as a quiet first course to the meal,
or step to the center of attention as a tantalizing entree.
Both are so easy to prepare and homemakers frequently keep
them on hand for unexpected guests.

Soups and eggs can be whisked out on short notice, prepared
in minutes and served as a delicious, satisfying meal.

The recipes in this section will give you many refreshing,
creative ideas for preparing egg or soup dishes.

BRUNCH EGG CASSEROLE

2 c. croutons
1 c. shredded Cheddar cheese
4 slightly beaten eggs
2 c. milk
1/2 tsp. salt
1/2 tsp. prepared mustard
1/8 tsp. onion powder
Dash of freshly ground pepper
8 slices bacon

Combine croutons and cheese in bottom of greased 10 x 6 x 1 3/4-inch baking dish. Combine eggs, milk, salt, mustard, onion powder and pepper; mix until blended. Pour egg mixture over crouton mixture. Cook bacon until crisp; drain and crumble. Sprinkle bacon over egg mixture. Bake at 325 degrees for 55 minutes to 1 hour or until eggs are set. Garnish with bacon curls, if desired. Yield: 6 servings.

Cmdr. John A. Landaker
NAS, Patuxent River, Maryland

MUSHROOM EGGS

2 slices American cheese
1 can cream of mushroom soup
2 tbsp. sherry
4 to 6 eggs
4 to 6 slices toast

Cut cheese in small pieces; place in electric skillet. Add mushroom soup and sherry and heat, stirring until cheese is melted. Break eggs into sauce; poach at 200 to 250 degrees until eggs are done to taste. Place eggs on toast; cover with mushroom sauce. Serve with bacon or sausage.

Capt. Kenneth F. Rowell
NAS, Barbers Point, Hawaii

EGGS MORNAY WITH MUSTARD

1 1/2 tbsp. butter
1 1/2 tbsp. flour
3/4 c. chicken stock
3/4 c. cream
3/4 c. grated sharp Cheddar cheese
1 tsp. salt
1/8 tsp. cayenne pepper
1/8 tsp. nutmeg
1/2 tsp. dry mustard
4 eggs
4 rusks

Melt butter in range-to-oven casserole over low heat; stir in flour until bubbly and smooth. Add stock, stirring constantly; bring to a boil. Boil for 1 minute; stir in cream and cheese until cheese is melted and mixture is smooth. Add salt, cayenne pepper, nutmeg and mustard; blend well. Break eggs into sauce. Bake at 350 degrees for 25 minutes or until eggs are set. Serve over rusks. Toast may be substituted for rusks, if desired. Yield: 2 servings.

Capt. Timothy Edward Danforth
Webb AFB, Big Spring, Texas

BIG SWEDE OMELET

4 lg. eggs
1/4 tsp. salt
Dash of pepper or lemon pepper
Hot sauce to taste (opt.)
4 tsp. milk
1/8 tsp. oregano
6 cherry tomatoes, quartered
2 to 3 tbsp. chopped onion
1/4 c. crisp bacon, crumbled
1 sm. dill pickle, diced
1/4 c. grated Cheddar cheese
3 sliced fresh mushrooms
2 tbsp. butter

Have all ingredients at room temperature. Combine eggs, salt, pepper, hot sauce, milk and oregano in blender container; mix well. Combine tomatoes, onion, bacon, pickle, cheese and mushrooms in bowl over hot water. Melt butter in omelet pan or 8-inch iron skillet over medium heat. Pour egg mixture into skillet; reduce heat. When egg mixture is just set, sprinkle tomato mixture evenly over egg mixture. Fold omelet over carefully; heat for 1 minute. Slide into heated serving dish. Yield: 2 servings.

Maj. Richard A. Erickson
Defense Lang. Inst., Monterey, California

CHEESE OMELET

4 eggs
1/4 c. milk
Salt and pepper to taste
Butter
Sliced American cheese
Chopped green chilies to taste
3/4 c. chili without beans
Tomato paste to taste

Place eggs, milk, salt and pepper in bowl and beat well. Melt enough butter in skillet to just cover bottom; pour in mixture. Cook over medium low heat until eggs are partially set. Place cheese slices on half the omelet; place green chilies, chili and tomato paste on cheese. Cook until omelet is set. Fold omelet over and cook over low heat for 6 minutes longer.

Lt. Charles D. Hamilton
NROTC Unit, U of Michigan, Ann Arbor, Michigan

FLAMED BRUNCH OMELET

1 med. onion
1 med. green pepper
4 tbsp. cooking oil
Salt and pepper to taste
1 tbsp. butter or margarine
4 oz. sharp Cheddar cheese, chopped
1 can cream of mushroom soup
1 sm. can chopped mushrooms, drained
6 eggs
4 to 6 tbsp. evaporated milk
6 drops of hot sauce
2 or 3 oz. brandy

Mince onion and green pepper; saute in 1 tablespoon oil until crisp-tender. Add salt and pepper to taste. Remove from skillet, drain. Melt butter in double boiler; add cheese, stirring until melted. Add soup; stir well. Stir in mushrooms. Set aside. Beat eggs in bowl; add milk gradually. Add salt, pepper and hot sauce. Heat brandy in small pot; keep warm. Pour remaining oil in skillet; heat until moderately hot. Add egg mixture; sprinkle sauteed vegetables evenly over egg mixture. Cook, tipping skillet occasionally to cover surface, until omelet bottom is browned and top is firm. Roll omelet up as for jelly roll, using spatula. Place on serving platter; cover with mushroom sauce. Pour brandy over omelet; ignite and serve. Yield: 4-6 servings. servings.

J. Robert Lucas
HQ USAREUR and 7th Army, Heidelberg, Germany

OMELETTE CHAMPIGNON

Butter
1 med. onion, chopped
1/2 lb. fresh mushrooms, halved
3 eggs
1/8 c. milk
Salt and pepper to taste
Diced sharp cheese to taste

Melt small amount of butter in large frypan; add onion and mushrooms. Saute until mushrooms and onion are golden brown. Remove from pan; drain on paper towel. Add small amount of butter to same frypan. Beat eggs with milk; season with salt and pepper. Add egg mixture to butter in frypan; cook until slightly solidified. Add cheese and mushroom mixture. Cook until cheese melts and omelet is firm enough to fold over. Fold omelet over in pan; reduce heat. Cook for 3 or 4 minutes on each side. Yield: 2 servings.

Capt. Barry R. Steinberg
Leighton Barracks, Wurzburg, Germany

LATE SCRAMBLED EGGS WITH
BACON

3 doz. eggs
1 1/3 c. half and half
3 tsp. salt
Pepper to taste
3 tbsp. butter
2 c. canned white sauce, heated
Toasted bread slices
Cooked sliced bacon

Beat eggs lightly with half and half, salt and pepper with wire whip. Melt butter in large iron skillet; pour in egg mixture. Cook over low heat till almost set, stirring constantly. Fold in white sauce and cook until eggs are set. Place over hot water or in 200-degree oven to keep warm. Serve on toast with 2 slices of bacon per person.

Lt. Col. F. Lee Early, Jr.
Ft. Campbell, Kentucky

CHEESE EGGS

1/4 c. grated Cheddar cheese
4 eggs
Salt and pepper to taste

Place cheese in skillet over low heat until cheese is melted. Beat eggs slightly; combine with cheese. Add salt and pepper. Scramble eggs, stirring constantly, to desired degree of doneness. Additional cheese may be added, if desired. Yield: 2 servings.

Capt. William R. Cotton, USN
Naval Dental Res. Inst., Great Lakes, Illinois

SPANISH OMELET

1/2 c. chopped green pepper
1/2 c. chopped onion
1/2 c. chopped celery
3 tbsp. butter
8 to 10 eggs
3/4 c. grated sharp cheese
Salt and pepper to taste
Dash of chili pepper
1 can green chilies, drained
Paprika to taste

Saute green pepper, onion and celery in 2 tablespoons butter for 5 to 10 minutes in 10-inch heavy skillet until pepper is cooked. Beat eggs; add 1/2 cup cheese, salt, pepper and chili powder. Mix well; add onion mixture. Spread green chilies in skillet; sprinkle with remaining cheese. Add remaining butter; cook until cheese melts. Pour egg mixture over top; sprinkle with paprika. Cover; cook over low heat for 15 to 20 minutes or until top is set. Yield: 4 servings.

Cmdr. Kelly E. Taggart
NOAA Hq., Rockville, Maryland

SUNDAY BRUNCH

1/2 lb. bacon
5 med. potatoes, grated
1 tsp. salt
1/2 tsp. pepper
1 tsp. garlic powder
1/2 med. onion, sliced in rings
8 eggs
1 c. grated sharp cheese

Fry bacon in skillet until crisp; remove from skillet. Add the potatoes to skillet and season with salt, pepper and garlic powder. Cook over medium high heat until potatoes are brown. Turn potatoes and brown. Reduce heat to medium and place onion rings on potatoes. Break eggs carefully over onions; sprinkle grated cheese over eggs. Add bacon; cover. Cook until eggs are set.

Lt. Cmdr. J. Michael Lents
Key West Naval Base, Key West, Florida

TART EGGS FOR TWO

1 can corned beef hash
3 eggs
1/4 c. milk
1/4 tsp. dry mustard
1 tbsp. bacon grease
1/4 med. green pepper
1/8 fresh lemon with peel, sliced
Dash of garlic powder
Salt and pepper to taste

Preheat oven to 400 degrees. Cut corned beef into 1-inch slices. Place slices in individual casseroles. Place remaining ingredients in blender container, blend for about 30 seconds, then pour over corned beef hash slices. Bake for 15 minutes; baked mixture will look like souffle.

Lt. Cmdr. Billy L. Heller
Naval Hosp., St. Albans, New York

CHICKEN CHOWDER

1   4 to 5-lb. stewing chicken
3 qt. water
5 tsp. salt
2 tsp. monosodium glutamate
4 med. carrots, diced
2 med. potatoes, cubed
3 stalks celery, chopped
2 sm. onions, chopped
1/2 lb. salt pork
1 No. 2 can whole kernel corn
1 1/2 c. noodles
1 1/2 qt. milk
1/2 tsp. white pepper

Disjoint chicken; place in 6-quart kettle. Add water, salt and monosodium glutamate; cover. Bring to a boil; reduce heat. Simmer for 3 hours or until chicken is tender when pierced with fork, skimming off foam as necessary. Remove chicken with slotted spoon; cool slightly. Strain liquid through fine sieve; cool. Remove chicken from bones; cut into pieces. Set aside. Skim off fat from chicken broth. Add carrots, potatoes, celery and onions to broth; cover. Bring to boiling point over moderate heat. Reduce heat; simmer for 20 minutes. Remove rind from salt pork; dice pork. Cook salt pork in skillet over medium heat, stirring occasionally with spoon, until lightly browned on all sides; drain on absorbent paper. Add to carrot mixture; add chicken, corn and noodles. Cover; bring to boiling point. Reduce heat; simmer for 10 minutes or until vegetables and noodles are tender. Add milk, stirring constantly; add pepper. Heat thoroughly.

Lt. Col. Vincent J. Pacer, Jr.
Hancock Field, Syracuse, New York

177 / Eggs and Soups

CHIP'S CHILI

3 lb. ground beef
3 onions, chopped
1 10-oz. can mushrooms, drained
3 tbsp. oil
4 15-oz. cans kidney beans
2 15-oz. cans stewed tomatoes
1 2-oz. can tomato paste
1 15-oz. can tomato sauce
2 pkg. chili mix
1 c. grated Parmesan cheese
1 1U-oz. can chopped ripe olives, drained
3 tbsp. hot sauce
2 tbsp. minced garlic
1 tsp. seasoned salt
1 tbsp. chili powder
2 tbsp. Worcestershire sauce

Brown beef, onions and mushrooms in oil in skillet; drain off excess fat. Mix remaining ingredients in a large pot; bring to a simmer. Add beef mixture; simmer for 1 hour, stirring occasionally. Yield: 25 servings.

Capt. Ronald R. Ravenscroft
616th A C and W Sq., Wasserkuppe, Germany

JAIL CHILI

1/2 lb. ground beef suet
2 lb. diced or ground beef
3 cloves of garlic, finely diced
3 chili peppers
1 1/2 tbsp. diced sweet pepper
1 tbsp. salt
1 1/2 tbsp. paprika
1 tbsp. cumin seed
1 tsp. white pepper

Fry out suet, then remove pieces from grease. Add beef, garlic, chili peppers, green pepper and seasonings. Add 3 cups water and cook over low heat for 5 hours, stirring occasionally and adding water for desired thickness.

Maj. Richard S. Ribinski
Wurtsmith AFB, Oscoda, Michigan

VERSATILE CHILI

1 lg. can mushrooms
3 or 4 slices bacon, chopped
3 tbsp. olive oil
2 med. onions, chopped
1/2 tsp. garlic powder
1 green pepper, chopped
2 lb. hamburger or ground chuck
1 16-oz. can tomatoes, chopped
2 cans tomato paste
1 tsp. oregano
1/2 tsp. sweet basil
2 tbsp. (heaping) chili powder
1 tsp. (heaping) cumin powder
2 cans red kidney beans, drained

Drain mushrooms; reserve liquid. Chop mushrooms. Cook bacon in large kettle until brown; remove from kettle. Drain bacon. Add olive oil to bacon fat. Add onions, garlic powder, green pepper and mushrooms; cook until onions are limp. Brown hamburger until almost burned in heavy frying pan while vegetables are cooking. Add 1 quart hot water, undrained tomatoes, tomato paste, reserved mushroom liquid, oregano, basil, chili powder and cumin powder to onion mixture; bring to a simmer. Add hamburger and bacon; simmer for 1 hour to 1 hour and 30 minutes or until of desired consistency. Add kidney beans; heat through. Kidney beans may be omitted and catsup added if spaghetti or pizza sauce is desired. Three finely chopped garlic cloves may be substituted for garlic powder. Caribou or moose meat may be used in place of hamburger. Yield: 6 servings.

Maj Lucius F. Hallett, III
Elmendorf AFB, Anchorage, Alaska

QUAHOG CHOWDER

4 thin sm. slices salt pork
3 lg. onions
4 potatoes, cut in cubes
1 qt. quahogs
1 sm. can evaporated milk
Salt and pepper to taste

Cut the salt pork into cubes and cook in kettle over low heat until browned. Slice the onions and place in kettle with salt pork. Cover and cook, stirring occasionally, until browned. Add 1 1/2 quarts water and potatoes to kettle and cook until potatoes are almost done. Drain the quahogs and reserve liquor. Grind the quahogs and add to kettle. Cook for about 5 minutes, then add reserved liquor. Add evaporated milk and heat through. Do not boil. Add salt and pepper. Any leftover chowder may be refrigerated for one day and reheated. Yield: 8-10 servings.

Capt. Stuart B. McCurdy
MacDill AFB, Tampa, Florida

COLD CURRY SOUP

2 cans cream of chicken soup
2 c. half and half
1 tbsp. curry powder
1/4 c. water
1/4 c. lemon juice
Salt and pepper to taste

Mix soup and half and half; bring to a boil. Reduce heat and simmer for 10 minutes, stirring frequently. Make paste of curry powder and water; add to soup mixture. Remove from heat; add lemon juice, salt and pepper. Let cool for 30 minutes, stirring frequently, then refrigerate until chilled. Yield: 6 servings.

Cmdr. Eugene M. Riddick
Naval Sta., Treasure Island
San Francisco, California

CRAB MEAT GUMBO

1/4 c. chopped onion
1/4 c. chopped celery
2 med. tomatoes, chopped
1 clove of garlic, finely minced
1/4 c. butter or margarine
1 1/2 c. sliced fresh or frozen okra
Hot sauce to taste
Salt and pepper to taste
Meat from 1 doz. crabs
Sherry to taste

Saute onion, celery, tomatoes and garlic in butter in heavy kettle for 5 minutes. Stir in okra and 1 1/2 cups water; bring to a boil. Reduce heat; add hot sauce, salt and pepper. Simmer, partially covered, for 10 minutes. Stir in crab meat and sherry. Serve with rice. Yield: 3 servings.

Adm. Thomas H. Moorer, Chm., Joint Chief of Staff
Pentagon, Washington, D. C.

RHODE ISLAND CLAM CHOWDER

1 3-in. cube salt pork, diced
1 onion, finely diced
1 qt. clam liquor
2 cans tomato soup
2 c. diced potatoes
1/8 tsp. thyme
Salt and pepper to taste
5 c. minced clams or quahogs
Butter to taste (opt.)

Fry out salt pork over low heat in large kettle. Add onions; fry over medium heat for 5 min-utes. Drain, if desired. Add clam liquor, tomato soup, potatoes and seasonings; mix well. Simmer for 40 minutes, adding 2 cups water gradually. Add clams, simmer for several minutes longer. Serve hot, topped with butter.

Capt. Donn L. Ashley, USN
Public Works Ctr., Pearl Harbor, Hawaii

SHOTGUN ITALIAN WEDDING SOUP

2 13-oz. cans chicken broth
2 5-oz. cans boned chicken
1 13-oz. can water
Salt to taste
Pepper
1 med. head fresh endive or escarole,
  chopped
1 lb. ground chuck
2 tbsp. grated Parmesan cheese
1 tbsp. ground oregano
1 egg
1/4 c. seasoned bread crumbs

Mix chicken broth, chicken, water, salt and pepper to taste in large Dutch oven or kettle. Wash endive well and drain; place in chicken mixture. Bring to a boil. Reduce heat and simmer. Mix remaining ingredients and 1/4 tsp. pepper; form into bite-sized meatballs. Place on cookie sheet. Bake in 375-degree oven till brown; drain well. Place meatballs in soup; cover. Simmer for 1 hour and 30 minutes to 2 hours. Double or triple recipe, place in containers and freeze, if desired. Yield: 6-8 servings.

Capt. Bruce Fredrick
Vint Hill Farms Sta., Warrenton, Virginia

VICHYSSOISE

4 or 5 leeks
1/4 c. butter
3 c. thinly sliced potatoes
1 c. hot water
4 chicken bouillon cubes
3 c. milk
1 tsp. salt
1/8 tsp. white pepper
1/8 tsp. paprika
1 c. cream
2 tbsp. finely chopped chives

Slice leeks thin, using only white and very light green portions; measure 1 1/2 cups. Melt butter in large, heavy saucepan. Add leeks; cook, stirring, until transparent but not brown. Add potato slices, water and bouillon cubes; cover.

Cook over moderate heat until potato slices are tender. Press through fine sieve or puree in blender. Return to saucepan; add milk, stirring rapidly to blend. Stir in salt, pepper and paprika. Add cream; heat just to serving temperature. Sprinkle with chives; serve hot. May be chilled quickly and served cold. One and 1/2 cups sliced onion may be substituted for leeks; minced parsley may be used instead of chives. Yield: 6 servings.

Photograph for this recipe is on page 172.

FRENCH ONION SOUP

12 onions, thinly sliced
4 tbsp. butter
14 c. beef bouillon
1 tsp. Worcestershire sauce
1/4 tsp. hot sauce
1 tsp. Kitchen Bouquet
Salt and pepper to taste
6   1-inch slices French bread
Grated Parmesan cheese

Saute onions in butter for 15 minutes or until golden brown. Add bouillon, sauces, salt and pepper. Bring to a boil, then reduce heat and cover. Simmer for 4 hours. Sprinkle bread with cheese and toast in oven until browned and crisp. Place piece of toast in each bowl of soup. Yield: 6 servings.

Cmdr. Robert D. Winters
NAS, New Orleans, Louisiana

GREEN PEA AND TOMATO ITALIANNE

1   11 1/4-oz. can green pea soup
1   10 3/4-oz. can tomato soup
1 1/2 soup cans water
2 tbsp. Chianti or other dry red wine
1/8 tsp. Italian seasoning
Saltines
Sliced mozzarella cheese
Crushed leaf oregano

Blend soups in saucepan. Add water, Chianti and Italian seasoning; cook over low heat for 10 minutes, stirring occasionally. Top desired number of saltines with cheese; sprinkle with oregano. Place on cookie sheet. Broil until cheese melts; serve with hot soup. Yield: 4 servings.

SALADS
AND VEGETABLES

In Europe, dinner is usually begun with a lavish tray of bite-size hors d'oeuvres or a bowl of taste-tempting soup. But here in America, we prefer to serve a crisp garden vegetable salad as the first course. And with good reason! No where else in the world is there a country so blessed with an abundance of fresh vegetables and garden greens, year 'round.

When you're at a party, what do you think of when the hostess asks if you'd like a vegetable salad? Do you think of a crisp tossed salad, cool and green with a tangy dressing? Or do you imagine a delicious congealed salad, chock full of fruits, nuts and cream, floating on a bed of lettuce. Main dish salads . . . quick and easy salads . . . seafood salads . . . slimming salads. All of these and many more are included for your eating pleasure in this section.

Vegetable recipes, from artichoke to zucchini are also included in this varied section. Not too many years ago, vegetables were considered regional and seasonal fare. Now, vegetables, the underrated step-child of many cook's in the kitchen, is making a stirring come-back. Baking, simmering, frying and sauteeing are just a few ways to prepare the many wonderful recipes included in this versatile section. "Eat your vegetables, dear", and enjoy them at your next party.

INSTANT TROPICAL FRUIT SALAD

1 No. 2 can pineapple chunks
2 or 3 ripe bananas
Shredded coconut

Pour pineapple and syrup into bowl. Slice bananas; stir into pineapple. Chill. Serve in sherbet glasses topped with coconut. Yield: 6-8 servings.

Col. Bernard J. Pankowski
Ft. Myer, Virginia

MRS. WILLIAMS' FROSTED GELATIN SALAD

2 3-oz. packages lemon gelatin
2 c. hot water
2 c. lemon-lime carbonated drink
1 20-oz. can crushed or chunk pineapple
2 bananas, sliced
1 c. miniature marshmallows
1/2 c. sugar
2 tbsp. flour
1 egg, beaten
2 tbsp. butter
2 c. whipped cream

Dissolve gelatin in hot water; stir in carbonated drink. Chill until slightly thickened. Drain pineapple; reserve liquid. Add pineapple, bananas and marshmallows to gelatin; place in 9 x 13-inch pan. Chill until firm. Combine sugar, flour, egg and 1 cup reserved pineapple juice; cook until thick, stirring constantly. Stir in butter until melted; chill. Fold in whipped cream; spread over gelatin mixture. Chill until served.

Col. Richard E. Chandler
George AFB, Victorville, California

SPICY BEAN-APPLE SALAD

1 1-lb. can cut Blue Lake green beans
3 tbsp. vinegar
1 tbsp. chopped candied ginger
1 2-in. stick cinnamon
6 whole cloves
1/4 tsp. salt
2 c. chopped tart red apple
1/4 c. raisins
1/3 c. red onion rings

Drain beans; reserve 1/2 cup liquid. Combine reserved liquid with vinegar, ginger, cinnamon, cloves and salt in saucepan; bring to a boil. Stir in apple and raisins; cook over medium heat for about 5 minutes or until apples are tender-crisp. Add beans and onion rings; bring to a boil. Pour into bowl; serve hot. May be covered and refrigerated to serve chilled. Yield: 5-6 servings.

ALLEN'S CAESAR SALAD

3 heads romaine
2 to 4 cloves of garlic
1 c. olive oil
Dash of cayenne pepper
Dash of hot sauce
1/2 tsp. sugar
3 anchovy fillets
2 egg yolks
Juice of 1 lemon
1/2 to 1 c. grated Parmesan cheese
1/2 to 1 c. croutons (opt.)

Tear romaine into bite-sized pieces; wash. Dry in perforated container. Crush garlic; add olive oil, cayenne pepper, hot sauce and sugar. Mash anchovy fillets; mix with garlic mixture. Pour oil mixture into salad bowl. Add egg yolks and lemon juice; stir gently. Place romaine in salad bowl; toss well. Add Parmesan cheese and croutons; toss. Use spinach instead of romaine for variety.

Lt. Cmdr. Allen R. Ruth
Public Works Ctr., Pearl Harbor, Hawaii

EASY CAESAR SALAD

1/2 c. salad oil
1 clove of garlic, pressed
1/4 c. lemon juice
1 tsp. Worcestershire sauce
1/4 tsp. pepper
1/2 tsp. salt
1 beaten egg
1/2 c. Parmesan cheese
1 2-oz. can anchovy fillets, chopped
1/2 to 1 head lettuce
2 to 3 tomatoes, quartered
1 c. croutons

Combine oil and garlic; let stand for several minutes. Add lemon juice, Worcestershire sauce, pepper, salt, egg, cheese and anchovies; stir well. Break lettuce into bite-sized pieces. Combine lettuce, tomatoes and croutons; pour dressing over all. Toss lightly. Serve immediately. Yield: 6-8 servings.

Lt. Cmdr. Roy O. Campbell
NAS, Glenview, Illinois

PARTY CAESAR SALAD

4 slices bread
1 lg. head romaine
6 anchovy fillets
1 tbsp. Dijon mustard
1/8 tsp. garlic powder
2 tsp. Worcestershire sauce
3 tbsp. lemon juice
1/8 tsp. coarsely ground pepper
Dash of hot sauce
1 egg
3/4 c. olive oil
1/4 c. grated Parmesan cheese

Cut bread into 1 1/2-inch cubes; place on cookie sheet. Bake in 225-degree oven for 1 hour or until well browned. Wash romaine; remove coarse ribs. Cut romaine into 1 1/2-inch strips. Line salad bowl with paper towels; place romaine on towels. Cover with paper towels. Chill for 1 hour. Wash anchovy fillets. Add mustard, garlic powder, Worcestershire sauce, lemon juice, pepper and hot sauce; mix thoroughly. Beat in egg. Remove paper towels from bowl. Toss romaine lightly with olive oil to coat leaves. Add dressing slowly; toss lightly. Add croutons and cheese; toss lightly. Crumbled bleu cheese may be substituted for Parmesan cheese.

Cmdr. James Brawley
USCG Air Sta., Brooklyn, New York

FIVE TEASPOON SALAD AND DRESSING

1/2 head crisp iceberg lettuce
1/2 head crisp romaine
1/2 c. diced green pepper
1 1/2 c. cubed fresh tomato
1 tbsp. diced onion or fresh scallions
1 tsp. monosodium glutamate
1 tsp. onion powder
1 1/4 tsp. salt
3/4 tsp. crushed parsley
1/2 tsp. garlic powder
1/2 tsp. pepper
2 c. buttermilk
2 c. mayonnaise

Tear lettuce and romaine into bite-sized pieces; mix with green pepper, tomato and onion. Place in plastic bag; seal. Refrigerate. Mix monosodium glutamate, onion powder, salt, parsley, garlic powder and pepper; add buttermilk and mayonnaise. Dressing may be prepared ahead; will keep in refrigerator indefinitely. Pour dressing over salad just before serving.

Maj. F. Cregg Crosby
Andersen AFB, Guam

MARINATED MUSHROOMS

1 lb. fresh mushrooms
6 tbsp. olive oil
3/4 c. dry white wine
1 1/2 tsp. salt
1/8 tsp. cayenne pepper
1/4 tsp. dried leaf oregano
1/4 c. chopped fresh parsley
2 tbsp. chopped fresh onion
3 tbsp. fresh lemon juice

Slice mushrooms; place in glass or earthenware bowl. Combine remaining ingredients in saucepan; simmer for 15 minutes. Remove from heat; pour over mushrooms. Cover; refrigerate for several hours. Yield: 8 servings.

Photograph for this recipe on page 180.

CHEESE-CAULIFLOWER SUPREME

1 med. head cauliflower
1/2 med. onion
1 clove of garlic, diced
2 eggs
3 tbsp. cornstarch
1 tsp. salt
2 c. milk
1 1/2 to 2 c. shredded mild Cheddar cheese
2 tbsp. butter or margarine

Break or cut cauliflower into flowerets; slice onion and cut into 1/2-inch pieces. Place cauliflower and onion in pan of water with garlic. Bring to a boil and cook for 10 to 15 minutes. Drain off liquid. Mix eggs, cornstarch, salt and milk in a saucepan until mixture is smooth. Heat, stirring, until thickened. Place a layer of cauliflower mixture in a baking dish; cover with sauce and shredded cheese. Repeat layers until all ingredients are used; dot with butter. Bake in a preheated 400-degree oven for 15 minutes. Yield: 4 servings.

Capt. Theodore R. Blasche
Fort Dix, New Jersey

CHINESE PEAS

3 tbsp. salad oil
1 c. diced pork
Salt and pepper to taste
1/2 tsp. sugar
2 tsp. soy sauce
1 tsp. sherry
2 1/2 tsp. cornstarch
1/2 c. chopped onion
1/2 c. chopped celery
1/2 c. mushrooms
1 pkg. frozen peas
1 c. stock or bouillon
1/2 tsp. monosodium glutamate

Heat oil in skillet until bubbly; add pork, salt, pepper, sugar, 1 teaspoon soy sauce, sherry, and 1/2 teaspoon cornstarch. Cook over high heat, stirring constantly, until pork is golden. Remove pork to warm dish. Fry onion in skillet until golden; add celery. Cook for 2 minutes. Add onions, celery and mushrooms to pork. Cook peas in stock to cover for 4 to 5 minutes. Drain; reserve liquid. Add peas to pork mixture; stir remaining cornstarch into reserved liquid. Add gradually to oil in skillet; cook, stirring constantly, until clear and thickened. Add remaining soy sauce and monosodium glutamate. Stir into pork mixture; serve immediately. Yield: 4 servings.

Capt. Keith Bennett
Pearl Harbor NSY, Hawaii

MISS BURTON'S SQUASH

2 lb. yellow squash
2 med. onions, chopped
2 med. green peppers, chopped
1/4 c. sugar
1 stick butter
3 eggs
Salt and pepper to taste

Cook squash until tender. Saute onions and peppers; mix with remaining ingredients. Place in small baking dish. Bake at 350 degrees for 1 hour.

Mrs. C. B. Nesbitt
Maxwell AFB, Alabama

WILD RICE CASSEROLE

3/4 c. wild rice
Salt
4 tbsp. butter
3/4 c. chopped onions
3/4 c. chopped celery
1 can cream of mushroom soup
1 2-oz. can mushrooms
2 tbsp. white wine
Pepper to taste
1/4 tsp. dried tarragon
1/4 c. chutney (opt.)

Place rice in bowl; cover with cold water. Stir and drain. Repeat washing several times. Cook rice over low heat in 1 quart water with 1 teaspoon salt for about 45 minutes or until rice is tender. Melt butter in small frying pan. Add onions and celery and saute over medium heat for 10 minutes. Place in 1 1/2-quart casserole; stir in salt to taste and remaining ingredients except chutney. Stir in rice; cover tightly with aluminum foil. Bake at 350 degrees for 45 minutes. Uncover and spread chutney over top. Bake for 10 to 15 minutes longer. Yield: 6-8 servings.

Lt. Col. Phil Serrin
Pentagon, Washington, D. C.

TUNA A LA GRECQUE

2/3 c. wine vinegar
1 2/3 c. salad oil
1 tsp. salt
1 tsp. sugar
1 tsp. dry mustard
1 tsp. paprika
1/2 tsp. ground coriander
1/2 tsp. hot sauce
1 tbsp. lemon juice
1 sm. clove of garlic, minced
1 1/2 c. celery, cut in 1/2-in. pieces
3/4 lb. very small white onions
3   6 1/2 or 7-oz. can tuna in
  vegetable oil
1   1-lb. 4-oz. can chick peas,
  drained
1   8-oz. can Greek or ripe olives,
  drained
1   6 or 8-oz. can sliced mushrooms,
  drained
3 med. tomatoes, cut in wedges
1/2 c. coarsely chopped parsley

Combine first 10 ingredients for marinade in large saucepan; bring to a boil. Add celery and onions; cook, covered, for 15 minutes. Place tuna, chick peas, olives, mushrooms and tomatoes in large bowl. Add hot vegetable mixture; mix well. Chill, stirring occasionally. Drain salad; sprinkle with parsley just before serving. Serve with drained marinade, if desired. Yield: 6-8 servings.

DESSERTS

Humm . . . It's Delicious! Compliments always abound
when a taste-tempting and eye-appealing dessert is placed
on the table. Wonderful things happen when a woman
decides to introduce a new dessert to her family —
and we have included some of the tastiest, most lavish
desserts to be introduced to you.

Each one of these desserts has been painstakingly
prepared, adapted and perfected just for you. Elegant
culinary creations of deliciously light and satisfying dessert
fondues, crepes and ice creams are presented in this section.
For those who prefer a more filling dessert, golden-
crusted pies, extravagantly filled with sweet and savory
fruits are included along with cakes and puddings,
long a tradition in American cookery.

When you serve a simply scrumptious dessert, chances
are your meal — or party — will be a big success. One glance
through this section and you'll want to try each and every
one. Some are for company fare, others for covered
dish suppers or family night at home. All are,
Humm . . . Delicious!

BANANAS FLAMBE

1 tbsp. butter
2 tbsp. brown sugar
1 ripe banana, sliced
Dash of cinnamon
1 tbsp. banana liqueur
1 tbsp. rum
2 scoops vanilla ice cream

Melt butter in chafing dish. Stir in brown sugar; blend well. Add banana and saute until golden. Sprinkle with cinnamon. Add banana liqueur and rum; ignite. Baste bananas with flaming liquid; serve over vanilla ice cream. Yield: 2 servings.

Lt. Robert M. Gillaspie
NAS, Barbers Point, Hawaii

CINNAMON-RAISIN RING

4 pkg. dry yeast
5 c. flour
1 tsp. salt
1 1/2 c. sugar
1 c. milk
3/4 c. butter
1/2 tsp. grated lemon rind
1 tsp. vanilla
3 eggs
1 tbsp. cinnamon
2/3 c. raisins
Powdered sugar icing

Mix yeast, 2 cups flour, salt and 1/2 cup sugar in large bowl. Heat milk and 1/2 cup butter in saucepan over low heat until warm; butter does not need to melt. Add lemon rind and vanilla. Add to dry ingredients and beat with electric mixer at medium speed for 2 minutes. Add eggs and 1 cup flour; beat for 2 minutes at high speed. Stir in remaining flour with wooden spoon. Knead on floured surface for 10 minutes, adding flour until dough no longer sticks to surface and is smooth and elastic. Place in bowl and let rise for 45 minutes. Punch down; divide in half. Roll out, half at a time, into 9 x 15-inch rectangle. Spread each rectangle with 2 tablespoons remaining butter and sprinkle with 1/2 of the remaining sugar and 1/2 of the cinnamon. Sprinkle half the raisins over each rectangle; roll as for jelly roll. Form each roll into circle on buttered cookie sheet; cut each circle almost through with scissors into 12 portions. Turn each portion on its side; cover with a clean towel. Let rise for 45 minutes. Bake at 350 degrees for 15 minutes or until golden brown; drizzle with powdered sugar icing. May be cooled, wrapped in foil and frozen before adding icing. Bake frozen ring in foil at 350 degrees for about 30 minutes to warm, then add icing.

Maj. Keith J. Minich
MacDill AFB, Florida

ED'S HOMEMADE BREAD

3 c. milk
2 pkg. dry yeast
4 tsp. salt
4 to 6 tbsp. sugar
4 tbsp. shortening, melted
16 c. flour

Scald milk. Dissolve yeast in 1 cup warm water. Combine salt, sugar, milk, melted shortening and 2 cups water in 8-quart mixing bowl, stirring until dry ingredients are dissolved; cool to lukewarm. Stir in yeast mixture. Sift flour 3 times. Add flour gradually to yeast mixture, blending well between each addition. Knead dough on lightly floured surface for 10 minutes or until smooth and elastic. Shape dough into ball; place in 8-quart greased bowl, turning to grease top. Let rise, covered, in warm place until doubled in bulk. Punch down; divide into 4 equal parts. Shape into loaves; place in lightly greased bread pans. Let rise, covered, in warm place until doubled in bulk. Preheat oven to 425 degrees. Bake for 15 minutes; reduce oven temperature to 350 degrees. Bake for 40 minutes longer or until bread tests done. Turn out on cooling racks. Brush tops with melted butter, if desired. Dough may be formed into rolls; bake for 25 minutes. May substitute 1/3 to 1/2 rye or whole wheat flour. Add 2 to 8 tablespoons molasses, if desired.

Maj. Edward B. Hanrahan
USAF Acad., Colorado

MONKEY BREAD

1 1/2 pkg. or cakes yeast
Sugar
1/4 c. warm water
1/2 c. butter
1 tsp. salt
3/4 c. scalded milk
5 c. flour
3 lg. eggs
Melted butter

Dissolve yeast and 1 teaspoon sugar in warm water. Combine the butter, 1/2 cup sugar and salt. Pour in scalded milk and stir to melt butter. Cool. Add yeast mixture and half the flour; mix. Beat in eggs thoroughly; stir in remaining flour. Turn out onto floured board and knead well. Place in buttered bowl; cover and let rise until doubled in bulk. Punch down and turn onto board again. Roll out to 1/4-inch thickness; cut into diamond shapes. Dip each diamond into melted butter and arrange in a buttered tube pan in staggered layers. Cover and let rise until almost doubled in bulk. Bake in a 375-degree oven for about 45 minutes or till browned. Yield: 8-10 servings.

Maj. Charles G. Simpson
Vandenberg AFB, California

RAISIN SCONES

2 c. flour
4 tsp. baking powder
1 tbsp. sugar
1/2 tsp. salt
1/4 c. butter or margarine
1/3 c. milk
2 eggs, beaten
1/2 c. raisins

Sift flour with baking powder, sugar and salt; cut in butter with pastry blender until of consistency of cornmeal. Stir in milk. Reserve 2 tablespoons egg; add remaining egg to flour mixture. Stir in raisins. Divide dough into 2 parts; knead gently on lightly floured surface. Shape dough into two 7-inch round loaves; place in greased 9-inch pie pan. Score tops into 6 wedge-shaped sections each; brush with reserved egg. Bake at 375 degrees for 15 minutes or until tops are golden. Break into sections; split sections. Fill with jam. Serve immediately. Yield: 12 scones.

Cmdr. Kelly E. Taggart
NOAA Hq, Rockville, Maryland

TANGIER ISLAND BREAD

1/3 c. wheat germ
7 c. unbleached flour, sifted
1 c. milk, scalded
1/2 c. honey
3 tbsp. (heaping) sugar
1/2 c. vegetable oil
1 tbsp. (or more) salt

2 eggs
2 pkg. yeast
Melted butter

Mix wheat germ and flour; combine milk, honey, sugar, oil and salt. Beat eggs in large bowl until foamy; add milk mixture to eggs. Add 2 cups flour mixture. Beat until smooth. Dissolve yeast in 1 cup lukewarm water; add to flour mixture. Add remaining flour gradually until dough can be kneaded by hand. Knead for 5 minutes. Place in greased bowl, turning to grease top; let rise, covered, until doubled in bulk. Punch down; knead for 5 minutes. Divide into 3 parts; shape into loaves. Place in well-greased bread pans. Bake at 350 degrees for 40 minutes or until bread tests done. Turn out on wire racks immediately; brush tops with melted butter. May be formed into rolls if desired. Yield: 3 loaves or 36 rolls.

Cmdr. William T. McMurry
Naval Safety Ctr., Norfolk, Virginia

PRUNE CAKE

2 c. flour
1 1/2 tsp. soda
1 tsp. salt
1 tsp. nutmeg
1 tsp. cinnamon
1 tsp. allspice
1 c. cooking oil
3 1/2 c. sugar
2 eggs
1 1/2 tsp. vanilla
1 1/2 c. buttermilk
1 c. chopped prunes
1 c. chopped nuts
1/2 c. butter
1 tsp. corn syrup

Sift flour, 1 teaspoon soda, salt, nutmeg, cinnamon and allspice together. Cream oil with 2 1/2 cups sugar and eggs; add 1 teaspoon vanilla. Add flour mixture and 1 cup buttermilk alternately to creamed mixture; beat until smooth. Stir in prunes and nuts. Pour into greased 9 x 12-inch baking pan. Bake at 325 degrees for 1 hour. Combine butter and remaining sugar, buttermilk, soda and vanilla with corn syrup in saucepan; bring to a boil. Boil, stirring constantly, for 2 minutes. Pour immediately over hot cake.

Capt. Olin C. Covington
Bamberg, Germany

GINGERBREAD SUPREME

1 egg, well beaten
1/2 c. sugar
1/2 c. light molasses
1/4 tsp. salt
1/2 c. melted shortening
1 1/2 c. flour
3/4 tsp. ginger
3/4 tsp. cinnamon
1 tsp. soda
3/4 c. boiling water

Combine egg, sugar, molasses, salt and shortening and mix well. Sift flour, ginger and cinnamon together, then stir into egg mixture. Add soda to boiling water and stir into flour mixture. Batter will be thin; do not add more flour. Pour into waxed paper-lined 10 x 7-inch pan. Bake at 350 degrees for 30 to 40 minutes. Delicious served warm and iced with slightly sweetened whipped cream to which a drop of vanilla has been added. Cut gingerbread into individual servings. Split each serving into 2 layers. Spread whipped cream between layers, then spread top and sides and serve immediately.

Maj. Gen. William W. Snavely
Hq. USAF, Washington, D. C.

CHOCOLATE FONDUE

3 8-oz. bars bittersweet chocolate
1/2 c. heavy cream
2 or 3 tbsp. kirsch or rum
Fresh banana slices, orange slices, cherries
    or pineapple, pear or apple chunks
Day-old sponge cake, cut in 1-in. cubes

Melt chocolate in top of double boiler. Add cream and kirsch and mix well. Add more kirsch if too thick; add more cream or chocolate if too thin. Place in fondue pot over warming candle. Spear fruit or cake with fondue fork; dip into chocolate mixture.

Capt. Paul A. Nicholson
Merrell Barracks, Nurnberg, Germany

PANCAKE FLAMBE

1 c. flour
1/4 tsp. salt
2 tbsp. sugar
1/2 tsp. cinnamon
1 c. milk
2 tbsp. melted butter
2 eggs, slightly beaten

1 c. apricot jam
Confectioners' sugar
2 tbsp. butter
4 tbsp. cognac or Cointreau

Sift flour, salt, sugar and cinnamon together. Add milk and melted butter to eggs, then stir into flour mixture. Beat till smooth. Grease 5-inch skillet; heat. Pour in 3 tablespoons batter; tilt skillet till bottom is covered. Cook till pancake is brown; turn and brown. Place in baking pan and keep warm in hot oven with door open. Cook remaining pancakes. Place 2 teaspoons jam in center of each pancake; roll. Dust with confectioners' sugar. Heat butter, remaining jam and 2 tablespoons cognac in chafing dish. Add pancakes; spoon sauce over pancakes for 2 minutes while sauce is boiling. Place pancakes on warm plates. Ignite remaining cognac in large serving spoon and stir into remaining sauce in chafing dish. Spoon flaming sauce over pancakes. Yield: 12 pancakes.

Capt. Walter T. Michnal
Kincheloe AFB, Michigan

LEMON BARS

1 stick soft butter
1 c. flour
1/4 c. confectioners' sugar
2 eggs, slightly beaten
1 tbsp. grated lemon rind
3 tbsp. lemon juice
2 tbsp. flour
1 c. sugar
1/8 tsp. salt

Cream together first 3 ingredients; pat into 6 x 8-inch pan. Bake at 350 degrees for 20 minutes. Mix remaining ingredients together; pour over crust. Bake for 20 minutes longer. Cool; slice and roll in additional confectioners' sugar.

Mrs. C. B. Nesbitt
Maxwell AFB, Alabama

LIGHT BATTER
FOR CREPES SUZETTE

1 c. cold water
1 c. cold milk
2 eggs
2 egg yolks
1 tbsp. sugar
3 tbsp. Grand Marnier
2 c. sifted all-purpose flour
5 tbsp. melted butter
1 recipe orange butter

Place all ingredients except orange butter in blender container in order listed. Cover and blend at top speed for 1 minute. If bits of flour adhere to the sides of blender, dislodge with a rubber scraper and blend for 3 seconds longer. Cover and refrigerate for at least 2 hours or overnight. This allows the flour particles to expand in the liquid and ensures a tender, light, thin crepe. Batter should be a very light cream, just thick enough to coat a wooden spoon. If batter seems too heavy after cooking first crepe, beat in additional water, 1 spoon at a time; each cooked crepe should be about 1/16 inch thick. Serve crepes with orange butter. Yield: 12-15 recipes.

Capt. Fred W. Coulter
Norfolk Naval Shipyard, Virginia

OLD-FASHIONED SOFT SUGAR COOKIES

2 c. sugar
1 c. shortening
2 eggs, beaten
1 tsp. baking powder
2 tsp. soda
1 c. buttermilk
1 tsp. vanilla
1 tsp. salt
6 1/2 c. flour
Raisins

Cream sugar and shortening until fluffy; stir in eggs. Add baking powder and soda and mix until well blended. Stir in buttermilk, vanilla and salt. Add flour, 1 cup at a time, beating after each addition until blended; dough will be quite stiff. Chill overnight. Roll out 1/4 inch thick on well-floured board; cut with round cutter. Place on greased cookie sheet. Place a raisin in center of each cookie and sprinkle well with additional sugar. Bake at 350 degrees for 12 to 14 minutes or until lightly browned.

Lt. Col. Richard C. Miller
Kincheloe AFB, Michigan

BROWNIES

1 1/2 c. sifted flour
2 c. sugar
4 oz. unsweetened chocolate, melted
2/3 c. soft shortening
1 tsp. salt
4 eggs
2 tsp. vanilla
1 c. broken nuts

Place all ingredients in bowl. Beat with electric mixer at medium speed until combined, then beat at high speed for 3 minutes. Spread in greased 15 x 11-inch baking pan. Bake at 350 degrees for 30 minutes; frost, if desired. Cut into bars or squares.

Maj. Keith J. Minich
MacDill AFB, Florida

CHERRY MELBA MERINGUES

Oil
4 egg whites, at room temperature
1/2 tsp. vanilla
1/4 tsp. salt
1/4 tsp. cream of tartar
1 1/3 c. sugar
8 fresh or canned peach halves, chilled
1 qt. vanilla ice cream
Cherry Melba Sauce

Cover baking sheet with brown paper. Draw 8 well-separated 3 1/2-inch circles on paper; oil area inside each circle. Combine egg whites, vanilla, salt and cream of tartar in large mixing bowl; beat with electric mixer at highest speed until soft peaks form. Reduce speed slightly; sprinkle 2 tablespoons sugar on whites every 30 seconds while beating continuously. Reduce beater speed as necessary as meringue thickens. Spread meringue, 1/4 inch high, inside circles with spatula; build up sides with additional meringue, using pastry tube or spoons. Bake in 250-degree oven for 45 minutes. Turn oven off; allow meringues to stand in oven for 30 minutes. Remove meringue to cooling rack; cool thoroughly. Place meringues on individual serving plates; top each with a peach half and a scoop of ice cream. Spoon some Cherry Melba Sauce on top of each; serve additional sauce in bowl.

Cherry Melba Sauce

1 8-oz. jar maraschino cherries
1 tbsp. water
1 tbsp. cornstarch
1/2 c. currant jelly
4 tsp. lemon juice
1/4 tsp. grated lemon peel

Puree maraschino cherries in blender at high speed until almost smooth; set aside. Mix water and cornstarch in medium saucepan. Add cherries, jelly, lemon juice and lemon peel; stir over medium heat until thickened and clear. Cool; chill thoroughly.

Photograph for this recipe on page 186.

BUTTERSCOTCH PIE

1/2 c. butter
3 c. sugar
1/2 c. milk
3 eggs
3 tbsp. (heaping) flour
3 c. milk
2 9-in. baked pie shells

Brown butter well in saucepan over medium heat; cool for 1 minute. Stir in sugar and milk; bring to a boil. Boil gently for 5 minutes; cool for 1 minute. Beat eggs, adding flour gradually; add milk, beating until smooth. Combine egg mixture with butter mixture; simmer, stirring constantly, until smooth and thickened. Pour into pie shells. Chill for at least 2 hours or until ready to serve. Yield: 12 servings.

Capt. Bob Buster, Jr.
Ft. Benjamen Harrison, Indianapolis, Indiana

MAPLE CHIFFON PIE

1 1/4 c. finely crushed vanilla wafers
1/4 c. finely chopped walnuts
2 tbsp. sugar
1/4 c. melted butter
1 env. unflavored gelatin
1/4 c. cold water
2 eggs, separated
1/4 tsp. salt
3/4 c. maple-blended syrup
1 c. milk
1/2 c. whipping cream
1 tsp. vanilla
Slightly sweetened whipped cream

Combine crumbs, walnuts and sugar. Add butter; mix well. Press firmly onto bottom and side of 9-inch pie plate. Bake in 375-degree oven for about 5 minutes; cool. Soften gelatin in cold water. Mix egg yolks, salt and 1/2 cup syrup in top of double boiler; beat to blend. Stir in milk gradually; place over hot water. Cook, stirring, until mixture coats metal spoon; remove from heat. Add gelatin; stir until dissolved. Chill until slightly thickened. Beat egg whites until foamy. Add remaining syrup gradually, beating until egg whites stand in stiff peaks. Fold into gelatin mixture. Whip cream until stiff; fold into gelatin mixture. Add vanilla; spoon into pie shell. Chill until firm; garnish with slightly sweetened whipped cream.

LIME-CHEESE PIE

15 slices zwieback
1/4 c. slivered almonds
1/3 c. sugar
1/3 c. margarine, melted
1/4 tsp. cinnamon

Place 1/3 of the zwieback and 1/3 of the almonds in blender container; blend on high speed until zwieback is finely crushed. Remove to bowl. Repeat process twice. Add sugar, margarine and cinnamon to crumb mixture; blend well. Press mixture into 10-inch pie pan, reserving 1 tablespoon mixture for garnish. Bake crust in preheated 375 - degree oven for 8 minutes.

Lime-Cheese Filling

1/2 c. milk
2 tbsp. unflavored gelatin
2 thin strips lime peel
Dash of salt
1/2 c. lime juice
3/4 c. sugar
2 eggs
Few drops of green food coloring
1 8-oz. package cream cheese
1 c. chopped ice
1 c. light cream
1 c. whipping cream, whipped

Scald milk. Combine milk, gelatin, lime peel, salt and juice in blender; blend, covered, on high speed for 1 minute. Add sugar, eggs, food coloring and cream cheese; blend, covered, on high speed for 15 seconds. With motor running, add ice. Add light cream; blend for 10 seconds or until well mixed. Let stand for 2 minutes or until slightly thickened. Pour into prepared crust; chill until set. Top with whipped cream sweetened with additional sugar. Garnish with reserved crumbs and lime twists, if desired. Yield: 6-8 servings.

Maj. David B. Bates
Minot AFB, North Dakota

CRUSTY APPLE PIE

1 recipe rich pastry
8 apples
1 c. sugar
1 c. hot water
Cinnamon to taste

Line a deep pie plate with pastry; flute edge. Prick pastry with a fork. Bake at 450 degrees for 10 to 12 minutes. Pare apples and cut into thick slices. Mix sugar and hot water in a saucepan; bring to a boil. Add apples; cook until tender but unbroken. Remove apples from syrup with a slotted spoon; place in pastry shell. Cook syrup until thick; pour 1/2 cup syrup over apples. Sprinkle with cinnamon; bake for 5 minutes longer. May be topped with slices of American cheese or scoops of vanilla ice cream.

Gen. William W. Momyer
Langley AFB, Virginia

PECAN PIE

1/4 c. milk
1/2 c. salad oil
2 c. sifted flour
1 1/2 tsp. salt
3 eggs, beaten
1 c. sugar
1 c. light corn syrup
1 1/4 c. chopped pecans
1 tsp. vanilla

Combine milk and oil; add flour and salt. Mix well. Roll out between sheets of waxed paper; line 9-inch pie pan, fluting edges. Combine eggs, sugar, corn syrup, pecans, vanilla and dash of additional salt; blend well. Pour mixture into prepared pie shell. Bake at 300 degrees for 1 hour. Yield: 6 servings.

Col. Thomas E. Wesson
Ft. Hood, Texas

HEAVENLY CHOCOLATE PIE

1 pkg. chocolate chips
3 tbsp. milk
2 tbsp. sugar
4 eggs, separated
1 tsp. vanilla
1 baked 9-in. pie shell
Sweetened whipped cream

Melt chocolate chips with the milk and sugar. Cool. Beat in egg yolks, one at a time. Beat egg whites until stiff peaks form, then fold in chocolate mixture and vanilla. Pour into pie shell. Top with whipped cream. Garnish with chocolate curls. Refrigerate for at least 2 hours or until thoroughly chilled.

Cmdr. Jerome Wiederholt
NAF, El Centro, California

CREAM PIE

3/4 c. sugar
1/3 c. flour
1/8 tsp. salt
2 eggs, separated
2 tbsp. butter
2 c. milk
1/2 tsp. vanilla
1 baked pie shell
Sliced bananas

Combine sugar, flour, salt, well-beaten egg yolks and butter in top of double boiler. Add milk slowly, stirring constantly. Cook over hot water, stirring constantly, until thick and smooth. Stir in vanilla. Line pie shell with sliced bananas. Spoon filling over bananas. Cool completely. Beat egg whites until stiff peaks form. Spread over cream filling, sealing to edge. Bake at 350 degrees for 15 minutes or until meringue is browned. One small can crushed pineapple, drained, may be stirred into cream filling for pineapple pie.

Cmdr. R. A. Esposito
NAS, Fallon, Nevada

PINEAPPLE TURNOVERS

1 No. 2 can crushed pineapple
Sugar
3 tbsp. cornstarch
4 c. sifted flour
2 c. shortening
1 tsp. salt
3 eggs, well beaten
1 cake yeast

Mix undrained pineapple, 1 cup sugar, cornstarch and 1/4 cup water; bring to a boil, stirring constantly. Cool. Mix flour and shortening in large bowl as for pastry. Add 2 tablespoons sugar, salt, 1/2 cup water and eggs and mix well. Dissolve yeast in 1/4 cup lukewarm water; stir into flour mixture. Cover and chill for 1 hour. Roll out dough, 1 tablespoon at a time, on a sugar-covered board or pastry cloth to a 6-inch round. May be rolled out to 1/4-inch thickness and cut with a sugared 6-inch soup bowl, if desired. Place 1 teaspoon pineapple filling in center of each round. Fold in half and press edges together. Place on cookie sheet. Bake at 400 degrees for 10 minutes or until lightly browned. Yield: 30-40 turnovers.

Lt. Cmdr. Edward R. Kuhn
DATC-Long Beach NS, California

GRANDMOTHER'S MARSHMALLOW PUDDING

1 1-lb. package marshmallows, cut up
1 No. 2 can crushed pineapple
1/2 c. chopped pecans
4 lg. bananas, sliced
2 c. whipping cream

Mix marshmallows and pineapple in 4-quart bowl. Chill for at least 8 hours or overnight. Stir occasionally. Add pecans and bananas. Whip cream until soft, smooth peaks form. Fold whipped cream into fruit mixture. Miniature marshmallows may be used, if desired.

Maj. Ben E. Killebrew
Fort Monmouth, New Jersey

PENNSYLVANIA DUTCH ICE CREAM

Crushed ice
Rock salt
1 lb. confectioners' sugar
2 13-oz. cans evaporated milk
3 beaten eggs
1 1/2 qt. half and half
1/4 tsp. salt
1 tbsp. vanilla

Place crushed ice and rock salt in mixer unit. Combine remaining ingredients in large bowl; mix well. Pour mixture into freezer container. Insert dasher; cover. Use additional ice and salt as needed. Freeze according to freezer directions. Crushed pineapple, chocolate, fruit or berries may be added near end of freezing process, if desired.

Maj. Chris Martin
Maxwell AFB, Alabama

HOT FUDGE SAUCE

2 1/2 oz. unsweetened chocolate
1/3 c. butter or margarine
1 c. sugar
1/3 c. milk

Melt chocolate in top of double boiler over hot water. Cream butter with sugar in bowl; add to chocolate. Add milk slowly; mix well. Cook over simmering water for 30 minutes. Serve over vanilla ice cream. May be refrigerated and reheated. Yield: 8 servings.

Capt. Sam S. Ryburn, Jr.
San Vito Air Sta., Brindisi, Italy

OUR MEN IN THE KITCHEN / INDEX

a la Jacque, 170
broiled, 170
cajun, 170
flambe, 170
herbed, diable, 171
scampi, 169
Shrimp, see Shellfish
Sole, see Fish
SOUPS
chili, see Chili
chowder
chicken, 176
clam, Rhode Island, 178
quahog, 177
crab meat gumbo, 178
curry, cold, 178
French onion, 179
green pea and tomato Italianne, 179
shotgun Italian wedding soup, 178
vichyssoise, 178

SPAGHETTI
and white clam sauce, 168
sauce with lobster, 170
with chicken creole, 163
with clam and anchovy sauce, 168
STEWS
beef
ground beef, 127
kidney and egg, 134
sweet and sour, 143
Sweet Breads
cinnamon-raisin ring, 188
raisin scones, 189
Veal Scallopini, 153
VEGETABLES
cauliflower-cheese supreme, 184
Chinese peas, 184
corn pudding and sausages, dixie, 145
mushrooms, marinated, 184
squash, Miss Burton's, 184

COLOR ILLUSTRATIONS

almond mushrooms, 162
Bahamian-barbecued chicken, 152
baked tangerines with orange-cranberry
relish, 131
black beans and rice, 151
crab meat quiche, 162
filbert torte with strawberry cream, 141
Florida grapefruit baskets, 131
grilled chicken with kraut relish, 142
herbed pinwheels, 152
hot potato salad with bacon, 141
lamb chop and tomato broil with sauce, 132

lobster barquettes, 161
old-fashioned strawberry shortcake, 142
orange crepes with orange sauce, 132
pate maison, 161
ripe olive quiche, 162
ripe olive rigolettos, 161
roast pork with sauerkraut and apple, 141
roast turkey with orange-rice stuffing, 131
seafood cream with avocado halves, 151
strawberry mocha cream tartlets, 151
tropical fruit bake, 152
vegetables vinaigrette, 162

PHOTOGRAPHY CREDITS: Florida Citrus Commission; American Lamb Council; National Kraut Packers Association; California Strawberry Advisory Board; Proctor & Gamble Company—Crisco Division; International Tuna Fish Association; Accent International; Olive Administrative Committee; Sterno Canned Heat; United Fresh Fruit and Vegetable Association; Grandma's West Indies Molasses; National Broiler Council; McIlhenny Company; California Avocado Advisory Board; Standard Fruit and Steamship Company: Cabana Bananas; Angostura-Wuppermann Corporation; R. C. Bigelow, Inc.; Brussels Sprout Marketing Program; National Macaroni Institute; National Cherry Growers & Industries Foundation; Pineapple Growers Association; National Association of Frozen Food Packers; American Lamb Council; National Livestock and Meat Board; Evaporated Milk Association; The American Spice Trade Association; Ocean Spray Cranberries, Inc.; U. S. Department of Commerce: National Marine Fisheries Service; McCormick & Company, Inc.; National Dairy Council; Campbell Soup Company; Keith Thomas Company.

Party Cookbook — Make every party a smashing success with hundreds of entertainment ideas and recipes. Everything is included from exotic drinks and punches to outstanding dinners ... along with special party tips for the host and hostess. **Fondue & Buffet Cookbook** — Hundreds of fondue, chafing dish and buffet recipes, sure to delight the most discriminating hostess. Colorful photographs and complete instructions give you great ideas for large or small parties, or even family fondue for two. **Meats Cookbook** — The way to a man's heart? Nothing beats roast beef, lamb, pork, veal ... or any other meat dish. Plain or fancy, mouth watering main dishes for every occasion and taste are included in this valuable recipe book.

Desserts Cookbook — Flaming crêpes to frosted cakes ... desserts are the crowning complements to every meal. And this marvelous cookbook contains hundreds of tempting desserts for every taste and fancy. Sure to bring smiles of delight from young and old alike.

Casseroles Cookbook — From poultry to sirloin tips, here are hundreds of delicious and timesaving casseroles. Mix and match vegetables, meats, pasta, seasonings ... and come up with a scrumptious meal — all in one dish. Fun to prepare and a breeze to serve. A family pleaser every time.

Holiday Cookbook — Prepare delicious and festive meals for all those special holiday events. Recipes are included for not only Christmas, Thanksgiving and New Year's Eve and Day ... but for Halloween, the Fourth of July, St. Patrick's Day ... every exciting occasion.

All-Purpose Cookbook — Desserts, main meals, salads, snacks ... recipes for every meal you can imagine. This happy combination cookbook makes meal planning and preparation fun and easy ... and guarantees success every time. **Quick & Easy Cookbook** — Here's the perfect answer to all those last minute meals — for families on the go! Hundreds of recipes to make delicious desserts, dinners, suppers, and snacks in a snap! Guarantees success with all your hurry-up meals. **Foreign Foods Cookbook** — Moo Goo Gai Pan, Baklava, Quiche Lorraine ... sound difficult? Well they're not! In fact all these foreign recipes are proven to be not only delicious but also easy to prepare. So, get exotic! Take your family on a tour of these mysterious lands with these great recipes.

Complete Your Cooking And Entertainment Library With Recipes On Parade Cookbooks!